How on Earth Did Jesus Become a God?

How on Earth Did Jesus Become a God?

HISTORICAL QUESTIONS ABOUT EARLIEST DEVOTION TO JESUS

Larry W. Hurtado

WILLIAM B. EERDMANS PUBLISHING COMPANY
GRAND RAPIDS, MICHIGAN / CAMBRIDGE, U.K.

© 2005 Wm. B. Eerdmans Publishing Co.
All rights reserved

Wm. B. Eerdmans Publishing Co.
255 Jefferson Ave. S.E., Grand Rapids, Michigan 49503 /
P.O. Box 163, Cambridge CB3 9PU U.K.

Printed in the United States of America

10 09 08 07 06 05   7 6 5 4 3 2 1

ISBN-10: 0-8028-2861-2
ISBN-13: 978-0-8028-2861-3

www.eerdmans.com

To Alan Segal,
scholar and friend

CONTENTS

In March 2004 I had the honor to give the inaugural lectures in the
Deichmann Annual Lecture Series at Ben-Gurion University of the
Negev (Beer-Sheva, Israel). Revised versions of these lectures form Chapters One through Four of this book. In response to requests from my Israeli colleagues, and with the encouragement of Eerdmans, I have also included several essays that originally appeared as articles in journals
(Chapters Five through Eight) and that are directly relevant to the issues in
view in the Deichmann lectures.

The annual lecture series at Ben-Gurion University, which I was privileged to inaugurate, forms part of the Deichmann Program for Jewish and
Christian Literature of the Hellenistic-Roman Era, a project that owes
much to the vision and generosity of Herr Dr. Heinz-Horst Deichmann. I
am pleased that Herr Deichmann's opening address for the lecture series is
included in this book (see appendix 1). The central aim includes promoting the academic study of the New Testament in Israel as an important historical resource for analysis of Jewish religion of the Roman period. I am
pleased to have been invited to participate in the formative stages of the
program, and I will watch with much interest the further developments.
For both my wife and me, one of the additional pleasures of the time in
Beer-Sheva was to make the acquaintance of Herr Deichmann and Frau
Deichmann, who honored the lectures with their faithful attendance.

The lectures represented now by Chapters One through Four of this
book were written originally for an audience made up largely of educated
and interested people but who might well not have much acquaintance
with either the early Christian texts or the approaches and conclusions of

the scholars concerned with them. My audience in Beer-Sheva was almost entirely Israelis from Ben-Gurion University and the wider community. In this published form, I have largely focused my efforts on stylistic improvements, clarification and slight expansion of some points, and some additional references in the footnotes for those who may wish to study issues further. So I trust that a rather wide readership will find these chapters accessible and informative. Chapters Five through Eight derive from journal articles originally addressed to fellow scholars in Christian origins, and reflect this in the many footnotes and references to other primary and secondary literature. I have included these studies here because they are particularly important in providing further support for positions that I present in Chapters One through Four (especially Chapters One through Two). I have limited myself to some small stylistic changes in refitting these essays for this book. But I hope that interested readers will have no trouble in following these discussions as well. Because Chapters Five through Eight represent some of the previous studies upon which I build in the earlier chapters, there are, unavoidably, some matters that get repeated. Usually, however, issues treated in more summary fashion in the earlier chapters are developed more fully in the later ones.

My hosts in Beer-Sheva received me and my wife so warmly that we felt as if we were family members returning home after a long time away, although it was our first visit to Ben-Gurion University and we were strangers to those who welcomed us. In particular, I thank Professor Zipporah Talshir (who was then serving as head of the Department of Bible and Near Eastern Studies) for coordinating many details locally (and for the enjoyable dinner party at her home during our visit). I also thank all those who attended the lectures and engaged me with questions and suggestions, which made me feel that I had been able to speak to matters of interest for them as well as for me. Dr. Cana Werner and Dalia Amara (a graduate student in the department) prepared Hebrew translations of my lectures, which were available for any in the audience who wanted them. After my revisions for publication, they reworked their translations and translated the four journal articles for publication of this book in Hebrew through Ben-Gurion University Press. My hearty thanks go to both of them for their generous contributions of their time and talents to the lecture series and the Hebrew edition of this volume.

My friend, Dr. Roland Deines (an impressive New Testament scholar in his own right), first approached me informally in May 2003 about giving the inaugural lectures in the Deichmann annual series. During our week-long visit to Israel, Roland also kindly guided my wife and me around several historic sites in the Negev, Jerusalem, and the Galilee, offering us the benefit of his extensive acquaintance with archaeological matters relevant to Second-Temple Judaism and early Christianity. Our whole time in Israel was informative, stimulating, and enjoyable, and Roland's generosity with his time is a major reason. He also was instrumental in arranging for the translation of the lectures and the publication of the Hebrew edition of this book.

I am also grateful to have been allowed to present some of the Deichmann lectures in other settings subsequently. In September 2004, I gave a version of Chapter One as a public/faculty lecture at the University of Lund, Chapters One through Two as the Broady Lectures at Stockholm, and Chapter Three as one of the Exegetical Day lectures at the annual meeting of the Uppsala Exegetical Society. I thank Kari Syreni for organizing that itinerary, as well as Thomas Kazen in Stockholm and Bengt Holmberg in Lund, who were involved in arrangements in their respective cities, and all the Scandinavian colleagues for their warm welcome.

I also gave Chapters One through Three as the Paddock Lectures at the General Theological Seminary, New York City, in October 2004. Dr. John Koenig nominated me for this, and I also thank his colleagues for electing me as a Paddock lecturer, and Dr. Robert Mullin in particular for overseeing arrangements and for making my visit comfortable and enjoyable. It is an honor to have been invited to join an illustrious line of previous lecturers in the Paddock series that includes William Temple and J. N. D. Kelly, and I am very pleased with the interest shown in my lectures by the numbers who attended and the animated discussions that followed each of them.

As already indicated, Chapters Five through Eight were previously published as journal articles. They are part of a number of publications on particular issues in a line of research that led to my large recent book, *Lord Jesus Christ: Devotion to Jesus in Earliest Christianity* (Grand Rapids/Cambridge: Eerdmans, 2003). The specifics of the original publications are given in a source note at the beginning of each of these chapters. I am very grateful to the several journals in which these essays first appeared (and their respective publishers) for their permission to include these articles in this book. I have made only slight changes to these studies. Because they were originally prepared as discrete studies, unfortunately certain points are dealt with in more than one of them.

All of the studies in this book reflect the enormous debt that I owe to many other scholars of previous and contemporary times, those with whom I disagree as well as those whose views I find more congenial. My sense of indebtedness and gratitude is reflected in the many footnotes. But I am sure that my debt extends much farther than I realize and have been able to credit in this way.

I dedicate this volume to my friend, Alan Segal, who has advocated and demonstrated serious engagement with the New Testament as comprising an important body of sources for historical analysis of Second-Temple Jewish tradition, which is also a key aim of the Deichmann Program.

Edinburgh
September 2005

The title of this book is deliberately provocative, but I do not wish to offend anyone. It expresses a *double entente* that captures two key emphases in the following pages. The one connotation in the title is how remarkable it is that Jesus of Nazareth came to be revered in the most exalted terms, and so early, in the religious movement dedicated to him that became what we call "Christianity." "How on earth" (to use a common English idiom of wonder) did this treatment of Jesus as divine happen? This reverence for Jesus included both grand claims about his significance and also a pattern of devotional practices in which he figured centrally and in ways that amount to him being treated as divine. In the Roman-era religious environment of the early churches, this devotion to Jesus effectively comprised treating him like a god. This is the premise for the following chapters, which reflect an effort to engage this keen devotion to Jesus as a subject for historical investigation.

This brings me to the other part of the *double entente*. How "on earth" — that is, how in *historical* terms — did Jesus come to hold such a status among early Christians? Of course, in traditional Christian faith, Jesus of Nazareth is the personal, human embodiment of the second person of the Trinity, and simply was divine from "before all time" (to use an ancient Christian creedal expression). But, whatever the validity of this traditional Christian view, the historical question remains: How did early Christians "on earth" come to see Jesus as divine and revere him as such? That is the key question that shapes the discussion in this book.

I am not primarily concerned here with considering the *legitimacy* of devotion to Jesus. That is a valid religious question, but more suitable for a study in Christian apologetics, or for a theological tome. Nor am I particularly concerned here with exploring the meaning of devotion to Jesus for contemporary Christian thought and practice. The latter likewise would be suitable for a theological treatise or perhaps a study intended to promote Christian reflection and piety. Christian apologetics, theological reflection, and the shaping and promoting of Christian piety are all, in principle, fully legitimate efforts. But these are not the focus or intention here.

Instead, this book represents an attempt to describe and understand *in historical terms* and *as a historical phenomenon* the devotion to Jesus that (as we shall see) characterized Christianity from a very (perhaps surprisingly) early point. To take this sort of historical approach does not necessarily signal or require either a disdain for questions about the validity and continuing meaning of devotion to Jesus or any particular answer to such questions. For example, one can certainly treat devotion to Jesus thoroughly as a historical phenomenon without denying thereby that it also may represent a response to the revelation of God. But, whatever the answers to religious and theological questions, I urge the validity and usefulness of the kind of historical analysis that I offer here.

For the past twenty-five years or so, I have devoted a good deal of effort to this historical investigation. In various publications, most recently in a large volume, *Lord Jesus Christ: Devotion to Jesus in Earliest Christianity,* I have offered the fruits of that effort.[1] In the present, much smaller book, I draw upon this work and those publications (as well as the work of a large number of other scholars of previous and contemporary time). I write here particularly (but not exclusively) for those who find the topic of interest and who would appreciate a more compact presentation of some of the important issues involved.

Early Christian devotion to Jesus certainly justifies attention, for it is remarkable in a number of respects. First, of course, this high reverence for Jesus in early Christian circles contrasts strongly with the very negative treatment of him by others, both during his historic lifetime and thereafter. Initially, Jesus was probably a follower of the fiery contemporary prophet of national repentance known as John "the Baptizer," but after

---

1. Larry W. Hurtado, *Lord Jesus Christ: Devotion to Jesus in Earliest Christianity* (Grand Rapids/Cambridge: Eerdmans, 2003). Among my prior publications, I regard as particularly important a smaller volume, *One God, One Lord: Early Christian Devotion and Ancient Jewish Monotheism* (Minneapolis: Fortress Press, 1988; 2d ed., Edinburgh: T&T Clark, 1998; reprint, London: T&T Clark International, 2003).

John's arrest and execution by Herod Antipas (the Roman client-ruler of Galilee), Jesus emerged more saliently as a prophet-like figure in his own right. He clearly and quickly became a controversial and polarizing figure for many, perhaps most, who had occasion to consider him seriously, and he remains so today.

By all indications, during his own historic lifetime Jesus became known in at least parts of Roman Judea through proclaiming the imminent arrival of God's "kingdom." To judge from many of the sayings attributed to Jesus in the New Testament Gospels, the coming of God's kingdom would comprise a genuine "regime change" (to borrow an expression from recent geopolitical discourse), and it represented values and purposes significantly different from those dominant in the religious and social structures of his day. In addition to proclaiming and teaching about God's kingdom, Jesus also seems to have engaged in other activities that had the effect of drawing further attention to him but were primarily intended to demonstrate something of the power and purposes of the divine kingdom that he announced. These other actions included calling a band of followers, pursuing an itinerant teaching activity, and taking controversial positions on some matters of religious practice. Both followers and opponents perceived Jesus as being able to perform miraculous healings and other deeds of supernatural power.

In view of the nearness of God's kingdom and the radical differences

---

2. This John ("the Baptizer") was sufficiently prominent in early first-century Roman Judea to be noted both in the Gospels (e.g., John's execution recounted in Mark 6:14-29) and by the ancient Jewish historian Josephus (*Jewish Antiquities* 18.116-19), but he is not always given sufficient attention in modern scholarly studies of Jesus' career. For basic information, see, for example, Paul W. Hollenbach, "John the Baptist," *Anchor Bible Dictionary*, ed. D. N. Freedman (New York: Doubleday, 1992), 3:887-99.

3. The contemporary interest in historical investigation of Jesus is vast, as is the body of recent publications addressing this interest. For one readable and soundly based portrayal of Jesus, see Scot McKnight, *A New Vision for Israel: The Teachings of Jesus in National Context* (Grand Rapids: Eerdmans, 1999). For a vigorous critical engagement with some tendencies in recent scholarship on Jesus, see Dale C. Allison, *Jesus of Nazareth: Millenarian Prophet* (Minneapolis: Fortress Press, 1998). Still more recent is the monumental study by J. D. G. Dunn, *Jesus Remembered* (Grand Rapids: Eerdmans, 2003).

4. Scholars have tended to focus on Jesus' teachings, and have been curiously shy of probing the traditions of Jesus' miraculous actions. One of the few recent exceptions is Graham H. Twelftree, *Jesus the Exorcist: A Contribution to the Study of the Historical Jesus* (Tübingen: J. C. B. Mohr; Peabody, Mass.: Hendrickson Publishers, 1993).

that it represented, Jesus seems to have urged his hearers to commence reordering their attitudes and behavior accordingly, and immediately: "The time is fulfilled, and the kingdom of God has come near; repent, and believe in the good news" (Mark 1:15). They were to live their lives in the "now" with a view toward, and their conduct shaped by, the future (but imminent) full manifestation of God's rule.

This is not the place to attempt a fuller account of Jesus' own message and aims, and it is not necessary to do so here. For the purposes of this book, the more crucial matter to note is that Jesus' activities clearly generated responses that ranged from a devoted following to mortal opposition, and these reactions to him became much more significant than was probably realized at first. The mortal opposition was manifest in Jesus' arrest, his denunciation by the Jerusalem Temple authorities, and his brutal execution under the authority of Pontius Pilate, the Roman governor of Judea. In the Roman arsenal of execution measures, crucifixion was the particular option for those of lower social orders, especially those deemed guilty of threatening Roman rule. The aim was not simply to terminate an offender's life; it was a public degradation and humiliation of the victim, and was intended to exhibit to all onlookers (and it was conducted as public spectacle) the consequences of daring to challenge Roman authority.[5]

But, against all odds, as it must have seemed at the time, in Jesus' case crucifixion did not have the result intended by his executioners. The form of his execution certainly indicated that he had generated severe hostility. But his grisly death did not by any means end the controversy that he had ignited over what to make of him and his message. Instead, with surprising rapidity, the controversy only became greater, and his followers exhibited a much more startling level of devotion to him. Perhaps within only a few days or weeks of his crucifixion, Jesus' followers were circulating the astonishing claim that God had raised him from death and had installed him in heavenly glory as Messiah and the appointed vehicle of redemption. Moreover, and still more astonishing, these claims were accompanied by an emerging pattern of devotional practices in which Jesus figured with an unprecedented centrality. For example, Jesus' name was invoked as part of the process of initiation into the early circles of those who identified them-

5. Martin Hengel, *Crucifixion in the Ancient World and the Folly of the Message of the Cross* (Philadelphia: Fortress Press, 1977).

selves with reference to Jesus.[6] In short, from a surprisingly early point after his death, Jesus' followers were according to him at a level of devotion that far exceeded their own prior and impressive commitment to him during his lifetime.[7] As I show later in this book (especially in Chapter Two), in the earliest extant artifacts of the Christian movement (texts written scarcely more than twenty years after Jesus' death), we see an amazingly exalted level of devotion to Jesus which at that early point was already commonplace among circles of his followers spread across a wide geographical area.

This devotion to Jesus was also momentous for all subsequent Christianity, which is another important reason to devote careful attention to questions about how and when it developed. Indeed, I contend that the energetic and sometimes complex early Christian efforts to articulate doctrines about Jesus and God in the next few centuries were practically demanded and significantly shaped by the intense devotion to Jesus that we see already expressed in our earliest evidence of the young Christian movement.

It is not possible in this volume to address all the texts and phenomena involved. Instead, I aim here to focus on some key historical issues, in the light of which I believe it will be easier to consider the significant body of remaining matters. I emphasize that I focus here on historical issues and questions, and that no particular personal stance is presumed on the part of the reader. The chronological scope is limited roughly to the first and early second centuries, with particular attention to the earliest evidence and the first-century developments.

The eight chapters of this book represent two collections of studies. The first four chapters (which derive from my four Deichmann lectures) form one collection, and the remaining four chapters derive from previously published journal articles that are devoted to some key issues raised in the first four chapters. It may be helpful for me to sketch a bit further how these studies hang together.

Of course, mine is by no means the first serious effort to deal with these important historical questions. Over the many years of modern

---

6. Lars Hartman, *"Into the Name of the Lord Jesus": Baptism in the Early Church* (Edinburgh: T&T Clark, 1997).

7. Larry W. Hurtado, "Homage to the Historical Jesus and Early Christian Devotion," *Journal for the Study of the Historical Jesus* 1 (2003): 131-46. Chapter Six of this book is a slightly modified version of this article.

scholarly investigation, a number of approaches have been tried. In Chapter One, I give a critical review of various historical approaches to understanding the emergence of Jesus-devotion, indicating the problems in those I find unsatisfactory, and sketching the main features of the approach that I favor. I focus on current scholarly alternatives and key exponents of them. This chapter will help readers to place my discussion on a "map" of current scholarly debate. My main point in this chapter is that earliest devotion to Jesus was a notable phenomenon that justifies a serious effort to understand it in historical terms.

In Chapter Two, I follow up on this by laying out the major evidence and factors that I believe require us to see the emergence of Jesus-devotion as a development initially *within* circles of Second-Temple devout Jews. That is, in this sense, devotion to Jesus initially appeared historically as an innovation in Second-Temple Jewish religion. I also emphasize in this chapter that in the crucial early decades of the young Christian movement, Jesus' exalted status was consistently affirmed in relation to the one God of biblical tradition. Devotion to Jesus was combined with a continuing monotheistic stance that promoted the disdain for participation in the worship of the many other deities of the Roman religious environment. In early Christian circles, however, this exclusivist stance also accommodated reverence for Jesus. But these early believers did not assent to the charge that they worshipped two deities. They insisted that Jesus' exalted status "at God's right hand" had been affirmed by the one God, and they saw their reverence of Jesus as obedience to the will of the one God who had given Jesus heavenly glory with the intention of all creation acclaiming Jesus as Lord.

In Chapter Three, I discuss some of the social and political consequences of devotion to Jesus for early Christians, particularly the negative consequences, the social costs of being a Christian in the earliest period. It is reasonable to suppose that the actual level of negative consequences experienced by Christians varied, and I do not intend to suggest that all believers were subject to any and all of the sorts of experiences and stresses that I refer to in this chapter. But it is fairly clear that a good many Christians did face the possibility of paying social costs for their faith, ranging from ridicule to much more painful opposition, whether from family members or wider social circles. And some Christians did find that their faith even led to trouble with the political authorities (usually local authorities). As I note, this was apparently rather more uncommon initially, but by the early second century things were looking a bit more widely ominous, at least for some Christian leaders.

In Chapter Four, I narrow the focus down to one particular text from a letter of the Apostle Paul, Philippians 2:6-11, which is widely acknowledged among scholars in Christian origins as one of the most important early expressions of devotion to Jesus. I engage here in a more detailed and sustained analysis of this one text, which I offer as a "case study" of a key passage that probably takes us back to within the first couple of decades of the Christian movement. This particular passage, widely thought to comprise the wording of an early Christian ode or hymn used in worship, has received an enormous amount of attention by scholars, which illustrates its historical importance. In spite of the many previous discussions of the passage, I hope to contribute something further to our appreciation of this fascinating text.

In my approach to early Christian devotion, I make frequent reference to ancient Jewish "monotheism" and its importance for relevant historical matters. "Monotheism" is a modern scholarly term, and not one used in the ancient sources. Moreover, there are controversies associated with the term in current scholarly debate. Some voices even question whether it is appropriate to ascribe "monotheism" to Roman-era Jewish religion. In Chapter Five I engage these controversies and try to indicate how and why it is appropriate to refer to Second-Temple Jewish religion as "monotheistic." If, as I contend, earliest Christianity emerged in the matrix of Second-Temple Jewish tradition, then it is important to have as accurate a grasp as we can obtain of what that religious tradition comprised. More particularly, I argue that the remarkable nature of earliest devotion to Jesus is more clearly appreciated when we see it in the context of ancient Jewish concerns about the uniqueness of the one God.

In Chapter Six I take up the question of how early Christian devotion might compare with, and be related to, the sort of stance toward Jesus that likely characterized his followers in the time of his own historical career. I analyze the way that the four canonical Gospels (our earliest narrative traditions about Jesus) portray people giving homage to Jesus, and I focus particularly on the use of the Greek term *proskynein* (meaning "to reverence, give homage, worship"). I contend that, although it is entirely likely that those who accepted Jesus' message about the kingdom of God gave Jesus homage and reverence, the level of cultic reverence that characterized early Christian churches represents a considerable further elevation of devotion.

Some scholars have expressed doubt, however, that the devotion to Jesus that I underscore really amounted to treating Jesus as divine in the earliest decades and in Jewish-Christian circles. Had early Jewish Christians treated Jesus as divine, had their devotion to him been seen to amount to "worship," this would have generated outrage and opposition from fellow Jews. But (so the argument goes) what indication do we have that this happened? In Chapter Seven I engage this question, showing that in fact we have clear indication that rather serious Jewish opposition to early Christian devotion to Jesus appeared early. Moreover, I argue that the level of opposition suggests that devotion to Jesus was perceived as a seriously outrageous phenomenon by some Jews concerned with protecting their religious traditions. This in turn confirms that what generated this kind of opposition likely involved treating Jesus as divine and in ways that represented a significant innovation in Jewish religious practice of the time.

How can we account for such a significant innovation in a religious tradition in historical terms? Some contend that any major innovation must be explained as the influence of beliefs and/or practices from another religion or religious tradition. It is entirely likely that some religious innovations are the result of such "syncretistic" processes. But for a number of years I have argued that some significant innovations in religious traditions can be traced back to powerful religious experiences that come with the force of new revelation to those who receive such experiences. In Chapter Eight I lay out the rationale for my view, drawing upon a variety of studies in the history of religions and in modern social-scientific studies of new/emergent religious movements. I offer this chapter in support of my contention that such powerful religious experiences are to be reckoned with as one important factor in the eruption of devotion to Jesus in earliest Christianity.

So, there you have the basic coherence of this volume and the rationale for what I have included in it. Above all, I hope that I have been clear in what I contend, fair to other scholars with whom I interact here, and successful in communicating how remarkable early devotion to Jesus is.

One final explanatory comment, especially for readers beyond the circle of scholars of religion. In the following chapters I will sometimes use the adjective "cultic" to designate certain kinds of devotion or reverence given to Jesus. I consistently use the term not in its popular and pejorative sense, as describing something unsavory pertaining to a "cult," but in its academic and technical sense, which derives from the Latin word *cultus*, which refers to worship (and particularly to sacrifice, which was typically the key action in ancient worship). That is, by "cultic" devotion/reverence/veneration, as I use the term, I mean devotional actions that form part of the corporate worship practices of a given group. It carries no negative connotation. The devotion given to Jesus in earliest Christianity is remarkable, and also a significant historical problem. To this we turn in the following chapter.

PART I

ISSUES AND APPROACHES

CHAPTER ONE

How on Earth Did Jesus Become a God?
Approaches to Jesus-Devotion in Earliest Christianity

About 112 C.E., while serving as special imperial legate in the Roman province of Bithynia, Pliny "the Younger" wrote a fascinating letter to the emperor Trajan. In it he describes how he handled people who were denounced to him as Christians, and what he learned about their religious commitments and activities. Among the information that he derived from his brutal interrogation of them, Pliny learned that a prominent feature of their gatherings was to "chant antiphonally a hymn to Christ as to a god."[1] Pliny's testimony to early Christian faith and practice is all the more notable because it comes from an obviously hostile witness. For our purposes, the crucial matters are that he attests the centrality of the figure of Jesus in early Christian piety and vividly reflects the further fact that in early Christian circles Jesus was a recipient of worship such as was given to a deity.

Moreover, Pliny says that he was also able to confirm that those who were truly Christians could not be persuaded to demonstrate reverence for the pagan gods and the image of the emperor, or to curse Jesus, even on threat of death. So the reverence given to Jesus was offered by people who sharply distinguished their religious orientation from the wider religious

---

1. Pliny (the Younger), *Epistles*, 10.96. English translation and commentary can be found in *A New Eusebius: Documents Illustrative of the History of the Church to A.D. 337*, ed. J. Stevenson (London: SPCK, 1974), 13-15. For basic information on Pliny, see, e.g., Michael P. McHugh, "Pliny the Younger," in *Encyclopedia of Early Christianity*, 2d ed., ed. Everett Ferguson (New York/London: Garland Publishing, 1998), 928. Pliny is usually cited as crucial evidence about the development of Roman imperial policy toward Christians. Trajan's reply to Pliny's letter is also interesting to note; see Stevenson, 16.

environment of the time, and who were ready to pay for this stance with their lives. Their refusal to reverence the pagan gods echoes ancient Jewish monotheistic practice, from which the Christian position was derived. Yet the early Christians whom Pliny interrogated also combined this negative stance toward the many deities of the Roman world with a distinctive readiness to include Jesus as a rightful recipient of worship. This makes their worship of Jesus all the more notable. For it did not simply represent an inclusion of Jesus as a new divine figure in the diverse circle of gods and demigods that made up the pagan pantheon. Instead, the devotion to Jesus described by Pliny amounted to a remarkable one-of-a-kind accommodation of Jesus to a level of reverence that the Christians otherwise fiercely reserved for the one God of biblical tradition.

Of course, belief that Jesus is somehow divine, and the accompanying practice of treating him as a rightful recipient of worship, characterize Christianity down through the centuries. But when did this faith and devotional practice first appear, and how are we to understand it in *historical* terms? Various answers to these questions have been proposed by scholars, and for a number of years I too have been heavily involved in searching for answers, and advocating the ones that I find most persuasive. In this chapter I want to review briefly some major approaches to these questions in contemporary scholarship and indicate in basic terms why I prefer the position with which I have associated myself.

I wish to emphasize that the views I advocate here reflect and build upon the work of a number of other contemporary scholars as well. The footnotes in my own publications make evident my dependence on, and agreement with, scholars in various countries who take a somewhat similar approach. So, although in what follows I will speak for myself, the views I advocate are by no means idiosyncratic, and I do not claim sole credit for them.

Worship of Jesus as Evolutionary Development

The first essential observation from which to proceed is that, in the context of ancient Jewish monotheistic scruples (inherited by earliest Christians from the Jewish religious matrix of the Christian movement), the worship of Jesus is truly an extraordinary phenomenon. It is entirely reasonable, thus, that various scholars have seen this devotion to Jesus as conceivable only as an evolutionary development that was somehow linked to the changing nature of the Christian movement across the first century C.E. The specifics vary from one scholar to another, but common to all of the evolutionary proposals is the claim that the worship of Jesus as divine cannot have been a part of the devotional pattern that characterized earliest strata and circles of Jewish Christians. In order to assess any such proposal, it is necessary to be acquainted with the basic shape of the development of earliest Christianity. For those who may not be familiar with the matter, I offer a very brief sketch before we proceed farther.

What became early "Christianity" originated as a small but vigorous messianic group among Jews in Roman Judea,[2] and then quickly spread to Jewish Diaspora locations where non-Jews, "Gentiles," were also among those recruited/converted (initially, perhaps, among those "God-fearing" Gentiles who had become interested in Jewish religion through contacts with Jews in the Diaspora).[3] Especially (but not exclusively) through the programmatic efforts of the figure known as the Apostle Paul (Saul of Tarsus), by about 60 C.E. (i.e., within the first three decades after Jesus' execution) small clusters of converts were established in various cities of Roman Asia and Greece, and (through the efforts of other, largely anonymous believers) in other key places such as Antioch, Damascus, Rome, and perhaps also Egypt. As well, especially in these Diaspora sites, the Christian movement included increasing numbers of Gentiles along with a continuing and influential core of Jewish believers. By the final decades of the first century, however, Gentile converts probably outnumbered Jewish believers by a significant margin, and developments within Judaism of the post-70 C.E. period included an increasingly sharp rejection of Jewish Christians.[4]

2. In the first century C.E., the Roman province of "Judea" was the area later renamed "Palestine," comprising the traditional component-areas of Galilee, Samaria, and Judea.

3. For a discussion of various responses of Gentiles to Jewish religion in the Roman period, see S. J. D. Cohen, "Crossing the Boundary and Becoming a Jew," *Harvard Theological Review* 82 (1989): 13-33. In the Acts of the Apostles in the New Testament, the stories of Philip and the Ethiopian eunuch (8:26-40) and of Peter at the house of the Roman centurion Cornelius (10:1-48) reflect the presence of Gentiles whose conversion to Christian faith had been preceded by their interest in Judaism.

4. It is widely thought that in the post-70 C.E. period Jewish Christians were put under great pressure by fellow Jews to renounce Jesus or to sever their connection with their Jewish community. There are references to Jewish believers being expelled from the synagogues in the Gospel of John (9:22; 12:42; 16:2). Scholars debate the question of whether the *Birkhat ha-Minim* (the "Benediction against the Heretics," the twelfth benediction of the synagogue

Essentially, in one way or another, proposals that the "divinization" of Jesus happened in an evolutionary manner all presuppose and invoke the geographical spread and increasingly large Gentile composition of Christianity, and the correspondingly decreased place and influence of Jewish Christians as the key context.

The most influential articulation of such a view emerged from the impressive body of scholarly work conducted by a group of scholars known as the *religionsgeschichtliche Schule*, who flourished in the closing decades of the nineteenth century and the early decades of the twentieth century. In particular, the oft-cited study by Wilhelm Bousset, *Kyrios Christos* (1913), located the emergence of the worship of Jesus in early "Hellenistic Gentile" circles, among whom a background of pagan reverence of demigods and divinized heroes could have provided the crucial atmosphere, model, and influence.[5] Bousset posited such circles of Gentile Christians in Syria in the early/middle decades of the first century C.E. In his view, it was the religious faith of these Hellenistic Gentile Christians that also shaped the beliefs of the Apostle Paul, through whose mission to the Gentiles the reverence of Jesus as divine then spread widely.

To his credit, Bousset understood that what he called the "Christ cult" (worship of Jesus as divine) actually emerged fairly early.[6] But he asserted that it did not go back to originating circles of Jewish Christians in Roman Judea. Bousset portrayed the "divinization" of Jesus as, instead, essentially produced under the impact of the larger pagan religious environment, which had this effect in Christian circles in major Diaspora locations such

---

prayer, the *Shemoneh Esreh*) was used against Jewish Christians. For a classic defense of the claim, see J. Louis Martyn, *History and Theology in the Fourth Gospel*, rev. ed. (Nashville: Abingdon, 1979), 37-62; and also William Horbury, "The Benediction of the Minim and Early Jewish-Christian Controversy," *Journal of Theological Studies* 33 (1982): 19-61. But cf. Reuven Kimelman, "The *Birkat Ha-Minim* and the Lack of Evidence for an Anti-Christian Prayer in Late Antiquity," in *Jewish and Christian Self-Definition*, vol. 2, ed. E. P. Sanders, A. I. Baumgarten, and A. Mendelson (Philadelphia: Fortress Press, 1981), 226-44.

5. Wilhelm Bousset, *Kyrios Christos: Geschichte des Christusglaubens von den Anfängen des Christentums bis Irenaeus*, Forschungen zur Religion und Literatur des Alten und Neuen Testaments, NF4 (Göttingen: Vandenhoeck & Ruprecht, 1913; 2d ed., 1921). Here I cite the English translation: *Kyrios Christos: A History of the Belief in Christ from the Beginnings of Christianity to Irenaeus*, trans. J. E. Steely (Nashville: Abingdon, 1970).

6. Scholars often use the word "cult" to mean formal worship of a deity (in the ancient world, usually involving sacrifice to the deity), and the word "cultic" to characterize actions associated with such formal worship. That is how I use these words in this book.

as Antioch. Moreover, he regarded this development as a regrettable deviation from what he claimed was the faith of the "Primitive Palestinian
Community," among whom Jesus was simply revered as the divinely appointed "Son of Man," a messianic figure who would return from his exalted place in heaven at some imminent moment to bring final redemption. He referred to "doubtful aspects" of the reverence given to Jesus in
these "Hellenistic Gentile" circles, and "the burdening and complicating of
the simple belief in God through the introduction of the cultic worship of
the Kyrios Christos." Yet, he allowed, "one will have to concede that it came
about with an inner necessity," for the religious environment demanded it,
and these "Hellenistic Gentile communities" had to compete in the religious marketplace of the time by introducing a deity of their own.[7]

The success of Bousset's view in influencing subsequent opinion was
due in part to his impressive scholarship, but also surely derived from the
intuitive appeal of his view. Granted, it is intuitively difficult to imagine
that devout Jews of the time could have accommodated a second figure
alongside God as a rightful recipient of worship in their devotional pattern. Consequently, in subsequent scholarly discussion, one finds confident exponents of Bousset's position, or variations on it. Indeed, it may be
that in some circles this sort of position is simply taken for granted as obviously offering the explanation that best accounts for things.

Over twenty years ago, however, I underscored some key problems in
Bousset's study and contended that the whole subject needed a fresh and
thorough analysis.[8] In subsequent publications over the last couple of decades, I have joined with other scholars in showing that the evidence demands a more satisfactory account than Bousset provided, and in Chapter
Two of the present book I sketch the case for another point of view that I
present in more extended form in a larger recent volume.[9] To be sure,
Bousset was a learned man, but for all his considerable learning, he worked
with a seriously inaccurate and somewhat simplistic view of earliest Christian history and also of Roman-era Jewish tradition.[10]

---

7. Bousset, *Kyrios Christos,* 151.

8. Larry W. Hurtado, "New Testament Christology: A Critique of Bousset's Influence,"
Theological Studies 40 (1979): 306-17.

9. Larry W. Hurtado, *Lord Jesus Christ: Devotion to Jesus in Earliest Christianity* (Grand
Rapids: Eerdmans, 2003). See esp. 5-18 for further comments on Bousset and other major
publications relevant to early devotion to Jesus.

10. See also my critique of Bousset's characterization of ancient Jewish interest in an-

Yet Bousset's view continues to be espoused with minor adaptations in current scholarly literature. To cite one example, Burton Mack posits anonymous circles of Christians in Syria, among whom the "Christ cult" supposedly had its origin, and Mack sharply differentiates these circles from the original follows of Jesus in Roman Judea, for whom Jesus was supposedly only an inspiring teacher.[11] On the surface, this may seem a plausible possibility. But, as I see the matter, Mack is able to maintain such a view only by resolute unwillingness to engage the full evidence concerning the origins of Christianity.

The British New Testament scholar Maurice Casey has offered what amounts to a somewhat more significant variation on Bousset's approach. Essentially, Casey contends that a view of Jesus as divine could have emerged only under the impact of "Gentile self-identification," the consequence of which, he alleges, included a greater readiness among Gentile Christians to accommodate more than one recipient of worship. In Casey's view, as Gentile converts, supposedly less sensitive to monotheistic concerns, came to make up an increasingly large and influential portion of Christianity in the later decades of the first century, they provided the crucial factor that enabled the divinization of Jesus.[12]

Casey contends that the full divinization of Jesus is really first evident in the Gospel of John, which is usually thought to have been composed sometime in the 80s of the first century c.e. So, like Bousset, Casey sees the worship of Jesus as basically due to the influence of pagan religious practice and ideas, mediated and enabled through significant numbers of inadequately converted Gentile Christians who were not sensitive to Jewish concerns about the uniqueness of the God of the biblical tradition. We should also note, however, that Casey locates the emergence of a genuinely divine Jesus several decades later than in Bousset's scheme, in the Christian circle reflected in the Gospel of John, not in Bousset's putative circles of "Hellenistic Gentile" Christians in Antioch.

To my mind, this is one of the major difficulties with Casey's position.

gels and "intermediary" figures in Larry W. Hurtado, *One God, One Lord: Early Christian Devotion and Ancient Jewish Monotheism* (Philadelphia: Fortress Press, 1988; 2d ed., Edinburgh: T&T Clark, 1998; reprint, London: T&T Clark International, 2003), esp. 24-27.

11. Burton L. Mack, *A Myth of Innocence: Mark and Christian Origins* (Philadelphia: Fortress Press, 1988).

12. Maurice Casey, *From Jewish Prophet to Gentile God: The Origins and Development of New Testament Christology* (Cambridge: James Clarke & Co., 1991).

As I shall show more fully in the next chapter, the chronological data do not readily support a claim that devotion to Jesus as divine first emerged in the late first century. More recently, Casey has granted that within the first few decades of the Christian movement we see "a serious development of monotheism," but he insists that "we have not yet reached the historical origins of the worship of Jesus, though some steps in that direction have been taken."[13] As I see things, however, the fine distinction that Casey tries to make is dubious, and his efforts to limit the significance of early phenomena are not persuasive. In my view, Casey has failed to recognize adequately the significance of the devotion to Jesus, involving both beliefs and devotional practices, that is already evident in our earliest Christian sources.

Like Casey, another contemporary British New Testament scholar, James Dunn, also claims that the worship of Jesus first emerged in the late first century C.E., and he too points to the Gospel of John as giving the first clear evidence of this development.[14] For Dunn, as for Casey, it is simply inconceivable that someone like the Apostle Paul could have countenanced the worship of a second figure alongside the one God. So, no matter how impressive the manifestations of devotion to Jesus that are reflected in Paul's letters (which come from the first few decades of the Christian movement), these simply cannot have been intended or understood as "worship" in the sense of reverence of a divine figure.[15]

In Dunn's view, however, the development of the worship of Jesus was not so much the product of Gentiles and pagan religious influence. Rightly, as I judge it, he is more ready than Casey to see the worship of Jesus as a distinctively Christian extension of religious dynamics and trends that were operative within Second-Temple Jewish monotheistic tradition,

---

13. P. M. Casey, "Monotheism, Worship, and Christological Developments in the Pauline Churches," in *The Jewish Roots of Christological Monotheism: Papers from the St. Andrews Conference on the Historical Origins of the Worship of Jesus,* ed. Carey C. Newman, James R. Davila, and Gladys S. Lewis (Leiden: E. J. Brill, 1999), 214-33.

14. But, in spite of broad similarity in their positions, Dunn has expressed strong criticism of Casey's scheme. See J. D. G. Dunn, "The Making of Christology — Evolution or Unfolding?" in *Jesus of Nazareth: Lord and Christ: Essays on the Historical Jesus and New Testament Christology,* ed. Joel B. Green and Max Turner (Grand Rapids/Carlisle: Eerdmans/Paternoster Press, 1994), 437-52.

15. See, e.g., James D. G. Dunn, *The Theology of Paul the Apostle* (Grand Rapids: Eerdmans; Edinburgh: T&T Clark, 1998), esp. 252-60.

in which there were interesting speculations about various figures portrayed as God's principal agent.[16] But he agrees with Casey that the unique extension of these trends that is involved in the worship of Jesus as divine is to be located in the Christian circles that are reflected in the Gospel of John, and that this development should be dated in the later decades of the first century C.E.[17]

In my view, however, Dunn, like Casey, underestimates the historical import of the pattern of devotional practice that we see already fully taken for granted in our earliest Christian sources, writings that take us back to the first couple of decades of the Christian movement. Dunn is correct in stating that the worship of Jesus would have been profoundly offensive to traditionally devout Jews. But his claim that there is no evidence of Jewish opposition to devotion to Jesus in Christian sources earlier than the Gospel of John is simply incorrect, as I will show in Chapter Seven of this volume.[18] From the earliest days of Jewish Christianity, it appears that devotion to Jesus was a cause of serious disputation and even persecution by some Jews who saw it as a disturbing threat to the uniqueness of the one God of Israel.

Worship of Jesus as Jewish "Cult" of Messiah and Martyrs

A very different position is taken by William Horbury, who proposes that the "cult of Christ" (the worship of Jesus as divine) is to be understood historically as an adaptation of the veneration of royal and messianic figures and martyrs in ancient Jewish tradition.[19] Horbury rightly sees that the worship of Jesus is not an incremental and evolutionary development that is to be attributed to Gentile converts and pagan religious influences. In-

---

16. I have myself discussed these phenomena and their relationship to the worship of Jesus in Hurtado, *One God, One Lord,* esp. 17-92. See also pp. 31 and 57-58 of the present book.

17. Dunn, "The Making of Christology," esp. 446-47. "The development within the NT is not so much from Jewish prophet to *Gentile* God, as from Jewish prophet to *Jewish* God; it is precisely that development and the problems it caused within Judaism which is reflected in the Fourth Gospel [Gospel of John]" (p. 447).

18. Chapter Seven appeared earlier as "Pre-70 C.E. Jewish Opposition to Christ-Devotion," *Journal of Theological Studies* 50 (1999): 35-58.

19. William Horbury, *Jewish Messianism and the Cult of Christ* (London: SCM Press, 1998).

stead, as he argues, the reverence given to Jesus represents the influence of precedents and dynamics already operative in Second-Temple Jewish tradition. Horbury claims that there was a tradition of "cult" given to royal and messianic figures and that the reverence of Jewish martyrs likewise is to be seen as a "cultic" precedent of devotion to Jesus. In short, Horbury presents the worship of Jesus as basically an early Christian variation on a religious outlook and practice well established in the ancient Jewish matrix of earliest Christianity.

Certainly, earliest Christian reverence for Jesus seems to have drawn upon pre-Christian Jewish tradition, especially ancient Jewish ideas about God having what we term a "principal agent." That is, typically in earliest Christian sources, Jesus is linked with God and is given a unique status in relation to God — for instance, as God's "Son" or "Messiah" (Christ) or "Word" or "Servant." In ancient Jewish sources, this sort of "principal agent" role is played sometimes by a great angel (such as Michael), sometimes by a great human figure of the past (such as Moses or Enoch), and sometimes by one of God's own attributes (such as divine Wisdom or God's Word, pictured in personified forms). Moreover, it is also clear that ancient Jewish messianic hopes were certainly appropriated and addressed in earliest Christian articulation of Jesus' significance. But, as I observed in a review of one of Horbury's publications,

> The problem is that Horbury defines "cult" so vaguely (and unhelpfully) that it includes any kind of respect or reverence, and then [he] treats all expressions and forms of respect/reverence as if they basically amount to the same thing and/or explain one another. In this, he ignores the very real Jewish (and Christian) concerns about differentiating God from other beings (even other heavenly, "divine" beings of God's entourage), especially in the kind of reverence given, and [he underestimates] the remarkable difference from contemporary Jewish practice constituted by the pattern of devotion given to Jesus in earliest Christianity.[20]

In short, in spite of his considerable learning in ancient Jewish evidence, Horbury seems to me to blur unhelpfully the very real differences between ancient Jewish reverence for martyrs, messiahs, or other figures,

20. Larry W. Hurtado, review of William Horbury, *Messianism among Jews and Christians* (London: T&T Clark International, 2003), in *Themelios* 29 (2004): 57-58.

and the distinctive pattern of devotion to Jesus in early Christian sources, and he fails in attempting to offer a historical explanation for the worship of Jesus. The fact is that we simply have no evidence that any figure, whether human or angelic, ever featured in the corporate and public devotional practice of Jewish circles in any way really comparable to the programmatic role of Jesus in early Christian circles. For instance, the praise of Judean kings reflected in some of the Psalms and the reverence later shown for Jewish martyrs do not provide genuine analogies or precedents, and cannot, thus, furnish an adequate historical explanation.

Worship of Jesus as Theological Inference

Yet another approach is to portray the worship of Jesus as basically a consequence of some theological conviction, which is posited as the really important matter. In short, the worship of Jesus is presented as essentially an inferential development that seemed to early Christians fully appropriate in light of their belief that Jesus held some uniquely exalted status.

For instance, in a recently published Ph.D. thesis, Timo Eskola proposes that the key factor which explains the worship of Jesus was the belief that Jesus had been enthroned in heaven. Drawing comparisons with Jewish *merkavah* mysticism, Eskola contends that early Christians came to the conviction about Jesus' heavenly enthronement.[21] Then, having come to believe that Jesus shared the divine throne, it seemed to them that worshipping him was the proper thing to do.

Richard Bauckham has proposed a more elaborate version of a similar point of view.[22] Bauckham contends that the worship of Jesus was a consequence and corollary of early Christians' belief that Jesus shared in what he calls the "divine identity," the key features of which were God's unique

21. Timo Eskola, *Messiah and the Throne: Jewish Merkabah Mysticism and Early Christian Exaltation Discourse*, WUNT, 2/142 (Tübingen: Mohr Siebeck, 2001). "Merkavah" means "chariot," and in some ancient Jewish mystical texts the term is used to refer to the throne of God, based on the vision in Ezekiel 1, where God is pictured as sitting on a wheeled throne, a chariot-throne. For discussion, see, e.g., Ithamar Gruenwald, *Apocalyptic and Merkavah Mysticism* (Leiden: E. J. Brill, 1980); Ira Chernus, *Mysticism in Rabbinic Judaism* (Berlin/New York: Walter de Gruyter, 1982).

22. Richard Bauckham, *God Crucified: Monotheism and Christology in the New Testament* (Carlisle, U.K.: Paternoster Press, 1998).

roles as creator of all and ruler of all. In Bauckham's view, the ancient Jewish monotheistic worship of God was predicated on the belief that the one God had created all things and was the one ruler of everything. So, when Christians became convinced that Jesus had uniquely participated in the creation all things (as reflected, e.g., in 1 Cor. 8:6; Heb. 1:2; John 1:1-3; Col. 1:15-17) and now shared the divine throne as ruler of all (e.g., Phil. 2:9-11), they felt free to extend worship to Jesus as well. For Bauckham, as for Eskola, the worship of Jesus, though a notable phenomenon, is secondary in historical importance to the theological convictions about Jesus' high status and significance, which form the center of attention in their studies.

To be sure, both Eskola and Bauckham see the theological beliefs that they highlight, and the consequential worship of Jesus, as having appeared very early, at or near the outset of the early Christian movement. So, no extended evolutionary development is involved, and they do justice to the very early evidence of cultic devotion to Jesus. Moreover, there were surely religious convictions involved in the extension of early Christian worship practice to include Jesus as recipient of such devotion. But some problems in the approach taken by Bauckham and Eskola make me hesitate to follow it entirely.

First, they do not offer an adequate explanation of how these key and very influential theological convictions appeared, for which the worship of Jesus was a supposedly logical and historical consequence. This lack is all the more curious given the historical importance that Bauckham and Eskola attach to these convictions, as essentially generating the worship of Jesus. Surely a fully satisfactory attempt at this sort of historical analysis must include some account in *historical* terms of how these supposedly crucial convictions arose.

Moreover, the credibility of the proposal would be enhanced considerably if we had an analogous development of the kind alleged by Eskola and Bauckham. If in ancient Jewish tradition the worship of a figure was essentially the logical corollary and consequence of holding certain theological convictions about the figure, then we would expect to find other examples of this. More particularly, we should hope to find one or more other examples of such a development *within Jewish monotheistic tradition of the Second-Temple period*. Indeed, it is rather essential to have precisely such analogies.

We do have indications that in ancient Jewish tradition certain figures were portrayed honorifically in ways that are analogous to some of the claims made for Jesus in earliest Christianity. Although Bauckham seeks to minimize the number of these analogies, he grants that divine Wisdom, for example, was sometimes portrayed as God's co-worker in the creation of the world, and God's throne-companion active in the governing of all things (e.g., Prov. 8:27-31; *Wisd. of Sol.* 7:21-22; 8:1-6; 9:1-4, 10-11; 10:1–11:20). If, however, for Roman-era Jews the cultic worship of a figure was simply the historical and logical consequence of belief that the figure shares with God in the creation and superintendence of all other things, then why do we have no indication of a cultic reverence specifically directed toward God's Wisdom or Word, each of which was certainly portrayed in highly personified and exalted terms?

In addition, I am not persuaded by the supposed logic asserted. To posit the origin of the worship of Jesus essentially as the consequence of understanding his exalted status in certain terms seems to me to reflect a failure to grasp how crucial worship practice was in defining all ancient religion, and especially how it defined and distinguished ancient Jewish religion. As I have shown in my 1988 book, *One God, One Lord,* devout Jews of Second-Temple time were often quite ready to portray this or that figure in astonishingly exalted terms (whether divine attributes such as divine Wisdom or the divine Word, or principal angels such as Michael or Yahoel, or revered ancestors such as Enoch or Moses).[23] Indeed, a number of the specific claims about Jesus in the New Testament have precedents and analogies in some of the claims made for these figures in sources that derive from or reflect Second-Temple Jewish circles. But what we do not find in the Second-Temple Jewish tradition is the further, momentous step of treating any such figure as a recipient of cultic devotion that in any way parallels the devotion given to Jesus in earliest Christianity.

The devotion given to Jesus was without true analogy, and so is a remarkable and puzzling historical phenomenon that requires more effort to account for it than has often been recognized. Just as it cannot accurately be taken as a late and evolutionary development influenced and prompted by pagan traditions of apotheosis of divine heroes and the welcome of new/additional gods for the pantheon, so devotion to Jesus cannot adequately be seen as simply the consequence of attributing to him a special place in relation to God in creation, governance, and redemption of the world. Though I agree that beliefs about Jesus were major components of

23. Hurtado, *One God, One Lord,* 17-92.

early Christian devotion to Jesus, I contend that for ancient Jewish Christians the worship of Jesus was far too momentous a step for it to have originated essentially as an inference from the theological convictions that Bauckham and Eskola underscore.

In summary, none of the sorts of approaches that I have referred to here seems to me to be fully accurate and/or adequate as giving a historical understanding of the origins of the kind of devotion to Jesus that is reflected in the New Testament. In the remaining part of this discussion, I sketch the basics of the approach that I prefer.

Worship of Jesus: A More Adequate Approach

To appreciate the need for a more adequate approach, we need to remind ourselves of a few basic facts. The first thing to highlight is how early the worship of Jesus originated. In the following chapter, I will discuss the evidence for this more fully. At this point, I simply want to emphasize that the origins of the worship of Jesus are so early that practically any evolutionary approach is rendered invalid as historical explanation. Our earliest Christian writings, from approximately 50-60 C.E., already presuppose cultic devotion to Jesus as a familiar and defining feature of Christian circles wherever they were found (e.g., 1 Cor. 1:2). So, instead of an evolutionary/incremental model, we have to think in terms of something more adequate. What we have suggested in the evidence is a more explosively quick phenomenon, a religious development that was more like a volcanic eruption.

Moreover, as I have emphasized already, the worship of Jesus is both remarkable and without real analogy in the ancient setting, and so requires particular effort to deal with it as a historical phenomenon. Certainly, various deities were reverenced in the Roman period, and it was in principle no problem to enfranchise another divine figure in the religious "cafeteria" of the time. But it was a major and unprecedented move for people influenced by the exclusivist monotheistic stance of Second-Temple Judaism to include another figure singularly alongside God as recipient of cultic devotion in their worship gatherings. That is, in the devotional practices and attendant beliefs of earliest Christian circles, Jesus was linked with God in astonishing and unprecedented ways. Indeed, it is rather clear that many contemporary Jews who did not share the faith of these early circles of

Christians regarded this elevation of Jesus as completely inappropriate, even blasphemous.[24]

This close association of Jesus with God is reflected in the way that earliest Christians understood Psalm 110, which seems to have been one of their most widely used biblical passages. They saw God and Jesus in the opening words where "the LORD says to my lord, 'Sit at my right hand . . .'" (110:1).[25] Similarly, as I emphasize in a later chapter, in Philippians 2:9-11 Jesus is linked with God as rightful recipient of the universal submission and reverence portrayed in Isaiah 45:23.

In fact, it is this pattern of cultic devotion, with Jesus included programmatically alongside the one God, that probably comprises the most characteristic and most notable feature of earliest Christianity. That is, we are dealing with a central, major, and absolutely crucial phenomenon. In the Roman era (as seems to have been the case generally in the ancient world), worship practice (usually sacrifice) was the key expression of religion, and the most characteristic way of affirming one's participation in and adherence to a religious position or group. In the Second-Temple period, devout Jews chose to express the distinctiveness of their religious stance most vividly and firmly in the area of worship, absolutely refusing to join in the worship of any figure but the God of biblical revelation.[26] From the Maccabean struggle onward into the Roman period, worship was the key area in which Jewish religious distinctiveness was most sharply exhibited (and was the feature of Jewish religion that often drew criticism from non-Jews). Those who persecuted Jews for their faith did not present them with a creedal statement to sign, but instead urged and demanded gestures of worship that signified acceptance of the other gods of the time, and in that setting the most sensitive concern of devout Jews was to maintain God's uniqueness in their worship practice (e.g., 1 Macc. 2:15-26).

Consequently, in view of its astonishingly early origins, the lack of valid precedent and analogy, and the crucial significance of scruples about worship among devout Second-Temple Jews, we require some serious and creative historical analysis to account for, and understand, the origins of

---

24. Again, I refer readers to my article "Pre-70 C.E. Jewish Opposition to Christ-Devotion," Chapter Seven of this book.

25. On earliest Christian use of this Psalm, see, e.g., Martin Hengel, *Studies in Early Christology* (Edinburgh: T&T Clark, 1995), 119-225; David M. Hay, *Glory at the Right Hand: Psalm 110 in Early Christianity* (Nashville: Abingdon Press, 1973).

26. See Chapter Five.

the worship of Jesus as divine in a religious movement that emerged in Second-Temple Judaism. These factors, which make devotion to Jesus so remarkable, will help to explain why I have devoted over twenty years of effort to this matter. In the final part of this discussion, I briefly itemize major features of the approach that I have helped to develop and advocate.

1. The focus of the approach includes devotional practice as well as religious beliefs. Other scholars have typically tended to concentrate more on "Christology," the beliefs about Jesus in early Christianity, and the terms used to express these beliefs; they have given surprisingly little attention to devotional practice. So, for example, much of this scholarly study of earliest Christology has focused on the honorific titles applied to Jesus, and on particular doctrines such as the belief in his resurrection or his miraculous birth or his "pre-existence" in heaven prior to his earthly existence. Likewise, study of early hymns about Jesus has tended to focus almost entirely on the contents, with little attention given to the significance of the *practice* of singing such hymns as a component of early Christian worship. Instead of "Christology," however, I focus on "devotion" to Jesus, a wider field of phenomena, within which I include "Christology" but also devotional practices as well. "Devotion" is my *portmanteau* term to designate all that was involved in the place of Jesus in earliest Christian belief and religious life. In particular, I emphasize the importance of the pattern of early Christian devotional *practice*, and I propose that it amounts to the worship of Jesus as divine.

2. In an effort to avoid both unhelpful abstractions and assertions that cannot easily be tested, I have underscored specific and demonstrable devotional actions attested in our earliest Christian sources, contending that these phenomena comprise a novel and significant pattern that signals Jesus' divine status. In several publications, from my 1988 book *One God, One Lord* onward, I have pointed to six specific practices that constitute this novel and remarkable pattern of devotion that is evident in our earliest Christian sources.[27] These are the follow-

27. Hurtado, *One God, One Lord,* 100-14; Larry W. Hurtado, "The Binitarian Shape of Early Christian Worship," in *The Jewish Roots of Christological Monotheism*, ed. Carey C. Newman, James R. Davila, and Gladys S. Lewis, JSJSup 63 (Leiden: E. J. Brill, 1999), 187-213 (esp. 192-211).

ing practices: (1) hymns about Jesus sung as part of early Christian worship; (2) prayer to God "through" Jesus and "in Jesus' name," and even direct prayer to Jesus himself, including particularly the invocation of Jesus in the corporate worship setting; (3) "calling upon the name of Jesus," particularly in Christian baptism and in healing and exorcism; (4) the Christian common meal enacted as a sacred meal where the risen Jesus presides as "Lord" of the gathered community; (5) the practice of ritually "confessing" Jesus in the context of Christian worship; and (6) Christian prophecy as oracles of the risen Jesus, and the Holy Spirit of prophecy understood as also the Spirit of Jesus.

Focusing on these specific phenomena more readily facilitates exploration for any precedents and analogies. The result of such exploration is that in Second-Temple Judaism there is no real analogy for these individual actions, and the cumulative pattern of devotional practice is even more striking. Indeed, I contend that these phenomena are properly understood as amounting to the "worship" of Jesus — that is, the unprecedented and unique inclusion of Jesus in the devotional life of Christian circles as recipient of the sort of reverence that they otherwise reserved for God.

3. Also, part of my concern has been to develop a conceptual model to use in trying to understand *how* such a remarkable pattern of devotion could have emerged in Second-Temple Jewish tradition. Although this devotion to Jesus is apparently unique in its own original time and setting (i.e., Jewish tradition of the first century), I have explored more widely instances of religious innovation across the centuries and, in particular, in the modern scene, and I have attempted to draw upon studies of these phenomena in framing an approach to earliest Christianity. Various social-scientific studies demonstrate that significant innovations in religious traditions can indeed appear, and that they are characteristically linked with powerful religious experiences that strike the recipients of these experiences as new revelations.[28] Usually these revelations amount to reconfigurations of beliefs and/or practices of the "parent" religious tradition in which the revelations are experienced. Such experiences can then generate suc-

28. Chapter Eight appeared earlier as Larry W. Hurtado, "Religious Experience and Religious Innovation in the New Testament," *Journal of Religion* 80 (2000): 183-205.

cessful religious innovations ("success" exhibited in the formation of a new religious movement that is able to grow and survive across time) when the reconfigured beliefs and/or practices are advocated with sufficient clarity, credibility, and appeal.

4. We can thus think of such major reconfigurations as significant "mutations" within religious traditions. Like major biological mutations in species, they are both distinguishable from and also clearly connected to their "parent" religious traditions. That is, major innovations can take place within religious traditions for reasons other than the influence or importation of foreign convictions or practices from other traditions.

Conclusion

The treatment of Jesus as a divine figure was most vividly and clearly manifested in according him the sorts of devotional reverence that I have cataloged briefly. Thus, at least in this sense, we can say that Jesus clearly "became a god" and "on earth" (i.e., expressed in historically observable phenomena) in early Christian devotional practice.

I have briefly described several different approaches to the questions about how and when this remarkable development originated and what it represents, and have tried to sketch the approach that I (and a number of other contemporary scholars in various countries) find most cogent. This pattern of devotion originated so early in the Christian movement that evolutionary approaches are simply not appropriate. In fact, so far as we can judge, such devotion to Jesus seems to have been a feature of circles of the Christian movement from their earliest moments. Yet the nature of the innovation involved is such that we cannot rightly portray it as simply an extension or minor adaptation of prior religious beliefs and practices. Nor can we posit this striking innovation in devotional practice as basically a logical inference that was made simply from early Christians having come to see Jesus as exalted to heavenly honor and status.

I contend that devotion to Jesus as divine was such a novel and significant step, and appeared so early as well, that it can only be accounted for as a response to the strong conviction in early Christian circles that the one God of biblical tradition willed that Jesus be so reverenced. Ancient Jewish scruples about worship were such that we cannot take devotion to Jesus as some sort of accidental development, or as indicative of a readiness of early Chistians to engage in liturgical experimentation. The circles of Jewish Christians among which devotion to Jesus as somehow divine originated must have reverenced Jesus as they did solely because they were convinced that it was the will of God for them to do so.

How would they have come to such an astonishing conviction? I submit that we have to posit powerful revelatory experiences of followers of Jesus early in the days after his execution that conveyed the assurance that God had given Jesus unparalleled heavenly honor and glory. Still more remarkable was the conviction also directly conveyed in powerful experiences that it was the will of God for people to honor him by giving devotional reverence to Jesus in the sorts of actions that are reflected in the writings of the New Testament.

As surprising as it may seem, the evidence indicates that Jesus was first given the sort of devotion that we associate with a deity *among the circles of devout Jews* who comprised the earliest adherents of the young Christian movement. Jesus was treated as worthy of divine honor initially because Christians were convinced that it was obedience to the one God to do so. Jesus' divine status was, however, not really an instance of apotheosis, but, instead, a rather novel religious innovation among circles deeply antagonistic to all such pagan ideas, and so unlikely to have appropriated them. So, in that sense we can say that Jesus did not really "become a god." Instead, he was given devotion that expressed the distinctively Christian recognition that Jesus was God's unique emissary, in whom the glory of the one God was singularly reflected and to whom God "the Father" now demanded full reverence "as to a god."

CHAPTER TWO

Devotion to Jesus and Second-Temple Jewish Monotheistic Piety

For those who are observers of Christian tradition from outside it as well as for adherents, devotion to Jesus is perhaps the most familiar distinguishing feature of Christian piety and belief. In particular, the characteristic reverence given to Jesus as divine is perhaps the most crucial distinction in belief and devotional practice between Christianity and its two sibling, "Abrahamic" religions of professed monotheistic stance. Indeed, down through the centuries, for many devout Jews and Muslims the reverence given to Jesus has probably been the most objectionable feature of Christian faith.[1] If candor be allowed, from the standpoint of devout Jewish and Muslim monotheistic scruples, Christian reverence for Jesus as divine may be regarded as ridiculous, and even blasphemous. In historical terms, it may seem very difficult to see how this devotion to Jesus as divine could have arisen in the Second-Temple Jewish matrix of earliest Christianity.

As we noted in the preceding chapter, the high status of Jesus in traditional Christian devotion is often explained in historical terms as essentially the result of pagan influences of the Roman period, especially the ancient pagan readiness to divinize human figures such as heroes and rulers (apotheosis). Under these influences, so a commonly recited theory goes, a supposedly "purer" monotheistic piety of the originating circles of Jewish followers of Jesus was transformed into the more familiar pattern of Christian belief and devotional practice. In a number of publications

---

1. E.g., from the second century C.E., note Trypho's characterization of devotion to Jesus as blasphemous (Justin Martyr, *Dialogue with Trypho* 38:1).

31

over many years, I have offered historical descriptions and analyses of early devotion to Jesus, and have emphasized its remarkable features.[2] As well, with a number of other scholars, I have argued that the historical evidence does not really permit the attribution of Jesus-devotion to pagan influences, and does not support an evolutionary model of development, with a divine Jesus emerging only at a secondary stage of the early Christian movement. In the following discussion, I draw upon these previous investigations, and I aim to show here why earliest devotion to Jesus as divine is best understood as a remarkable innovation within (and as a novel expression of, the monotheistic piety characteristic of Second-Temple Jewish tradition.[3]

Chronology Matters

The first thing that I wish to underscore and expand upon here is that this devotion to Jesus developed very early and quickly. Early in my own research, it was particularly Martin Hengel (of Tübingen University) who in an essay focused this point for me with his characteristically forceful argumentation.[4] The earliest extant historical sources for studying the origins of Christianity are letters of the one-time Pharisee Saul of Tarsus, who is more familiarly known today as the Apostle Paul.[5] These letters form part

2. See esp. Larry W. Hurtado, *Lord Jesus Christ: Devotion to Jesus in Earliest Christianity* (Grand Rapids: Eerdmans, 2003), and *One God, One Lord: Early Christian Devotion and Ancient Jewish Monotheism* (Philadelphia: Fortress Press, 1988; 2d ed., London: T&T Clark, 2003).

3. In his stimulating book *Rebecca's Children: Judaism and Christianity in the Roman World* (Cambridge: Harvard University Press, 1986), Alan F. Segal explores more broadly the origins of rabbinic Judaism and Christianity as "sibling" movements developing out of the biblical/Jewish tradition of the early Roman period.

4. Martin Hengel, "Christologie und neutestamentliche Chronologie," in *Neues Testament und Geschichte, Festschrift O. Cullmann*, ed. H. Baltensweiler and B. Reicke (Zürich/ Tübingen, 1972), 43-67. Here I cite the English translation: "Christology and New Testament Chronology," in *Between Jesus and Paul* (London: SCM Press, 1983), 30-47.

5. The scholarly literature on Saul/Paul is immense. For introductory purposes, the recent book by Calvin Roetzel is worth noting: *Paul: The Man and the Myth* (Minneapolis: Fortress Press, 1999). For a major mine of information, see *Dictionary of Paul and His Letters*, ed. G. F. Hawthorne, R. P. Martin, and D. G. Reid (Downers Grove, Ill.: InterVarsity Press, 1993).

of the New Testament, "Scripture" for Christians, but they are also invaluable for historical inquiry into earliest Christianity. Scholars commonly agree that seven of the New Testament letters ascribed to Paul were certainly written by him, and these are usually dated roughly between the late 40s and the early 60s of the first century C.E. As Hengel observed, it is striking that Paul's extant letters fully *presuppose* the high estimation of Jesus as Messiah (Greek: *Christos*), "Lord" (Greek: *Kyrios*), and God's "Son," and also the devotional pattern of according Jesus a reverence that amounts to him being treated as in some sense divine.[6] Yet the time span between the probable date of Jesus' execution (30-33 C.E.) and the earliest of Paul's extant letters (ca. 50 C.E., perhaps a few years earlier) is scarcely twenty years.[7] To cite Hengel's vivid statement, "In essentials more happened in christology [beliefs in/about Jesus] within these few years than in the whole subsequent seven hundred years of church history."[8]

In fact, a little further reflection will quickly lead us to a still more astonishing chronological conclusion. The figure known as Paul the Apostle is also perhaps the most famous convert to early Christian faith. By any reckoning, his conversion is to be dated within a very few years at most after Jesus' execution (i.e., sometime in the early to mid 30s C.E.). Moreover, in an autobiographical passage in his letter to his converts in Galatia (an area within what is now Turkey), we learn that prior to his conversion he had been zealously devoted to Jewish traditions, and, prompted by his zeal, he had sought vigorously to destroy the young Christian movement (Gal. 1:13-14).[9] Obviously, he must have found something seriously objection-

---

6. I have discussed the evidence for devotion to Jesus in Paul's letters at much greater length in *Lord Jesus Christ*, 79-153.

7. First Thessalonians is commonly dated ca. 48-51 C.E. On dates for Paul's activities as debated by scholars, see, e.g., L. C. A. Alexander, "Chronology of Paul," in *Dictionary of Paul and His Letters*, 115-23.

8. Hengel, *Between Jesus and Paul*, 39-40.

9. Galatians 1:11–2:21 is the most extensive autobiographical passage in Paul's undisputed letters, and it includes the most explicit reference to his conversion from a violent opponent of the Jesus movement to a dedicated proponent of devotion to Jesus. In this passage he attributes his religious change to a revelation from God (Gal. 1:11-17). Other important autobiographical passages include Philippians 3:1-11, where he also refers to his very traditional Jewish background and his pre-conversion religious stance, including his claim to have been a Pharisee. In 1 Corinthians 15:8-10, there is another and briefer reference to his conversion. For further discussion, see, e.g., Martin Hengel, *The Pre-Christian Paul* (London: SCM Press, 1991), and, more briefly, Roetzel, *Paul: The Man and the Myth*, 8-43.

able in it, so objectionable that he sought strenuously to suppress it. To prevent misunderstanding, I must emphasize that his violent opposition was directed against some *fellow Jews*. We must realize that the "church" that drew the ire of this zealous Pharisee Saul was then still a new religious movement entirely within the Jewish community/tradition of the day. So, the concern of this devout Pharisee appears to have been to protect the religious integrity of his ancestral religion against what he regarded as inappropriate, even dangerous developments manifested in early circles of Jewish believers in Jesus.

Paul does not say explicitly what it was about the followers of Jesus that drew his zealous opposition, and so scholars have considered a few possibilities.[10] Some have proposed that Saul was concerned that Jewish Christians were not adequately observant of the Torah, or that they associated too freely with Gentiles. But there is no evidence for either of these possibilities as characteristic of the Jesus movement in the very earliest years when Saul's zealous efforts were underway. It seems to me likely that prominent among his reasons for proceeding against the early Jewish Christians was his outrage over their claims about Jesus and their reverence of him. I think that it is particularly significant that Paul describes his religious re-orientation as caused by a divine revelation to him of Jesus as God's unique "Son" (Gal. 1:15). This suggests that the key cognitive component in Paul's conversion was his realization that Jesus (whom till then Paul had probably regarded as a false teacher) held a unique and exalted status. *That is, at its heart, Paul's conversion appears to have been a radical change in his view of Jesus.*

Indeed, we may get hints of just how radical this change in his view of Jesus was from other passages in his letters. In Galatians 3:13-14 (in the midst of an argument involving subtle and complex references to passages in several biblical books), Paul refers to Jesus as having redeemed believers by "becoming a curse for us," and Paul then cites a line from Deuteronomy 21:23: "Cursed is everyone who is hung upon a tree." It is an intriguing possibility that here Paul is re-interpreting in a positive direction a very negative reference to Jesus as "accursed" that may have originated from those Jews who regarded Jesus as a false teacher/prophet. For them, Jesus' execution was just punishment and signaled that he fell under God's curse for

---

10. See, e.g., Arland J. Hultgren, "Paul's Pre-Christian Persecutions of the Church: Their Purpose, Locale and Nature," *Journal of Biblical Literature* 95 (1976): 97-111.

his misbehavior.[11] If Saul the Pharisee, the "pre-Christian" Paul, was among those who judged Jesus to have been an accursed false teacher/prophet, and thus regarded the Jesus movement's devotion to Jesus as outrageous, this would certainly account for his heated efforts to eradicate the movement. Further, if subsequently he came to believe that God had directly shown him that he had been completely wrong, and that Jesus actually bore God's own supreme approbation and unique favor, this would certainly explain Paul's sudden and significant shift from opponent to advocate of the Christian movement and its message about Jesus.

In another passage in one of his letters, Paul attributes a spiritual blindness to those fellow Jews who are unable to perceive that the risen and exalted Jesus bears the glory of God, and that Jesus is rightly to be acclaimed as "Lord" (2 Cor. 3:7–4:6, especially 3:12-18). Here also, it seems to me quite likely that Paul is drawing upon his own past, his own previously negative view of Jesus and the radical reappraisal of Jesus that he believed had come to him by divine revelation. In the light of that revelation, Paul quickly came to see his previous opposition to the proclamation of Jesus' glorious status as blind and misguided.

So, let us summarize matters at this point. Paul refers to his own conversion as primarily focused on his realization of Jesus' glorious significance. Furthermore, after his conversion, he quickly associated himself with the religious movement and faith in Jesus that he had been seeking to destroy. The reasonable inference, therefore, is that his previous opposition had been directed against just the sort of view of Jesus that he felt divinely directed to embrace in his conversion. This in turn means that, between the emergence of a Jewish movement in Jesus' name almost immediately after Jesus' crucifixion and Paul's conversion (perhaps within a year or two, and certainly no more than a few years), devotion to Jesus was already a prominent feature of the movement. Moreover, *already at that point* devotion to Jesus must have been sufficiently striking (even au-

---

11. Graham N. Stanton, "Jesus of Nazareth: A Magician and a False Prophet Who Deceived God's People?" in *Jesus of Nazareth, Lord and Christ: Essays on the Historical Jesus and New Testament Christology,* ed. Joel B. Green and Max Turner (Grand Rapids: Eerdmans, 1994), 164-80, discusses early evidence of such polemical charges about Jesus in ancient Jewish sources. Paul's statement that God's Spirit would never prompt someone to pronounce an "anathema" upon Jesus (1 Cor. 12:3) may be another allusion to what he knows to be the negative view of Jesus held by some fellow Jews, the view that he once shared before he believed himself to have been given a revelation of the truth.

dacious) that it could draw the determined efforts of this formerly zealous Pharisee to destroy what he regarded as an unacceptable innovation in Second-Temple Jewish religion. It had to be some major offense by Jewish Christians to have elicited the kind of Phinehas-like zeal with which Saul/Paul attacked the Jesus movement.[12] Consorting with Gentiles socially or even being less observant of the Torah than Pharisees would have preferred is not likely to have generated this sort of action. There was considerable diversity in Second-Temple Judaism, and Pharisees had neither the authority nor the power to police some uniform expression of Jewishness. But, apparently, for the dedicated Pharisee Saul/Paul, the young Jesus movement went far beyond the acceptable limits of variation, and in his eyes demanded forceful and urgent action.

It is also important to note that after his conversion Paul never indicates that the devotional claims and practices that he affirms and reflects in his letters represent anything innovative from him. Indeed, he insists that in these matters he and other Jewish Christians of the Jerusalem church share a common faith and devotional pattern (e.g., 1 Cor. 15:1-11). So there is really no basis for thinking either that Paul was particularly responsible for inventing the view that Jesus is to be reverenced as divine, or that this view of Jesus distinguished the churches that he established. In fact, all the evidence points to the opposite conclusion: that the devotion to Jesus that Paul affirms in his letters was manifest already in the very earliest circles of Jewish Christians, including those of the very first years (perhaps months) in Roman Judea.

It is widely accepted among scholars that we even have a linguistic fragment or actual artifact of the devotional practice of Aramaic-speaking circles of Jewish Christians preserved in 1 Corinthians 16:22. The untranslated expression found here, *"Marana tha,"* is commonly taken as a prayer or an invocation formula, and is probably to be translated something like "O Lord, come!" It is also now commonly accepted that it was the exalted Jesus who was addressed as the "Lord" in this formula. It is interesting that Paul does not bother to translate the expression here for his Greek-speaking church in Corinth, probably because he expected his readers to recognize it. This is likely because it was one of the devotional formulas

---

12. Paul's reference to his "zeal" suggests an allusion to the tradition associated with the vigilante action of Phinehas (Numbers 25). See Torrey Seland, "Saul of Tarsus and Early Zealotism: Reading Gal 1,13-14 in Light of Philo's Writings," *Biblica* 83 (2002): 449-71.

from Aramaic-speaking circles of the early Christian movement that he conveyed to his Greek-speaking Gentile converts, as a gesture of their religious solidarity with believers in Judea, whom Paul refers to as predecessors of his Gentile converts (e.g., 1 Thess. 2:13-16; Rom. 15:25-27). Other examples of devotional expressions that derive from Semitic-speaking Christian circles and were circulated by Paul among the congregations that he established include *"Abba,"* as a devotional expression used to address God in prayer (Rom. 8:15; Gal. 4:6), and *"Amen."*

To repeat the point for emphasis, the *"Marana tha"* expression must have been conveyed to Paul's Greek-speaking converts as already a standardized devotional formula, which confirms that the devotional stance reflected in the expression was a familiar feature of Aramaic-speaking circles of Christians well before the date of 1 Corinthians. Indeed, as I have argued here (and more extensively in previous publications), it seems most likely that this kind of devotion to Jesus erupted with amazing force and rapidity.[13] As Hengel contended in that important essay which I have mentioned earlier, the really crucial period for the origin of remarkable beliefs about Jesus' significance is "the first four or five years" of the early Christian movement.[14]

Such an extremely early and short period of time does not allow for an evolutionary process of multiple stages, with pagan religious influences seeping in and having their supposedly crucial effects across several decades. The chronological indicators seem instead to require us to think that the devotion to Jesus reflected in Paul's letters came about more as an explosion than an evolution, at least in its most crucial components. The chronological data make totally false any idea of a slow "seepage" of pagan ideas of multiple deities and/or deified heroes as the historical cause of devotion to Jesus. Likewise, against some widely cherished suppositions, it is not consistent with the chronological data to imagine some distinguishable later stage of early Christianity that was more prone to such religious influences as the decisive setting in which devotion to Jesus as divine first appeared.

In short, proper historical method requires us to take seriously the chronological data. However uncomfortable it may be to some popular notions, and however difficult it may seem to account for, a rather robust

---

13. E.g., Hurtado, *Lord Jesus Christ*, 134-53.
14. Hengel, *Between Jesus and Paul*, 44.

devotion to Jesus rather clearly appeared early and was widely characteristic in the first years of the Christian movement.

Demographics

My second key point is a demographic one. We have to remember that we are dealing with a religious movement of *Jewish* provenance, especially in the crucial first couple of decades of what became "Christianity." The religion that by (or during) the second century of the Common Era was dominantly composed of Gentiles unquestionably began in Roman Judea, and, at least initially, seems to have been composed entirely of Jews (and perhaps a few proselytes to Judaism, such as the Nicolaus of Acts 6:5). Moreover, so far as we can tell, they were devout Jews who identified themselves closely with the distinguishing features of biblical/Jewish tradition of the time.

When we examine particularly those named figures who seem to have been prominent and influential, we find them to be such Jews. The named disciples who made up Jesus' own entourage (men and women) were all Jews from Roman Judea (mainly Galileans, it appears).[15] The early named figures associated with the Jerusalem church, such as Shimon bar Yona (nicknamed "Kephas" and more well known as "Simon Peter"), Yakov ("James," the brother of Jesus), and the two sons of Zebedee (Yohanan, "John," and Yakov, "James"), and Jesus' mother Mary (Miriam) were Jews as well.[16] There were other Jews from the Roman-era Diaspora, such as Barnabas (from Cyprus), probably Stephen, and others identified as leaders among Greek-speaking Jewish Christians in Jerusalem, and, most famously of course, Saul/Paul (reportedly from Tarsus).[17] Still other figures

---

15. These figures are all referred to as Galileans in the New Testament Gospels and in Acts 1:12-14. Against previous assertions that first-century c.e. Galilee was populated with significant numbers of Gentiles and that pagan religious influences were strong there, see Mark A. Chancey, *The Myth of a Gentile Galilee*, SNTSMS, 118 (Cambridge: Cambridge University Press, 2002).

16. These names are among the most popular names borne by Judean Jews of the time. See Tal Ilan, *Lexicon of Jewish Names in Late Antiquity, Part 1: Palestine 300 b.c.e.–200 c.e.*, TSAJ, 91 (Tübingen: Mohr Siebeck, 2002).

17. The Acts of the Apostles (New Testament) gives information on these figures and others: e.g., Jesus' mother, Mary (Acts 1:14); Barnabas (e.g., Acts 4:36-37; 13:1); James, the

named in our earliest sources, such as Silas/Silvanus, John Mark, and Philip, are all Jews. Named Gentiles of the earliest years include proselytes to Jewish religion, such as Nicolaus and still others such as the Ethiopian of Acts 8:27 and Cornelius (Acts 10:1-2), who are portrayed as attracted to Jewish religion but appear not to have made a full proselyte conversion.[18]

Even if we confine ourselves to the activities and circles of Saul/Paul, the "Apostle to the Gentiles," the named figures (i.e., those in prominent roles) are mainly fellow Jewish Christians such as Barnabas, Priscilla (Prisca) and Aquila, Apollos, and Andronicus and Junia, Jason, and Sosipater.[19] These Jewish Christians are all (or mainly) from the Diaspora, but nevertheless are firmly identified by Paul as fellow Jews.[20] Moreover, we have no reason to think that either they or the Jewish Christians from Roman Judea had been apostates from Judaism, or were particularly more prone than other Jews of the time (among those who identified themselves with their people and their religious tradition) to accept ideas or practices from the pagan religious environment that represented a major departure from the religious stance of Jewish tradition. This is another reason to dispute the notion that the striking devotion to Jesus that emerged so early and so quickly in earliest Christianity can be explained as the massive influence or appropriation of pagan religious ideas and practices.

To be sure, in the Roman period, and perhaps especially in the Diaspora,

---

brother of Jesus (e.g., Acts 15:13); Stephen (e.g., Acts 6:5-6), and Saul/Paul (e.g., Acts 7:58; 9:1-9). As well, Paul mentions a number of these figures in his letters: e.g., Kephas/Peter in Galatians 1:18; 2:11; 1 Corinthians 9:5; James (brother of Jesus) and John (Zebedee) in Galatians 2:9-10; Barnabas in Galatians 2:13; 1 Corinthians 9:6; and several are also named in 1 Corinthians 15:3-7.

18. There were various gradations of Gentile relationship to Judaism and the Jewish people in the Roman period. See Shaye J. D. Cohen, "Crossing the Boundary and Becoming a Jew," *Harvard Theological Review* 82 (1989): 13-33; and Paul F. Stuehrenberg, "Proselyte," *Anchor Bible Dictionary,* ed. D. N. Freedman, 6 vols. (New York: Doubleday, 1992), 5:503-5.

19. Paul identifies Barnabas as a Jewish Christian in Galatians 1:13. On Aquila and Priscilla, see Acts 18:2; on Apollos, Acts 18:24. Paul's references to several people named in Romans 16 as "kindred" (Greek: *sungeneis*) — Andronicus and Junia (16:7), Herodion (16:11), Lucius, Jason, and Sosipater (16:21) — probably means that they were fellow Jews. In this passage from Romans there are probably also others whose names signal their Jewish descent, such as the Mary of 16:6.

20. Paul's letters refer to a large number of named individuals (well over thirty in Romans 16 alone), all of whom were referred to because apparently they were active and prominent in disseminating the Christian faith of the time. For a survey, see E. E. Ellis, "Coworkers, Paul and His," in *Dictionary of Paul and His Letters,* 183-89.

Jews were confronted with the larger religious environment, with its poly-theistic character and its readiness to accommodate new deities and even de-ified humans. Moreover, some Jews readily saw worldly advantages to assim-ilating to the dominant culture, even in religious matters/practices (such as Tiberius Alexander, the nephew of Philo of Alexandria), and we even hear of a few male Jews who underwent surgery to mask their circumcision.[21] In the Hellenistic and Roman periods, many Jews obviously adapted themselves to the larger culture in various ways, such as by using Greek language and by appropriating features of Greek philosophical tradition, dress, and certain dining customs. Philo of Alexandria is usually cited by scholars as the most prominent example. The popularity of Greek translations of Tanach (the Christian "Old Testament") in the Second-Temple period is clear proof that there were many Jews whose primary language was Greek.[22] But such cul-tural adaptations did not by any means signal a readiness to adopt pagan re-ligion.[23] It is also a plausible guess, however, that there were other Jews of the time who did not commit apostasy but may well have made various kinds of compromises with, or appropriations of, features of the larger religious cul-ture. For example, it is clear that some Jews, as well as many others of the Ro-man period, dabbled in practices associated with "magic," such as the invok-ing of various powerful names and divine beings.[24]

But it is important to note that we do not have evidence that Jews who identified themselves with their ancestral religious tradition openly em-braced the appropriation of deities other than the God of Israel, or that they were ready to accede openly to the idea that deified humans should share in the reverence that their tradition reserved for the one God alone.

21. Josephus refers to Tiberius Alexander in *Antiquities* 20.100 and *Jewish War* 2.220. Ancient references to Jews who underwent surgery to hide their circumcision include 1 Maccabees 1:15. See R. G. Hall, "Circumcision," *Anchor Bible Dictionary*, 1:1025-31, esp. 1029.

22. Scholars often refer to the Greek translation of the "Old Testament" as the "Septua-gint." For an accessible introduction, see Karen H. Jobes and Moises Silva, *Invitation to the Septuagint* (Grand Rapids: Baker Academic, 2000), and for advanced study, Emanuel Tov, *The Text-Critical Use of the Septuagint in Biblical Research*, 2d ed. (Jerusalem: Simor Ltd., 1997).

23. See, e.g., Alan Mendelson, *Philo's Jewish Identity*, Brown Judaic Studies, 161 (Atlanta: Scholars Press, 1988); Ellen Birnbaum, *The Place of Judaism in Philo's Thought: Israel, Jews, and Proselytes*, Studia Philonica, 2 (Atlanta: Scholars Press, 1996).

24. See, e.g., Peter Schäfer, "Magic and Religion in Ancient Judaism," in *Envisioning Magic: A Princeton Seminar and Symposium*, ed. Peter Schäfer and Hans G. Kippenberg (Leiden: E. J. Brill, 1997), 19-44.

Indeed, to judge by the Jewish evidence of the time (and the non-Jewish references as well), this scruple about the uniqueness of the one God seems to have been perhaps the most widely known and most fervently held feature of Roman-era Jewish religious practice.[25] In fact, there is good reason to think that, from the Maccabean crisis onward, Jewish reaction to pagan religious influences became, on the whole, more hostile, and that Jewish concern to maintain ethnic and religious particularities was more robust than in earlier times.[26]

It is simply not very credible, therefore, to allege influence of the pagan religious environment as the crucial factor generating devotion to Jesus as divine. As I have emphasized already, earliest "Christianity" was originally a Jewish religious movement, and it remained dominated by Jews through the crucial first few decades. Jews who identified themselves firmly with their people and their religious tradition, such as those named Jewish Christians of the earliest years, were scarcely likely to accommodate Jesus in such lofty terms under the influence of pagan notions of apotheosis or because in the larger religious environment multiple deities were reverenced. By all accounts, loyal Jews of the time, whether in Judea or the Diaspora, found precisely these features of the Roman religious environment particularly repellent.[27] In the crucial earliest years, exactly when the most remarkable key developments of devotion to Jesus happened, there simply were not significant numbers of former pagan converts to the young Christian movement. The demographics of the crucial earliest years do not allow us to suppose that Gentile converts could have made pagan ideas influential upon Christian circles of that time. In any case, Gentile converts to the early Christian message, just like proselytes to Roman-era Judaism and other Gentiles referred to as "God-fearers," were expected to regard their pre-conversion religious beliefs and practices as foolish at best, and as reverence of demons at worst.[28] So, it is entirely improbable to

25. See, e.g., Lester L. Grabbe, *Judaic Religion in the Second Temple Period: Belief and Practice from the Exile to Yavneh* (London: Routledge, 2000), 210-31, esp. 216-19.

26. See, e.g., Victor A. Tcherikover, Alexander Fuks, and Menahem Stern, *Corpus Papyrorum Judaicarum,* 3 vols. (Cambridge: Harvard University Press, 1957-1964), 1:1-110.

27. Note, e.g., Philo of Alexandria's extended critique of apotheosis of rulers, *The Embassy to Gaius.* For introduction, text, and translation, see F. H. Colson, *Philo,* Loeb Classical Library, vol. 10 (Cambridge: Harvard University Press, 1971).

28. Note, e.g., Paul's characterization of the pre- and post-conversion religious stances of his Gentile converts in Thessalonica (1 Thess. 1:9-10), and his exhortations to his Corin-

suppose that somehow Gentile converts would have missed the firmly established concern to avoid idolatry and any compromise in the reverence due to the one God, and would also have been able to influence Jewish-Christian devotional practice on such a crucial matter.

To summarize the discussion to this point: both the chronological and the demographic data make it extremely dubious to attribute the level of devotion to Jesus that characterized earliest Christianity to syncretistic influences from the pagan religious context. Devotion to Jesus appeared too early, and originated among circles of the early Jesus movement that were comprised of — or certainly dominated by — Jews, and they seem no more likely than other devout Jews of the time to appropriate pagan religious influences.

Monotheism in the New Testament

But we do not have to confine ourselves to the sort of educated guesswork that I have been developing to this point. Our earliest extant historical sources exhibit an emphatic rejection of pagan religion and a corresponding monotheistic affirmation of the exclusive validity of the one God.[29] That is, in these sources the devotion given to Jesus in earliest Christianity is never justified or articulated with reference to the pagan polytheism of the day, with its many deities and its divinized heroes. Instead, in a novel and astonishing move that we will examine more closely later, reverence for Jesus is consistently and firmly expressed in the context of commitment to a recognizably traditional Jewish monotheism of the Roman period.[30] This is further reason to approach Jesus-devotion as a phenomenon to be understood historically *within* Second-Temple Jewish monotheism. As I have noted in a recent book, "This hardly requires substantiation for anyone acquainted with the New Testament and the majority of extant early Christian writings."[31] I restrict myself here to a few illustrative examples.

---

thian converts not to continue in their former religious practices (1 Cor. 10:14-22). In the next section of this chapter, I discuss these passages further.

29. See, e.g., Robert M. Grant, *The Gods and the One God* (Philadelphia: Westminster Press, 1986).

30. Larry W. Hurtado, "First-Century Jewish Monotheism," *Journal for the Study of the New Testament*, no. 71 (1998): 3-26 (Chapter Five of this book); Hurtado, *Lord Jesus Christ*, 29-53.

31. Hurtado, *Lord Jesus Christ*, 48.

I shall focus on examples from the letters of Paul, as they are our earliest extant Christian sources.[32] Moreover, these writings are particularly important for this discussion, precisely because they are directly connected with Paul's mission to the Gentiles to win their obedience to the gospel. If there were any readiness to take on board pagan religious influences in earliest Christianity, we should perhaps more readily hope to find signs of this in these Christian circles rather than in those that were composed of Jewish believers. As I shall illustrate in the following remarks, it is, thus, all the more interesting to see that there is in fact no sign of such an open attitude toward the pagan religious scene.

In the letter that is widely thought by scholars to be the earliest extant Christian writing, 1 Thessalonians, the Apostle Paul addresses the little circle of Christians that was the result of his own missionizing work in Thessalonica. In 1:2-10, Paul applauds his Thessalonian converts for their exemplary faith and describes them as having converted "to God from idols, to serve a living and true God, and to wait for his Son from heaven, whom he raised from the dead — Jesus, who rescues us from the wrath that is coming" (1:9-10). The most obvious sociological implication is that these are Gentiles who have now renounced their former pagan religious life in favor of exclusive service to the one God. Jewish Christians could not have been described as turning from idolatry.

But the still more obvious import of this statement is that Paul affirmed and promoted in his churches a sharp distinction between the polytheistic character of the larger Gentile environment and the exclusivist monotheistic stance that was a major requisite in accepting his gospel message. Moreover, the language used here, the pagan deities designated as "idols" and contrasted with "a living and true God," can only derive from Jewish monotheistic religious discourse of the time.[33] To be sure, also woven tightly into the statement is the reference to Jesus as God's unique Son whom God raised from death and who brings deliverance from (God's) es-

---

32. See also Karl-Wilhelm Niebuhr, "Jesus Christus und der eine Gott Israels: Zum christologischen Gottesgalauben in den Paulusbriefen," in *Glauben Christen und Muslime an denselben Gott?*, ed. Reinhard Rittner (Hannover: Lutherisches Verlagshaus, 1995), 10-29; and Charles H. Giblin, "Three Monotheistic Texts in Paul," *Catholic Biblical Quarterly* 37, no. 4 (1975): 528-47.

33. See, e.g., Ernest Best, *A Commentary on the First and Second Epistles to the Thessalonians* (London: A. C. Black; New York: Harper & Row, 1972), 82-83, for references and discussion.

chatological "wrath." But this perfectly illustrates my point that, characteristically, earliest Christian devotion to, acclamation of, and claims about Jesus are all framed with reference to the one God. They all have a clear monotheistic tone, although this unquestionably is a monotheism with a novel feature for which we have no genuine analogy elsewhere in Jewish tradition of the time: Jesus as the unique principal agent of God.[34]

Let us look at another relevant passage, this one from one of Paul's letters to the Corinthian church. In 1 Corinthians 8-10, Paul is obviously addressing Gentile converts about questions that have to do with their pagan religious setting and former religious activities in Corinth. These questions were scarcely peculiar to Corinth, but were instead the sort of matters that Gentile Christians of the time living in any Roman city (outside of Judea at least) had to face. Essentially, Paul directs his converts to shun any overtly pagan religious activity and practice, and he does so in the strongest kind of terms.

From the outset of the discussion, he refers to offerings to the pagan deities as *eidōlothyta*, "things offered to idols" (8:1, 4), an obviously scornful characterization. He then goes on to draw a sharp contrast between the many deities of the Roman religious environment and the "one God, the Father, from whom are all things and for whom we exist, and one Lord, Jesus Christ" (8:6). We shall return to this latter statement later in this discussion. For now, I want simply to note that it expresses an exclusivist stance and a resolute rejection of the polytheistic character of the pagan religious world from which Paul sought to win Gentile converts. The "one God" here is not one among others, but instead the *only* true deity.

In 10:1-22, Paul again directly engages the question of whether Gentile converts can continue to participate in the religious ceremonies of their former life, and he utterly rejects this in the strongest terms. The comparison that he draws (10:6-13) with the biblical story of Israel's apostasy in Numbers 11 surely makes it clear how Paul regards the matter. Paul's complete disdain for pagan worship is reflected in his reference to it as "the worship of idols" (10:14). Indeed, he even claims that "what pagans sacrifice, they sacrifice to demons and not to God" (10:20). Therefore, he insists, participation in the worship of these pagan deities is completely incompatible with participation in the Christian fellowship: "You cannot drink the cup of the Lord [alluding to the Christian Eucharistic meal] and the

34. See esp. Hurtado, *One God, One Lord,* passim.

cup of demons [alluding to the cult meals of the pagan environment]" (10:21). Clearly, Paul's own readiness to adapt himself on some matters to the practices of Gentiles, "those outside the Law" (1 Cor. 9:21), did not extend to allowing any continued participation in their pre-conversion religious practices.

We could extend our examination to further examples from the New Testament writings, but it would only reinforce the clear conclusion that the fundamental standpoint taken in these historical sources of first-century Christianity is an emphatic monotheism. Equally clearly, the one God who is affirmed over against the polytheism of the Roman era is the God of biblical Israel. That is, the monotheism reflected in these writings is derived from the Jewish matrix in which the Christian movement had its origins.

The firmness of the monotheistic commitment reflected in the New Testament and the emphatic disdain for all forms of pagan religion combine to make another serious difficulty in attributing any readiness of earliest Christians to absorb and appropriate pagan beliefs and religious categories of thought. Of course, the early Christian circles of believers were shaped in many ways by their historical setting, just as were all Jews of the Roman period, and just as people of any time are shaped by their cultural environment. But, as characteristic of devout Jews of the Roman era, in the known first-century circles of the Christian movement, whether comprised of Jews or Gentiles, a monotheistic position was promoted, and participation in pagan religious observances was directly condemned as incompatible with Christian baptism. We have, thus, another reason that it is not credible to attribute the devotion to Jesus that appears in these earliest years to pagan religious ideas and practices. The religious rhetoric of early Christianity is overwhelmingly monotheistic, and the rhetoric was matched with firm expectations about behavior too.

Jesus and God

It is, therefore, all the more amazing to find the exalted place occupied by the figure of Jesus in earliest Christian religious belief and practice. The huge significance of Jesus and the devotion in which he shares a unique status with God comprise a remarkable phenomenon that cannot be explained simply as one instance of a common sort of development for which we have additional examples of that time. I certainly support the effort to understand this phenomenon historically, but it is not as easy to do so as some have imagined.

In fact, in my judgment, there is no full contemporary analogy. Putative analogies from the larger Roman-era religious scene, such as deified heroes/humans and the emergence of new deities, fail as genuine analogies, precisely because they require the "logic" of pagan polytheism. It is one thing to make room for a new additional deity, or to imagine some human figure being made a divinity worthy of worship, in a polytheistic scheme in which multiple deities, new deities, and apotheosis are all legitimate and inherent features of the religious outlook. It is quite another thing, however, in a fervently monotheistic stance, in which one God is exclusively the rightful recipient of worship and all else is distinguished as creation of this one God, to accommodate a second figure in cultic devotional practice and to conceive of a second figure as somehow sharing uniquely and genuinely in the attributes and exalted status of the one God.

In the preceding discussion we have noted that the religious outlook of earliest Christianity was not at all sympathetic to the polytheistic nature of the larger religious environment, and that chronological and demographic factors further make it extremely improbable that early Christian faith could have involved the appropriation of pagan notions such as apotheosis. Indeed, if such notions had an effect upon earliest Christianity, it is likely that it was to reinforce the concern of early Christians to distinguish devotion to Jesus from the accommodation of new deities and divine heroes in the Roman scene.[35]

Principal Agents of the One God

There is also no full analogy within Roman-era Jewish tradition for the level of devotion given to Jesus in early Christian circles. Certainly, Second-Temple Jewish tradition was able to accommodate various figures who were portrayed as agents of God's purposes, including some figures portrayed with a specially assigned role and status. Of course, prophets, angels, and messiah figures are all agents of God with various responsibili-

---

35. This is also the conclusion reached many decades ago in a major study by Stephan Lösch, *Deitas Jesu und antike Apotheose: Ein Beitrag zur Exegese und Religionsgeschichte* (Rottenburg: Bader'sche Verlagsbuchhandlung, 1933).

ties. But also in ancient Jewish tradition, we have instances of this or that particular figure described in the most amazingly exalted terms. We can think of such a figure as God's "principal agent," distinguished from all other beings in God's large retinue. I have discussed major examples and the relevant ancient texts more fully in my book *One God, One Lord,* so I shall simply summarize very briefly the results here.

I have proposed that there are three main types of "principal agent" figures in ancient Jewish texts. There are examples of personified attributes of God portrayed as his principal agent, especially God's Wisdom and God's Word (Greek: *Logos*).[36] There are also revered ancestor-figures from the biblical narratives, such as Enoch, Jacob, and especially Moses, who sometimes are ascribed a status that seems to amount to them being God's special, principal agent.[37] In still other cases, a particular angel is portrayed in such a status and role.[38]

Indeed, these figures can be ascribed an amazingly exalted status. For example, they can be portrayed as sharing in the creation and superintendence of the world and as sitting beside God in heaven (Wisdom), as a "second god" through whom God reveals himself to the world (Logos), as endowed with the divine name (the angel Yahoel), as the one for whom the world was created (Moses), or as the captain set over all God's other angels (Michael). Essentially, although the details vary, each of these figures appears to function as God's vizier, distinguished from all other beings and second only to God.

But, although a number of the specific ways that Jesus is charcterized in early Christian writings have interesting similarities and parallels in the references to these "principal agent" figures, there is a crucial difference that makes them all fall considerably short of serving as an adequate/full analogy for the place held by Jesus in early Christian circles. None of the principal agent figures in the relevant Jewish texts functions in the way that Jesus does in the devotional practice of earliest Christians. More specifically, as I have argued elsewhere and shall illustrate later in this discussion, in early Christian circles Jesus is recipient of the sorts of expressions of devotion that are otherwise reserved for God alone, and which simply have no analogy in Jewish tradition of the Second-Temple pe-

---

36. Hurtado, *One God, One Lord,* 41-50.
37. Hurtado, *One God, One Lord,* 51-69.
38. Hurtado, *One God, One Lord,* 71-92.

riod.[39] Put simply, this worship of the risen/exalted Jesus comprises a radical new innovation in Jewish monotheistic religion.

Devotion to Jesus as "Binitarian" Monotheism

So, it appears that earliest extant Christian writings reflect the religious stance of people who expressed a stridently monotheistic position in the Roman-era religious scene, and yet who also incorporated a second, distinguishable figure (Jesus) into their beliefs and devotional practice in a novel and unparalleled way. That is, there is a remarkable "two-ish" shape to this particular type of avowedly monotheistic devotional stance and practice. Elsewhere I have characterized this as a "binitarian" form of monotheism, and I have also proposed that it should be seen as a distinctive "mutation" or "variant form" of exclusivist monotheism. This "binitarian" monotheism obviously derives from, and is related to, the strong monotheistic stance of Roman-era Jewish tradition. Yet it also rather clearly represents something new and even astonishing.

My use of the term "binitarian" is intended to reflect the clear concerns registered in earliest Christian writings to avoid "di-theism," that is, conceiving of Jesus as a second god. Instead, the early Christians whose faith is reflected in these writings rather consistently express Jesus' divine status with reference to the one God of the ancient Jewish tradition. Let us look at a few examples of this, beginning once again with a couple of key passages from the letters of the Apostle Paul. As we have already noted, Paul's letters give us our earliest access to Christian devotion.

Earlier in this discussion we considered passages in 1 Corinthians where the Apostle Paul gives instructions to Gentile converts about religious/cultic behavior, especially about whether they can continue to participate in the worship of the many deities of the Roman world. There we noted 1 Corinthians 8:5-6, where Paul insists that for Christians there can be only the one God, "the Father" *from* whom all things are created and *to*

---

39. Hurtado, *One God, One Lord,* 93-128; Hurtado, "The Binitarian Shape of Early Christian Worship," in *The Jewish Roots of Christological Monotheism: Papers from the St. Andrews Conference on the Historical Origins of the Worship of Jesus,* ed. Carey C. Newman, James R. Davila, and Gladys S. Lewis (Leiden: E. J. Brill, 1999), 187-213. The latter essay also appears as a chapter in Larry W. Hurtado, *At the Origins of Christian Worship: The Context and Character of Earliest Christian Devotion* (Carlisle: Paternoster, 1999; Grand Rapids: Eerdmans, 2000), 63-97.

whom believers ("we") belong (or "to/for whom we are intended or directed"). Then, in the very next line, Paul immediately also posits Jesus as the "one Lord" *through* whom all things have been created and through whom "we" are (or are redeemed and/or related to God).[40] This passage is widely regarded by scholars as a striking interpretative adaptation of the wording of the *Shemaʿ* (Deut. 6:4), in what we may refer to as a novel "binitarian" direction.[41] Paul's phrasing here certainly affirms an exclusivist monotheism, rejecting the many pagan deities such as characterized Roman-era Jewish religion. But the tight inclusion of Jesus along with "the Father" in the same statement clearly indicates a major religious development, in comparison with other known examples of Roman-era Judaism.

Yet we must also notice that the bold inclusion of Jesus here as the "one Lord" is expressed in a way that maintains a clear distinction between him and "the Father." More specifically, this distinction involves a functional subordination of the "Lord" (Jesus) to the one God. God here is the creator-source of all things, and the one to whom all belong and for whom they exist, and the "one Lord, Jesus Christ" is then explicitly portrayed as the unique *agent* of divine purposes of creation and redemption. Through a deft use of Greek prepositions, Paul distinguishes Jesus' role from that of God "the Father." All things are *from* (Greek: *ek*) and directed *to/for* (Greek: *eis*) "one God the Father," and all things are *through* (Greek: *dia*) the "one Lord Jesus Christ" (1 Cor. 8:6).

In Paul's letter to the church in Philippi, we find another bold statement of Jesus' high significance. On account of its being both an early and a comparatively extended statement about Jesus, Philippians 2:6-11 has received an enormous amount of scholarly attention directed to a wider variety of issues than we can consider here.[42] It is worth noting, however, that the passage is widely thought to be (or to be derived from) an early

---

40. There is no verb in 1 Corinthians 8:6, and so we have to try to express the sense of the phrasing as best we can in light of the context.

41. E.g., Richard A. Horsley, "The Background of the Confessional Formula in 1 Cor. 8:6," *Zeitschrift für die neutestamentliche Wissenschaft* 69 (1978): 130-34. The *Shemaʿ* is traditionally the key confession of Judaism.

42. Ralph P. Martin, *Carmen Christi: Philippians 2:5-11 in Recent Interpretation and in the Setting of Early Christian Worship* (Cambridge: Cambridge University Press, 1967; rev. ed., Grand Rapids: Eerdmans, 1983); *Where Christology Began: Essays on Philippians 2*, ed. Ralph Martin and Brian Dodd (Louisville: Westminster/John Knox Press, 1998). I return to this passage for more extended analysis in the final chapter of this book.

Christian hymn.[43] This means that in this passage we have a presentation of Jesus that was embraced and affirmed *corporately and liturgically,* a "popular" expression of devotion to Jesus (i.e., not an individual's speculative effort, or a formal theological statement). The hymnic nature of the passage is reflected in the very compressed nature of the phrasing. This requires some commentary to "unpack" the meaning of expressions that may have been more familiar to first-century Christians.

My particular interest in the passage here is the thrust of the final lines, verses 9-11. In these lines, Jesus is portrayed as having received from God a uniquely exalted status, which is indicated both in the intensive form of the verb "highly exalted" (Greek: *hyperypsōsen,* v. 9) and in the following statement that God gave Jesus "the name that is above every name" (v. 9). Moreover, the next lines adapt phrasing from Isaiah 45:23 to depict Jesus as being reverenced by every creature "in heaven and on earth and under the earth" (v. 10). This is yet another astonishing example of how far early Christians went in expressing Jesus' high status. In particular, we have here a biblical passage that is among the most fervent expressions of God's uniqueness, adapted (and apparently interpreted) to affirm Jesus as supreme over all creation.

Indeed, the climactic lines in verse 11 predict a universal acclamation, "Jesus Christ is Lord," which almost certainly confirms that "the name above every name" given to Jesus (v. 9) is the divine name itself. "Lord" (Greek: *Kyrios*) most likely functions here as the Greek equivalent of *Adonay,* the familiar reverential substitution for the sacred Tetragrammaton in Hebrew. In short, Jesus is here linked with God in ways that, rightly understood, are startling and unequaled. The monotheistic thrust of Jewish tradition that is stridently expressed in Isaiah 45:23 is adapted to express in equally strong terms a new and remarkable "binitarian" form of monotheism, with *two* closely linked but distinguishable figures: God and Jesus.

---

43. This and several other passages in New Testament writings are widely thought by scholars to be derived from early Christian hymns. See, e.g., Leonard L. Thompson, "Hymns in Early Christian Worship," *Anglican Theological Review* 55 (1973): 458-72; Klaus Wengst, *Christologische Formeln und Lieder des Urchristentums,* SNT, no. 7 (Gütersloh: Gerd Mohn, 1972); Larry W. Hurtado, "Philippians 2:6-11," in *Prayer from Alexander to Constantine,* ed. Mark Kiley (London: Routledge, 1997), 235-39; Robert J. Karris, *A Symphony of New Testament Hymns: Commentary on Philippians 2:5-11, Colossians 1:15-20, Ephesians 2:14-16, 1 Timothy 3:16, Titus 3:4-7, 1 Peter 3:18-22, and 2 Timothy 2:11-13* (Collegeville, Minn.: Liturgical Press, 1996).

Whatever others thought of this sort of affirmation, for the Christians whose faith is represented in this passage this is not really di-theism, and Jesus is not advocated simply as another or new deity alongside the one God. Along with the explicit reference to two figures, there is also a pronounced concern to present Jesus' significance as expressing and furthering the unity of God. It is God (*ho Theos,* v. 9) who supremely exalted Jesus and bestowed on him the unsurpassable name, and the universal acclamation of Jesus as "Lord" that is thereby required is intended to promote "the glory of God the Father" (v. 11). That is, Jesus' divine status is portrayed with reference to the will and actions of the one God, and his exaltation is really intended to express and serve the glory of God.

On the one hand, it is entirely understandable that many devout Jews of the time and subsequently as well have found this sort of expression of Jesus' divine status objectionable and incompatible with Jewish monotheism, even blasphemous, appearing to jeopardize the uniqueness and unity of God. It is particularly important to note that, in the case of the early Christian circles whose devotion is reflected in the passages that we have been considering, we see indications of *devotional practice,* and not simply religious rhetoric. It is clear, thus, that we have before us a genuinely radical development. Nevertheless, I contend that in terms of its historical derivation, and also with reference to the intentions of those for whom such expressions of devotion to Jesus were central in their religious life, this religious development represents a new "binitarian" form of *monotheism.*

If we now turn to the New Testament writings that are widely considered to have been written toward the end of the first century, several decades later than the letters of Paul, and at a time when a large percentage of Christians were Gentiles, we see basically the same pattern of belief and devotion. The Gospel of John, for example, is usually regarded as reflecting a very "high" view of Jesus, his divine status explicit from the outset of the writing in a statement well known in Christian tradition: "In the beginning was the Word [*Logos*], and the Word was with God, and the Word was God" (John 1:1). Certainly, this statement is notable both for explicitly positing the "pre-existence" of Jesus and for the designation of Jesus as the divine "Word" and even as "God."

Yet, even in this astonishingly exalted view of Jesus, he is still defined with reference to the one God. The "Word" is there at the beginning (of the cosmos) *with God.* Moreover, in the next lines of the passage, the Word is posited as the one through whom (Greek: *dia*) all things were created (1:2).

That is, the Word is the unique *agent* through whom God's creation of all things took place. This certainly amounts to an impressive claim. But my point here is that this claim is expressed with a concern to "locate" the Word/Jesus, so to speak, in a way that reflects a monotheistic stance, with the role of the Word implicitly (but clearly) subordinate to the one God.

Indeed, this concern to affirm Jesus' exalted status and to avoid charges of di-theism is reflected explicitly in other passages in the Gospel of John. In some passages, controversies over divine claims for Jesus are situated within the time of Jesus' own activities, but scholars widely agree that these particular controversies more likely (and directly) emerged in the historical context of early Jewish-Christian efforts to promote claims about Jesus among fellow first-century Jews.[44] Note, for example, John 5:18, where Jewish voices accuse Jesus of "making himself equal to God," and 10:31-33, where Jews are portrayed as preparing to stone Jesus for blasphemy because, they say, "though only a human being, you are making yourself God [or a god]."[45] We cannot linger over the other sensitive issues involved in such passages. I restrict myself here to the point that in each case the context makes it rather clear that the author presents these accusations as unfair and incorrect. The author of the Gospel of John certainly affirmed Jesus' divine status, linking Jesus with God so directly that it is not difficult to see how such a view of Jesus could generate the judgment that it amounted to making Jesus a rival to God, or a second god. But we must also note that, as emphatic as this author is about Jesus' divine status, he is equally clear that Jesus' divine glory derives from the one God.

In another passage in the Gospel of John, Jesus is pictured offering a final prayer before the looming ordeal of his arrest and execution, and he refers to the divine glory that he shared with God "before the world existed"

44. There is also wide scholarly support for the view that the Gospel of John reflects vigorous Jewish opposition to the Jewish Christians whose faith is reflected in this text. Some passages are commonly taken as reflecting the expulsion of Jewish Christians from the larger Jewish community/communities of the time, esp. 9:22; 12:42; and 16:2. See esp. J. Louis Martyn, *History and Theology in the Fourth Gospel* (1968; rev. ed., Nashville: Abingdon Press, 1979).

45. The Greek word for "god" here has no definite article. I personally suspect that we are intended to understand the statement as the accusation that Jesus is compromising God's uniqueness in making extravagant claims for himself. That is, Jesus is accused of making himself "a god." But commentators and translators are divided on exactly how to render the accusation.

(17:5). Yet in the same passage Jesus is also pictured as positioning himself in service to God, the glorification of God being his sole purpose (e.g., 17:4, 25-26), and he acknowledges that everything that he has (or has a right to) is given to him by God (e.g., 17:7-8). Indeed, another statement here, and familiar in subsequent Christian tradition, defines eternal life simply as "that they may know you, the only true God, and Jesus Christ whom you have sent" (17:3). Both the constitutive significance of Jesus and the monotheistic language combine to make this statement remarkable. But it is simply indicative of the whole fabric of religious affirmation in the Gospel of John. Scholars agree that one of the striking features of the Gospel of John throughout is this combination of an incredibly high view of Jesus as divine along with an equally clear subordination of Jesus to the one God.[46]

In short, in their own minds, early Christians were not taking on conceptions of apotheosis in portraying Jesus in such exalted terms, and they were not betraying the monotheistic concern to maintain that the God of ancient Israel is the only true God. These devotees to Jesus (who, in the earliest years, please remember again, were overwhelmingly *Jews* who identified themselves with their ancestral religious tradition and its values and hopes) proclaimed his supreme status as God's unique "Son" and their "Lord" entirely in terms of the actions and will of the one God. Their faith and devotional practice, thus, represent what we may call a "binitarian mutation" in Roman-era Jewish monotheism. Jesus is linked with God in their beliefs and in their devotional life in ways that made their religious stance genuinely novel, and problematic for monotheists who did not share their own religious experiences and convictions. But, in historical terms, this religious stance can rightly be seen as initially appearing as a striking development *in Jewish religious tradition of the Second-Temple era.*

Subsequent Doctrinal Development

We have focused here on the earliest extant expressions of devotion to Jesus, and within the limits of this discussion it is not possible to consider at

---

46. See, e.g., C. K. Barrett, "'The Father Is Greater than I': John 14:28: Subordinationist Christology in the New Testament," in *Essays on John* (London: SPCK, 1982), 19-36; Barrett, "Christocentric or Theocentric? Observations on the Theological Method of the Fourth Gospel," in *Essays on John*, 1-18; Paul N. Anderson, *The Christology of the Fourth Gospel*, WUNT, 2/78 (Tübingen: J. C. B. Mohr, 1996).

any length the subsequent developments in early Christian faith. Across the decades and first few centuries after the date of the texts that we have looked at here, there certainly were further developments. Indeed, there was considerable diversity, and there were sharp controversies as well, over how best to express Jesus' significance, and even over who the God was with whom Jesus was to be linked.[47] On the latter issue, the most popular position, and the one that became the "orthodox" view, was always basically the one advocated in the New Testament: the one true God with whom Jesus is to be linked is the God of the biblical tradition, the God of Abraham, Isaac, and Jacob, the creator of heaven and earth. As to doctrines about Jesus, these too involved controversies and massive struggles to find adequate expressions of his divinity, while also doing justice to his human nature and preserving a monotheistic stance.[48]

Had Christians been ready to regard Jesus simply as a prophet, or had the view become dominant in which Jesus was thought of as entirely a heavenly/divine being like an angel, his earthly existence an elaborate disguise (somewhat similar to the way the earthly appearance and activity of the angel Raphael are presented in the book of Tobit), they would not have needed the time and effort that they spent on their Christological concerns. Likewise, had they been ready to adopt the apotheosis model, the human Jesus understood as made a new god in his own right, deified on account of his exceptional merit, their doctrinal efforts would have been much simpler. But no previous model seemed adequate, at least to those Christians whose efforts framed what became more classic Christological doctrine. What came to expression in the prolonged doctrinal explorations of the early Christian centuries was a remarkable, new conception: Jesus as remaining genuinely human and also genuinely divine and worthy of cultic devotion.

In these doctrinal struggles, especially in the second through the fifth centuries, Christians drew upon a wider body of conceptual categories, from biblical traditions, Jewish writers of the Second Temple period (especially Philo of Alexandria), and philosophical traditions of the day. But rarely did they simply appropriate religious or intellectual terms and categories, whether from Jewish or philosophical traditions of the time. More

---

47. See, e.g., Hurtado, *Lord Jesus Christ,* esp. chaps. 8-10.

48. William R. Schoedel, "A Neglected Motive for Second Century Trinitarianism," *Journal of Theological Studies* 31 (1980): 356-67.

often they adapted traditions to express their convictions about Jesus, which, in the main, were decisively prompted and shaped by the earliest devotion to Jesus such as we have been considering here, this devotion to Jesus of Nazareth that seems to have erupted within the earliest moments of the Christian movement. It not only fueled fervent communication of the gospel message in the subsequent decades; this devotion also shaped and, indeed, required the considerable efforts of the next several centuries toward formulation of further Christian doctrine about Jesus and God. Moreover, in what became the dominant view, Jesus' real human and historical activity remained as crucial as the heavenly glory that he was believed to share.

In the process of trying to articulate a view of Jesus, Christians also elaborated a new interpretation of the unity of the one God of the biblical tradition, a unity in which Jesus, "the Son," is integral. In the doctrinal language that began to be favored in the second century and thereafter, the Son shares the same divine "nature/being" (Greek: *ousia*) with "the Father." Of course, in the classic expression of Christian teaching about God, the doctrine of the Trinity, the "Holy Spirit" comes to be included as well, as the third constituent of the divine triadic unity.[49] But the main concerns in this long and complex disputation and development of the Christian doctrine of God were to express Jesus' genuinely divine significance and status, and, equally firmly, to maintain that God is "one." In this latter concern especially, which remained crucial in the early centuries, we see the continuing influence of Second-Temple Jewish monotheism.

---

49. The term "constituent" is my attempt to use a nontechnical term for what early Christians meant in referring to the "Father," the "Son," and the "Holy Spirit" as the three "persons" (Latin: *personae*; Greek: *hypostases*) of the Trinity.

CHAPTER THREE

To Live and Die for Jesus: Social and Political Consequences of Devotion to Jesus in Earliest Christianity

Typically, religion involves a significant social dimension. Beliefs, rituals, ethical/moral scruples — these all characteristically find expression socially, whether in participation in the religious acts of a given group, or through interpersonal relations shaped by religious convictions and teachings. Moreover, religion often is part of what comprises and identifies a given social group, such as a people, a nation, or a tribe. We typically are members of such "traditional" social groups by birth, and the religion of such groups is typically "inherited" along with the rest of what it means to be part of them.

Even "voluntaristic" religion — that is, religion that people subscribe to by personal choice (through conversion, for example) — characteristically involves a social dimension. To make this or that religious affirmation typically involves associating with others who share one's particular religious stance. The social entity with which the convert associates might be small, such as a localized circle of fellow adherents, or it might be larger, perhaps a religious movement, a sect, or a denomination. The geographical extent of such a larger social entity may be local or trans-local, perhaps even international. In some cases, the social composition of a voluntaristic religious group, whether local or broader in scope, may cross lines of ethnicity, gender, age, economic level, and social status.

But, whether a person's religion is an inherited tradition or a voluntary choice, there is a social dimension, and there are social and even political consequences involved that are to be reckoned with in understanding any particular religious affirmation. To join in expressing the religious stance of a given group affirms and reinforces it, and each participant also receives, whether implicitly or explicitly, affirmation as part of the group and the benefits of participation in the group.

On the other hand, to dissent or to withhold participation in the religious stance of a given group can have more negative consequences. In the case of a traditional religion, it can mean that a dissenter, or merely someone who does not openly show observance of the religion, can be regarded by the group as behaving suspiciously, and perhaps can be seen as subversive, a threat to the solidarity and cohesion of the group, or at least a bit of a troublemaker. In the case of a voluntaristic religious group, those who are not adherents are typically considered in some way outsiders, whether they be regarded more kindly as lost souls who might come to see the validity of the group's religious stance, or are viewed more negatively as infidels, unbelievers, enemies of the truth, perhaps even a spiritually inferior form of humans.

If the religious stance or practice from which one is seen to dissent has an official status or is somehow especially linked with the political structures of the setting, then (whether by intention or not) religious dissent can also be taken as having political implications and can have political as well as social consequences. As I will use the terms in this discussion, "political" consequences involve specifically the actions and attitudes of government officials/representatives (whether local or wider), and "social" consequences have to do with the effects of a religious behavior upon relations with family, neighbors, friends, associates, and the rest of those who make up one's social world.

In the following pages, I wish to focus on the social and political consequences of devotion to Jesus for earliest Christians, particularly negative consequences, the social and political costs of being a Christian in the early years of the movement that came to be called "Christianity." As we shall see, the social and political costs involved make it remarkable that the young faith proved as attractive as it obviously was for some, and also may help us understand better the limits of its attraction for others.

The Roman Religious Environment

Before we consider the specific phenomena of earliest Christianity, however, it may be helpful to take basic stock of some features of the religious environment of the Roman period.[1] I shall begin with the wider "pagan" environment and then take special notice of the particular environment of Second-Temple Judaism.

What we have come to call "earliest Christianity" first emerged as a new religious movement in Second-Temple Judaism, and then quickly became a trans-local and trans-ethnic movement that won adherents of various backgrounds. As Arthur Darby Nock emphasized in a justly respected study many decades ago, the Roman period was a time of considerable religious diversity, with new and reformulated religious ideas and groups, along with the traditional deities and religious observances of the various peoples who made up the Roman Empire.[2] The impressive amount of travel, trade, and communication around the Mediterranean Basin and beyond facilitated the export and sharing of various traditional deities and attendant beliefs and practices; and the Roman period seems to have been a time of unprecedented religious voluntarism, with numerous people ready to consider religious options beyond their traditional deities and practices.[3] So, we could view early Christian faith as one of numerous religious options that were circulating in that time and to which one could "convert."

But it is also important to remember a crucial difference. As Nock emphasized, in general it is misleading to use the word "conversion" to designate the winning of adherents by the many religious groups that were active in the Roman world.[4] For most people in the Roman period, joining a

---

1. In an earlier publication, I have surveyed some features of the religious "environment" of earliest Christianity, drawing upon the work of numerous specialists in Roman-era religion: Larry W. Hurtado, *At the Origins of Christian Worship: The Context and Character of Earliest Christian Devotion* (Carlisle: Paternoster, 1999; Grand Rapids: Eerdmans, 2000), 7-38.

2. A. D. Nock, *Conversion: The Old and the New in Religion from Alexander the Great to Augustine of Hippo* (London: Oxford University Press, 1933).

3. See, e.g., Robert Turcan, *The Cults of the Roman Empire*, trans. Antonia Nevill (Oxford: Blackwell Publishers, 2000), who emphasizes the success of religious movements from the eastern parts of the Roman Empire. For wider treatments of Roman-era religion, see also Ramsay MacMullen, *Paganism in the Roman Empire* (New Haven: Yale University Press, 1981); and Mary Beard, John North, and Simon Price, *Religions of Rome*, vol. 1: *A History* (Cambridge: Cambridge University Press, 1998). Also worth noting is the collection of essays edited by A. H. Armstrong, *Classical Mediterranean Spirituality: Egyptian, Greek, Roman* (New York: Crossroad, 1986).

4. Nock, *Conversion*, 13-16.

new religious group did not mean forsaking their previous religious associations. However, unlike nearly all the other religious options of the time (but directly reflecting the Roman-era Jewish tradition in which it emerged), earliest Christian faith involved an *exclusivist* religious claim upon adherents. In all the earliest sources, the Christian message was about the one God of biblical tradition, and all other purported deities were regarded as mere "idols" and worse. Thus, for non-Jews, "pagans," a proper conversion to early Christian faith involved a radical *disassociation* from their previous traditional religious groups and practices.[5] For early Christians of Jewish background, of course, this rejection of the many deities of the Roman period was nothing new. But, as we shall see shortly, for Jews as well as for Gentiles, there were nevertheless often social consequences of associating with the emergent Christian movement.

Although Jews who identified themselves religiously with Jewish tradition seem characteristically to have shared some beliefs and concerns, there was also considerable diversity in Second-Temple Judaism.[6] The limitation of extant evidence requires some caution in what we can posit with confidence, but it seems reasonably clear that this diversity included several identifiable religious parties, each with a somewhat distinguishable emphasis.[7] For example, there were Pharisees, a group who represented a particularly strong concern to observe the Torah themselves and to promote observance of the Torah among other Jews as well. We also find references to Sadducees, a group about which we actually know very little, but which seems to have been particularly made up of Jews from priestly and quasi-aristocratic sectors of Roman Judea, and likely conservative in atti-

---

5. I use the word "pagan" without any pejorative connotation, simply as a shorthand designation of the vast majority of people of the Roman period, who were neither Jews nor Christians.

6. Two recent scholarly efforts to describe matters are the following: E. P. Sanders, *Judaism: Practice and Belief, 63 B.C.E.–66 C.E.* (London: SCM Press; Philadelphia: Trinity Press International, 1992); and Lester L. Grabbe, *Judaic Religion in the Second Temple Period: Belief and Practice from the Exile to Yavneh* (London: Routledge, 2000). Among many other useful studies, note also *The Jewish People in the First Century*, ed. S. Safrai and M. Stern, 2 vols., CRINT (Assen: Van Gorcum; Philadelphia: Fortress Press, 1974, 1976).

7. See, e.g., Grabbe, *Judaic Religion in the Second Temple Period*, 183-209. One of the crucial ancient sources is Josephus, *Jewish Antiquities* 18.11-25, who gives descriptions of three "philosophies," those of the Essenes, the Sadducees, and the Pharisees, and also that of a fourth group which Josephus credits Judas the Galilean with founding, and which engaged in violent, religiously motivated opposition to Roman rule.

tude.[8] With the discovery of the texts linked to the Qumran community, we have direct evidence of yet another identifiable expression of Jewish piety of the time.[9]

Then, as now, devout Jews differed in religious matters, sometimes sharply, even denouncing fellow Jews over differences of belief and practice deemed significant. For example, in the extra-canonical writing known as The Psalms of Solomon, there is strong criticism of "sinners," who appear to include fellow Jews whose behavior the author regards as seriously violating the Torah.[10] So it should not be entirely surprising that early Jewish Christians experienced some controversy and suffered some negative social consequences for their faith. Let us now turn to consider some of the specific sorts of tensions, both social and political, to which earliest Christians were subject as particular consequences of their devotion to Jesus.

Family Relationships

The evidence suggests that for both Gentiles and Jews, becoming an adherent of the early Christian movement could result in tensions with that most intimate social circle, one's family. A saying attributed to Jesus (Matt. 10:34-36; Luke 12:51-53) warns his followers of the divisive effects of their faith upon their immediate family relations (e.g., those with parents and children and in-laws). The stark prediction is that "one's foes will be members of one's own household" (Matt. 10:36), and in an associated saying, Jesus' followers are warned that they may have to choose between their commitment to him and their own family (Matt. 10:37-39; Luke 14:26-27).

8. In particular, the Sadducees are portrayed as refusing belief in bodily resurrection, a teaching especially promoted by the Pharisees. New Testament references are among the most important for our knowledge of these Second-Temple Jewish groups: e.g., Matt. 22:23/ Mark 12:18/Luke 20:27; Acts 23:6-7.

9. The literature on the Qumran texts and community is now enormous, and I limit my citation here to one excellent collection of studies by major scholars: *The Dead Sea Scrolls in Their Historical Context*, ed. Timothy H. Lim et al. (Edinburgh: T&T Clark, 2000).

10. The Psalms of Solomon comprise a collection commonly thought to have been composed in Hebrew (though the text is preserved only in some Greek and Syriac manuscripts) sometime in the latter half of the first century B.C.E. For an English translation, see, e.g., *The Apocryphal Old Testament*, ed. H. F. D. Sparks (Oxford: Oxford University Press, 1984), 649-82.

These sayings are widely thought to derive from an early collection of Jesus' sayings that was used as a source by the authors of Matthew and Luke.[11] Whatever the prior history of the sayings, it is likely that they were preserved and circulated in early circles of Jesus' followers because they reflected the experiences and expectations of these people.[12]

In another saying ascribed to Jesus (Mark 13:8-13; parallel versions in Matthew 24:9-14; Luke 21:12-19), his followers are warned that they may be delivered up to examination before "councils" (Greek: *synedria*) and synagogues, and may be arraigned before governors and rulers on account of faith in Jesus ("for my sake"). Then comes the stark warning that "brother will deliver up brother to death, and the father his child, and children will rise against parents and have them put to death, and you will be hated by all for my name's sake." This saying seems to address the situations of Jewish Christians in particular (only members of a Jewish community could have been arraigned before synagogues), but Gentile Christians as well could have seen themselves addressed in warnings about being brought before government officials and about betrayal by members of one's own family.

If early followers of Jesus held the sort of strong convictions about his unique significance that we see reflected everywhere in our earliest sources, and if they were zealous in advocating these convictions among other members of their families, it is not difficult to see how tensions could have arisen. The references to the sufferings involved as "for my [name's] sake" (e.g., Mark 13:9, 13) probably reflect the early Christian view that their devotion to Jesus was the provocation of the enmity from family and society and the issue on which they would be pressed when arraigned before authorities.

Among Gentile Christians, their advocacy of Jesus would characteristically have been accompanied by their refusal to participate in traditional religious practices of the family and the wider social group (e.g., worshipping deities of their city, guild, and other groups, and associated religious observances), providing a further basis for antagonism. Given that partic-

---

11. This sayings collection is often referred to by scholars as "Q." Though hypothetical, it is widely accepted as a good explanation for the 200-250 verses of Jesus' sayings common to Matthew and Luke.

12. Among the few studies relevant to the matter, see Stephen C. Barton, *Discipleship and Family Ties in Mark and Matthew*, SNTSMS 80 (Cambridge: Cambridge University Press, 1994).

ipation in the religious observances of one's city, for example, indicated solidarity in seeking the protection and blessings of the civic deities for the city, a deliberate withdrawal from such observances and an accompanying disdain for these deities would have provoked an understandable level of ire. Indeed, one could be seen as endangering the welfare of the city by failing to reverence its tutelary deities. As Elizabeth Castelli puts the matter,

> Sacrifice keeps the tenuous balance between the human world and the divine realm intact, assures that the dramatic vagaries of divine dissatisfaction will be held in check. In the Roman context, where sacrifice serves as a first line of defense in the preservation of political stability, the refusal to sacrifice or the perversion of the carefully balanced sacrifical relations produces threatening seismic fissures running underneath the foundations of society.[13]

For Jewish Christians as well, devotion to Jesus was likely the key polarizing issue that provoked antagonism and opposition, in their case from fellow Jews, including their own families. But here we must suspect that the more precise nature of the offense that drew such negative consequences was different. Jewish Christians were likely viewed by at least some fellow Jews as practicing and advocating an inappropriate reverence for a figure whom Jewish religious authorities had judged to be a false teacher, and whose violent death by crucifixion reflected his accursed standing.[14] Indeed, early Jewish-Christian reverence for Jesus may well have been seen by at least some other devout Jews as a dangerous infringement upon the uniqueness of the one God.[15] I shall return to this topic a bit later in this discussion.

---

13. Elizabeth A. Castelli, "Imperial Reimaginings of Christian Origins: Epic in Prudentius' Poem for the Martyr Eulalia," in *Reimagining Christian Origins: A Colloquium Honoring Burton L. Mack,* ed. Elizabeth A. Castelli and Hal Taussig (Valley Forge, Pa.: Trinity Press International, 1996), 179 (173-84).

14. Paul's contrast of the characteristic expression of Christian faith in Jesus, "Jesus is Lord," with its opposite, "Jesus is anathema," in 1 Corinthians 12:3, may reflect the cursing of Jesus in some Jewish circles of his day. For further discussion and evidence, see Chapter Seven of this book, which appeared earlier as Larry W. Hurtado, "Pre-70 C.E. Jewish Opposition to Christ-Devotion," *Journal of Theological Studies* 50 (1999): 35-58 (esp. 55-57).

15. See, e.g., Larry W. Hurtado, *Lord Jesus Christ: Devotion to Jesus in Earliest Christianity* (Grand Rapids: Eerdmans, 2003), esp. 155-216, "Judean Jewish Christianity."

Christians Married to Non-Christians

The New Testament also reflects the particular situation of early Christians married to "unbelievers," especially, it appears, "pagan" spouses. Our earliest reference to such relationships is in a letter of the Apostle Paul to the church at Corinth (1 Cor. 7:12-16).[16] It is worth noting that Paul here addresses both Christian men married to non-believing wives and Christian women married to non-believing husbands. That is, Paul seems to anticipate (and perhaps he even has direct knowledge of) both kinds of marital situations. If so, then the passage could offer interesting evidence that acceptance of Christian faith was, in at least some cases, very much an individual choice, and that marriage partners did not always simply follow the actions of their spouses in this matter.

Paul's specific instruction here is that the Christian husband or wife should not divorce the non-Christian spouse, but instead should continue to treat the marriage as valid and binding, and the children of the marriage as "holy."[17] Paul also mentions the possibility that the non-Christian spouse might choose to dissolve the marriage, in which case the Christian husband or wife is no longer "bound" to try to maintain the relationship (1 Cor. 7:15). But his final statement holds out another possibility: that the Christian partner might be able to "save" his or her non-Christian spouse, which probably means that the Christian partner may be able to influence the non-Christian spouse to adopt Christian faith.

In another passage from a somewhat later writing attributed to the Apostle Peter (but commonly thought by scholars to be written in his name posthumously), Christians are exhorted about how to conduct themselves in marriage, including those who may be married to non-Christians (1 Pet. 3:1-7).[18] Here again, there is no difference in what is expected of the Christian partner. Christian wives in particular are urged to

16. For more detailed analysis of this passage, see, e.g., Gordon D. Fee, *The First Epistle to the Corinthians,* NICNT (Grand Rapids: Eerdmans, 1987), 296-306.

17. In the context, the opposite of "holy" is that the children could be "unclean," a term that seems to reflect Levitical categories. So, "holy" here most likely means "legitimate" or religiously "clean." See Yonder Moynihan Gillihan, "Jewish Laws on Illicit Marriage, the Defilement of Offspring, and the Holiness of the Temple: A New Halakic Interpretation of 1 Corinthians 7:14," *Journal of Biblical Literature* 121 (2002): 711-44, for interesting comparisons of Paul's directions about interfaith marriage with rabbinic views.

18. For further discussion of this passage, see, e.g., Paul J. Achtemeier, *1 Peter,* Hermeneia (Minneapolis: Fortress Press, 1996), 205-19.

"submit" themselves to their own husbands, whether they be fellow believers or non-Christians. Obviously, however, in this passage the submission of Christian wives to pagan husbands could not entail submitting in matters of religious faith. Indeed, the passage holds out the hope that the unbelieving husband may even be won over to Christian faith by the impressive conduct of his Christian wife, and "without a word" (3:1). This last phrase suggests a concern that Christian wives should avoid generating a counterproductive response to their faith through unwisely propagandizing their husbands.

But the potential cause for tension and hostility from the non-Christian husband was not simply unwise nagging about religion by a Christian wife. In the eyes of those who represented Roman cultural traditions of the time, the proper wife was expected to worship and acknowledge only the deities and rites endorsed by her husband, and, as the Roman author Plutarch urged, she should avoid all "outlandish superstitions."[19] Paul Achtemeier has observed that this limitation on the religious choices open to wives in the Roman period rather obviously placed the Christian wife married to an "unconverted" husband in "a most difficult situation." For, particularly in the matter of religious commitment, as a Christian married to a pagan husband, "she may *not* be subordinated to him, thus [potentially] incurring his disapproval as well as that of his family and acquaintances."[20] Precisely because the Christian wife could not follow the demand to reverence only her non-Christian husband's deities, the passage urges her to make extra effort to demonstrate exemplary wifely behavior in all other areas of domestic life (1 Pet. 3:3-5). In the final word in the passage that Christian wives should not be influenced by fear (1 Pet. 3:6), we probably have an implicit reference to the real possibility that the pagan husband might employ fear and intimidation to try to compel acquiescence in religion, exactly what the Christian wife could not offer.[21]

---

19. Plutarch, *Moralia, Coniugalia praecepta*, 140D. For further discussion, see Achtemeier, *1 Peter*, esp. 208-11, with additional references to Roman-era sources. In Roman usage of the time, "superstition" could designate any kind of religion that seemed to deviate from the ancestral tradition, especially if it involved practices deemed extreme or bizarre in the eyes of advocates of Roman traditionalism such as Plutarch.

20. Achtemeier, *1 Peter*, 208.

21. On women's religious activities and interests in the Roman era generally, see, e.g., Ross Shepard Kraemer, *Her Share of the Blessings: Women's Religions among Pagans, Jews, and Christians in the Greco-Roman World* (New York/Oxford: Oxford University Press, 1992),

Christian Slaves

Before we turn to considering wider social circles, there is one more feature of the Roman-era household to consider, and, thankfully, one that, for
most of the likely readers of this book, does not form part of our experience today: slavery.[22] It is difficult to develop firm estimates, but it appears
that slave ownership was fairly common in the Roman period among
those with the financial means to own property.[23] We have direct references to indicate that slaves were among those who adopted the Christian
faith in the early decades and thereafter. For example, in 1 Corinthians 7:17-
24, the Apostle Paul includes a reference to Christian slaves in his exhortation to each believer to "lead the life which the Lord has assigned to him,
and in which God has called him" (7:17). Several other passages in New
Testament writings urge Christian slaves to obey their masters faithfully —
indeed, to render their service as done "unto the Lord" (e.g., Eph. 6:5-8;
Col. 3:22-25; Titus 2:9-10), from whom they may hope for a reward for
their good conduct.[24]

In some cases, the conversion of slaves may have come as a result of
their household master adopting Christian faith, as may be implied in the
story of the conversion of the Philippian jailer and "all his household" in

---

esp. 128-90 for her treatment of women's involvement in early Christianity. But, unfortunately, Kraemer does not seem to deal with the question of what particular opportunities
and consequences there were for married women who became Christians, especially if they
refused to participate in the (pagan) religious orientation favored by their husbands.

22. Tragically, slavery does continue to be practiced in some areas of the world, and
was, of course, a major social and economic phenomenon in societies such as Britain and
the United States well into the nineteenth century.

23. See Keith Bradley, *Slaves and Masters in the Roman Empire* (Oxford: Oxford University Press, 1987). Slaves were acquired in Roman wars, and thereafter were also bred and sup-
plied by dealers. Bradley (p. 14) observes, "To the extent that many of the accomplishments
of the upper classes depended upon the leisure time which accompanied the exploitation of
a servile labour force, slavery was a fundamental component of Roman society."

24. Bradley (*Slaves and Masters in the Roman Empire*, 38) is correct to note that the
early Christian sources exhibit an implicit acceptance of slavery, or at least offer no direct
challenge to the institution as such, and that exhortations to slaves to be obedient reflect the
dominant values of the Roman period. But he fails to note that in the early Christian sources
these exhortations are not in fact linked with fear of punishment, which he shows was the
characteristic motivation for slave behavior that was encouraged by Roman-era pagan writers. Instead, Christian sources exhort Christian slaves to render their obedience out of sin-
cerity and devotion to Christ (e.g., Eph. 6:5-8).

the Acts of the Apostles (16:30-34).[25] But there are also exhortations directed to Christian slaves of pagan masters and mistresses, and we must presume that these slaves somehow learned of Christian faith and adopted it individually as their own choice. Even more the case than with wives, such a move represented an interesting exercise of volition on the part of people whose status did not encourage it.

It is interesting to ask how slaves of pagan households might have learned of Christian faith on their own, and how and where they had opportunities to take instruction, be baptized, and meet with fellow believers. There were legal Roman holidays when slaves were supposedly to be free from their regular duties, and in cities especially slaves may have had opportunities for use of any free time given to them by their masters/mistresses. But, as Keith Bradley complains, our knowledge of the lives of slaves is in fact very limited and tentative, on account of the relative dearth of any extensive sources.[26]

The situation of a Christian slave in a pagan household would have been very difficult, probably even more difficult than that of a Christian wife married to an unbeliever. The exhortation in 1 Timothy 6:1-2 that Christian slaves should be obedient and should aim to make their service a testimony to their faith also includes a special encouragement not to show any less respect to Christian masters, the latter statement an implicit indication that there were also Christian slaves in pagan households. First Peter 2:18-19 urges Christian slaves to show obedience both to good and reasonable/kind masters and to harsh masters, the latter perhaps more likely to have been masters who did not share the faith of their Christian slaves.

Given that Christians were characteristically expected to avoid participation in religious rites directed to any deity other than the one God of the biblical tradition, slaves who adopted Christian faith on their own choice

---

25. Slaves were considered part of the household, and so the references in Acts 16:31-34 to the entire "house(hold)" (*oikos*, 16:31), "all those in his house" (16:32), and "all who belonged to him" (*hoi autou pantes*, 16:33) are almost certainly to be taken as inclusive of the jailer's family and any slaves owned by him.

26. Bradley, *Slaves and Masters in the Roman Empire*, 18-19. In a recent study, Dale B. Martin reviews intriguing inscriptional evidence about slaves in households, showing that they could sometimes be treated as a member of the family and could exercise significant responsibilities, including oversight of other slaves or nonslaves in the household. See "Slave Families and Slaves in Families," in *Early Christian Families in Context: An Interdisciplinary Dialogue*, ed. David L. Balch and Carolyn Osiek (Grand Rapids: Eerdmans, 2003), 207-30.

and then sought to distance themselves from the religious rites of their pagan household would likely have experienced some trouble. Aside from the question of what right slaves had to make their own religious choices without the approval and consent of their masters, especially if slaves demurred from further participation in the religious rites of the household, this may well have been taken as an offensive and disrespectful stance by their masters/mistresses.

Moreover, in a recent provocative study, Jennifer Glancy has focused on the difficult situation of Christian slaves of pagan masters, underscoring another particularly acute problem. The common Roman-era view was that slaves were the economic and *sexual* property of their masters and mistresses, mere "bodies" to be used as their owners saw fit, for labor or for pleasure.[27] Indeed, slaves were commonly referred to in Greek as mere "*sōmata*" ("bodies"), indicative of this attitude.[28] Insofar as a slave (male or female) may have been required to perform sexual services for his or her master or mistress, the Christian slave would have been put in a particularly difficult situation. Of course, such sexual exploitation and abuse would have been a grievous degradation for anyone. But for Christian slaves there was another problem. If they obeyed in such a matter, they would commit a grievous sin, fornication (Greek: *porneia*), violating the strict sexual teaching promoted in earliest Christian circles. If they attempted to refuse the sexual demand of their master/mistress, they could have been subject to extremely harsh treatment such as flogging.

We simply do not know much about the extent of the problem and what kinds of harsh consequences were suffered by Christian slaves, especially those in pagan households. But it is clear that Christian slaves of pagan masters/mistresses were in an especially vulnerable situation, and that some likely suffered for their faith, on account of the conflict between its behavioral demands and those pressed upon them by their owners.

---

27. See Jennifer A. Glancy, *Slavery in Early Christianity* (New York: Oxford University Press, 2002). But not all of Glancy's claims are equally persuasive. For another analysis, see Carolyn Osiek, "Female Slaves, Porneia, and the Limits of Obedience," in *Early Christian Families in Context*, 255-74.

28. Note, e.g., the use of this term in Revelation 18:13, in a list of goods bought and sold by the evil system referred to as "Babylon," the name the author uses to designate Rome. But note also that the author's use of *sōmata* here is immediately followed by his critique and rejection of what the term represents in his statement that the trafficking in these "bodies" is actually trading in "human souls."

Wider Social Relations

We turn now to survey briefly the wider social context in which early Christians experienced consequences of their devotion to Jesus. All the extant evidence suggests that from the earliest years (i.e., within the social context of Second-Temple Jewish religion), Jesus' followers encountered tensions over their faith.[29] The earliest direct evidence is testimony from someone who himself once had been involved vigorously in opposing the new movement of Jewish Christians.

In several letters written to groups of Christians whom he had established as "Apostle to the Gentiles," Saul/Paul refers to his previous opposition to Jewish Christians. The language he uses to portray his actions suggests that his opposition involved harsh, even violent actions (Gal. 1:13-14; 1 Cor. 15:9; Phil. 3:6).[30] This is especially so in Galatians 1:13-14, where he refers to having "violently" persecuted the young Christian movement, seeking to "destroy" it, as an expression of his great zeal for "the traditions of [his] fathers." Neither here nor in his other brief references, however, does Paul elaborate on his specific actions. The Acts of the Apostles refers to Saul/Paul "ravaging the church by entering house after house, dragging off both men and women, and committing them to prison" (8:3), "breathing threats and murder against the disciples of the Lord [Jesus]," and, with authorizing letters from the high priest, going to Damascus also to arrest followers of Jesus and bring them back to Jerusalem (9:1-2, 14). In the speech before Herod Agrippa in Acts, Paul depicts his pre-conversion aim as "to do many things against the name of Jesus of Nazareth" (26:9). As these passages in Acts are all secondhand reports, however, scholars have wondered how much to credit them. In the judgment of most schol-

---

29. In the following paragraphs, I draw upon my earlier study entitled "Pre-70 C.E. Jewish Opposition to Christ-Devotion" (Chapter Seven of this book). See also Claudia J. Setzer, *Jewish Responses to Early Christians: History and Polemics, 30-150 C.E.* (Minneapolis: Fortress Press, 1994).

30. See esp. Martin Hengel, *The Pre-Christian Paul* (London: SCM Press, 1991), 62-86, esp. 70-72; A. J. Hultgren, "Paul's Pre-Christian Persecutions of the Church: Their Purpose, Locale, and Nature," *Journal of Biblical Literature* 95 (1976): 97-111. Cf. Justin Taylor, "Why Did Paul Persecute the Church?" in *Tolerance and Intolerance in Early Judaism and Christianity,* ed. G. N. Stanton and G. G. Stroumsa (Cambridge: Cambridge University Press, 1998), 99-120, who suggests that Paul was a revolutionary zealot and opposed Jewish Christians because they would not take part in the national struggle for independence from Rome, a view of the pre-Christian Paul that seems to me entirely without foundation.

ars, we are safer in giving our primary attention to what Paul says about himself. Based on other uses of the Greek terms in Jewish writings of the period, Martin Hengel concluded that Paul's own description of his actions implies "brute force," the young Pharisee Saul acting perhaps in the tradition of Phinehas, the biblical vigilante praised for his forceful actions in defense of the Torah.[31]

As I have argued more fully elsewhere, it is likely that at least one major factor prompting Saul/Paul to act so aggressively against Jewish Christians was the level of the reverence that they gave to Jesus.[32] In the eyes of the "pre-Christian" Saul/Paul, Jesus was probably a justly executed false prophet, and so reverencing him as Messiah was altogether inappropriate. Indeed, this zealous Pharisee may have interpreted early Jewish-Christian devotion to Jesus as amounting to a serious compromise of the uniqueness of the one God, a violation of the First Commandment, and, if so, he was likely not unique in this judgment.

Other New Testament texts offer what appears to be evidence that first-century Jewish Christians experienced sharp opposition from within their Jewish communities. Several decades ago, Douglas Hare studied references to this in the Gospel of Matthew, and he concluded that Jewish opposition in this time was likely provoked by the kinds of reverence directed to Jesus by Jewish Christians, which must have struck many other Jews as idolatrous.[33] As we have already noted, Matthew includes warnings that Jesus' followers will be persecuted specifically "because of me [Jesus]" and "because of my [Jesus'] name" (e.g., 10:18, 22). The Gospel of Matthew is

---

31. Hengel, *The Pre-Christian Paul*, 71-72, discusses use of the Greek verb *portheo* in other New Testament writings (Luke and Acts), Josephus, and 4 Maccabees (4:23; 11:4). The story of Phinehas appears in Numbers 25:1-13, and his example is urged as a model for devout Jews by Roman-era Jewish writers such as Josephus (*Ant.* 4:145-58) and Philo of Alexandria (*Spec. Leg.* 1:54-57), and in 1 Maccabees 2:23-26 Mattathias's violent actions are praised as manifestations of a zealousness comparable to that of Phinehas. See the full discussion of the Phinehas tradition esp. in Torrey Seland, *Establishment Violence in Philo and Luke: A Study of Non-Conformity to the Torah and Jewish Vigilante Reactions* (Leiden: E. J. Brill, 1995), esp. 42-74.

32. Hurtado, "Pre-70 c.e. Jewish Opposition to Christ-Devotion," esp. 50-57 (Chapter Seven of this book, 168-77).

33. Douglas R. A. Hare, *The Theme of Jewish Persecution of Christians in the Gospel according to St. Matthew*, SNTSMS 6 (Cambridge: Cambridge University Press, 1967), paraphrasing his statement on p. 17. See also, Hurtado, "Pre-70 c.e. Jewish Opposition to Christ-Devotion," 155-60 herein.

commonly seen by scholars as reflecting circles with a particularly strong heritage in at least one kind or group of first-century Jewish Christians. These references to opposition in Matthew most likely reflect the sort of conflicts over devotion to Jesus that the readers had experienced specifically as members of their Jewish community, or knew of through reports of such experiences by Jewish Christians.[34]

Other texts support the likelihood that Jewish Christians at least sometimes generated sharp social conflict with fellow Jews over their devotion to Jesus. In the earliest narrative of the first-century Christian movement, the Acts of the Apostles, there are numerous references to such opposition from within the larger Jewish communities in which Jewish Christians sought to live and promote their convictions about Jesus' significance.[35] For example, Jewish-Christian leaders in Jerusalem are arraigned by the Jerusalem Temple authorities and warned to cease their speaking about Jesus (Acts 4:17-18; 5:40). Also, among the most dramatic and extended scenes in Acts is the account of Stephen, the Jewish-Christian leader whose controversial preaching leads directly to his death by stoning at the hands of fellow Jews, apparently enraged over what they see as his blasphemous claims about Jesus (Acts 6:8–8:1, esp. 7:54-60). Although this narrative may well reflect some dramatic heightening by the author, it is not entirely unthinkable that Jewish Christians may have generated the sort of violent antagonism that this episode depicts. But we must presume that the level of mortal violence portrayed in this narrative was rare.

Since the influential study by J. Louis Martyn, scholars are also well aware of the several references in the Gospel of John about Jewish Christians being excluded from the *synagogē* (John 9:22; 12:42; and particularly 16:1-3).[36] (It seems to me likely that in these references *synagogē* connotes the Jewish *community*, the sense of the word in a number of other ancient uses.) These statements in John, which are set in the narratives of Jesus' activities, are now commonly taken by scholars as actually reflecting the ex-

---

34. See, e.g., Graham N. Stanton, *A Gospel for a New People: Studies in Matthew* (Edinburgh: T&T Clark, 1992).

35. Helpful (though very brief) is the essay by Ernst Bammel, "Jewish Activity against Christians in Palestine according to Acts," in *The Book of Acts in Its First-Century Setting*, vol. 4: *Palestinian Setting*, ed. Richard Bauckham (Grand Rapids: Eerdmans, 1995), 357-63.

36. J. Louis Martyn, *History and Theology in the Fourth Gospel* (Nashville: Abingdon Press, 1979).

periences of the Jewish Christians whose traditions are preserved in John. That is, the sharp conflicts and punitive actions against Jewish followers of Jesus that are referred to in the Gospel of John actually took place in the period after Jesus' execution, and probably should be dated anywhere from a few years to a few decades earlier than the date of the composition of the Gospel of John as we now have it (which is usually dated sometime around 85-90 C.E.).

The expression of antagonism to Jewish Christians within the larger Jewish communities is likely to have varied. The references in John concern expulsion from the Jewish community, and one passage even raises the possibility of death at the hands of devout fellow Jews who see themselves as acting in service to God (John 16:2). Again, the story of the death of Stephen may preserve remembrance of the earliest such incident (which would help explain why the incident is then given such significance in Acts). However, to repeat the point: for various reasons we must presume that the deaths of Jewish followers of Jesus at the hands of fellow Jews were very few.[37] But it would take only one or two incidents to raise the specter of such violence among Jewish Christians, who must have felt very vulnerable on account of their limited numbers.

Both the narratives in Acts and firsthand statements by Paul indicate that Jewish Christians could certainly generate antagonism from fellow Jews (both in Roman Judea and in the Diaspora). But the more frequent expressions of this sort of attitude were probably verbal abuse, denunciation, and other measures by which members of a social group indicate strong disapproval of fellow members whom they see as in some way acting in an outrageous or offensive manner.

The more severe expressions of antagonism are likely to have been directed against those Jewish Christians who were more visible and active in pressing the claims of the young movement. In the catalog of personal costs that he suffered as a leading proponent of the Christian gospel (2 Cor. 11:22-29), Paul includes various punitive actions, some (but by no means all) at the hands of local Jewish authorities in some of the Diaspora cities in which he was active. His claim to have received floggings five times

---

37. Jews were no more given to violence than any other group. Moreover, in addition to a probable reluctance felt by many Jews to kill fellow Jews, Roman officials would likely have taken a dim view of any sector of the population of cities feeling free to carry out executions of their own. So, if the Stephen episode reflects an actual vigilante action, it must have been rare.

at the hands of fellow Jews (2 Cor. 11:24) is particularly interesting. Paul's reference to these as "forty lashes minus one" obviously indicates the punishment based on Deuteronomy 25:2-3 (and for which we have later legal discussion in the Mishnah, *Makkoth* 3.1-16). It bears noting that this punishment, which was most likely carried out by local synagogue authorities, could be inflicted only upon members of the Jewish community, and probably only if the perceived offender willingly submitted to it. So, Paul's willingness to submit to this rather severe punishment on at least five occasions during his itinerant ministry as "Apostle to the Gentiles" is a powerful testimony to his strong personal desire to continue to function as a member of his ancestral people. If Paul's reference in this same passage to being stoned (2 Cor. 11:25) likewise harks back to punishment at the hands of fellow Jews, then on that occasion his religious crime was seen as particularly severe, perhaps in terms of the charge of idolatry/apostasy based on Deuteronomy 13:1-11; 17:2-7.[38]

There is also rather clear evidence that Gentile Christians were subject to abuse of various types from fellow Gentiles, in addition to the possibility of opposition within their own households. In a letter to the Thessalonian church probably written about 51 C.E., Paul makes several references to such experiences. After rehearsing briefly his missionary visit that produced the conversion of the Thessalonian Christians (rather clearly identified as Gentiles in 1 Thess. 1:9-10), Paul then congratulates them for their steadfastness in the face of local opposition from their own people, comparing their experiences to those of Jewish believers in Judea who had experienced trouble from fellow Jews (2:14). Just a bit later in the letter, Paul urges his readers not to be deterred from their new faith by "these persecutions," and he reminds them of his previous warnings that suffering for their faith is simply a part of the lot of believers (3:3-4).

In Paul's letter to the Philippian congregation (also almost certainly Gentile converts, at least mainly), we have further allusions to the vulnerable situation of the small Christian circles in their larger social setting. He urges the Philippian believers to stand firm and together in their religious

---

38. For a survey of biblical background, see Raymond Westbrook, "Punishments and Crimes," *Anchor Bible Dictionary*, ed. D. N. Freedman, 6 vols. (New York: Doubleday, 1992), 5:546-56. Acts 14:19-20 portrays Paul being stoned in Lystra by enraged fellow Jews. Note, however, that in Acts 14:5 a mixed group of Gentiles and Jews are portrayed as aiming "to mistreat and stone" Paul and Barnabas.

profession, and not to be intimidated by their (unspecified) "opponents" (Phil. 1:27-28), remaining strong in the assurance that God has "graciously granted you the privilege not only of believing in Christ, but of suffering for him as well" (1:29).

These references are important but also frustrating in their lack of specificity as to what precisely were the troubles experienced by these early groups of Gentile Christians. The most specific firsthand information is, as noted already, from Paul, particularly in 2 Corinthians 11:22-29. In addition to his references here to trouble from fellow Jews, he also mentions numerous imprisonments, "countless floggings" (which appear to go beyond those attributed to Jewish authorities in 11:24), three times being beaten with rods (presumably punishment meted out by civil authorities), and unspecified and varied dangers "from Gentiles" and others. Earlier in the same letter, Paul refers to severe affliction that he experienced in the Roman province of Asia (2 Cor. 1:8-11). Although he does not specify what happened, his rather candid description of the effects upon him and his missionary companions indicates something traumatizing, from which he is grateful to have been rescued by God: "We were so utterly, unbearably crushed that we despaired of life itself. Indeed, we felt that we had received the sentence of death . . ." (1:8-9).

The narratives in Acts set in the various cities of Paul's missionary efforts likely incorporate some dramatic license on the part of the author, and they also focus particularly on the leading characters, Paul and his close companions. But we may get some further glimpses of the sorts of tensions and social disturbances that early Gentile Christians could encounter, especially those who were more active in promoting their faith. We have scenes of public disputation and polarization of residents of some cities (e.g., in Lystra, Acts 14:1-7). In one of these scenes, an uproarious mob attacks the house where Paul was thought to be staying and drags the Jewish owner, named Jason, before the city authorities on accusations of complicity in violating imperial decrees by claiming that Jesus is the true king (Acts 17:1-9). In the famous scene of Paul addressing Greek philosophers in Athens (Acts 17:16-34), people refer to him derisively as "a babbler" who appears to proclaim "foreign divinities" (17:18). In an even more dramatic and hostile scene, Ephesian artisans for whom the sale of images of the goddess Artemis was a major economic concern are pictured as inciting a major disturbance leading to a near-riot in the city theater (Acts 19:23-41). This suggests a possible relationship of economic and religious concerns in the antagonism generated by early Christianity, a matter to which I return briefly later in this chapter.

As I have already noted, the author of Acts probably selected (and perhaps enhanced) scenes that were more useful for dramatic purposes, particularly in portraying Paul and his companions in heroic terms. For most ordinary Gentile believers, the social tensions experienced likely involved mainly their own immediate social circles of friends, neighbors, co-workers, fellow members of their guilds, and so forth. But, to repeat another point made previously, given that virtually every area of social life was marked with religious acts and connotations, the early Christian scruple against reverencing any deity but the one God of biblical tradition would have comprised a wide basis for potential tensions and antagonism.[39] Libations to tutelary deities were a regular part of many social occasions such as guild dinners or the meetings of city authorities. Gentile Christian converts would have had to consider whether they could in good conscience continue to participate in any of a number of social occasions that involved such overtly religious features and implications. Of course, this means also that they would have considered ways of negotiating their social life, trying to find events and venues in which they might continue to participate without compromising their religious scruples.

In a very useful recent study, Philip Harland has emphasized two points important to my discussion: (1) there was a diversity of early Christian judgments about how to negotiate their lives socially, and (2) a good many Christians sought to continue and demonstrate their participation in society in ways that they could see as avoiding involvement in the worship of the pagan deities.[40] Of course, early Christians appear not always to have made the same decisions about how to negotiate these concerns.

Perhaps the most interesting discussion of this topic is in 1 Corinthians (especially chapters 8 and 10), where Paul advises the Corinthian Christians (who were at least mainly Gentiles) about what they could and should not do with reference to the pagan deities and the foods that had been offered to these deities. It requires some close attention to follow the intricacy of Paul's discussion, but I shall confine myself here to the major points. Essentially, there are two issues. First, there were concerns about

---

39. I refer again to my discussion in *At the Origins of Christian Worship*, 7-38.

40. Philip A. Harland, *Associations, Synagogues, and Congregations: Claiming a Place in Ancient Mediterranean Society* (Minneapolis: Fortress Press, 2003).

the eating of food (especially meat) sold in the market, as it may have been part of a sacrificial offering to a pagan deity *(eidōlothyta)*. Second, there was a question about participation in ritual activities that were overtly in honor of a pagan deity *(eidōlolatria)*. It is not clear whether the Corinthians treated these as distinguishable issues, or if, instead, it was part of Paul's contribution to make this distinction. In any case, he distinguishes these two issues, with instructions about each.

As to the one question, Paul advises the Corinthians that they can freely "eat whatever is sold in the meat market" in good conscience, even if this includes food that may have come from sacrifices in the pagan temples, for (quoting Psalm 24:1) "the earth and its fullness are the Lord's" (1 Cor. 10:25-26). That is, he urges his converts to think of the food available in the market not in terms of its possible use in pagan sacrifice, but in terms of the universal scope of the dominion of the Lord whom they serve as believers. He then also allows Christians to accept invitations to dine with "unbelievers" (pagans) and to "eat whatever is set before you" with a good conscience (10:27). In the Roman period, this is a significant position, in principle allowing Christians to continue at least some level of participation in social life outside of their Christian fellowship. But Paul also advises that, at such dinners, if the food is specifically identified as sacrificial food, then Gentile Christians are not to partake, lest those at the table, or fellow Christians who observe the event, take the eating of the food on such an occasion as a participation in the cultic reverence of a pagan deity (10:28-30) — that is, as joining in idolatry.

In 1 Corinthians 8, Paul seems to take basically the same stance. But in this passage he more explicitly indicates that there were differences among Christians about such matters. Some of the Gentile converts in Corinth appear to have taken the view that, if the pagan deities were merely idols (i.e., illusory things, not really gods), then Christians could treat sacrificial food with complete indifference, and could even partake of meals in pagan temples without fear of any sin.[41] Others, however, insisted that Christians should distance themselves entirely from pagan worship, and (as we have noted already) some were even troubled about eating any food from the market that had originated in sacrifices to the pagan deities. Paul certainly

---

41. A similarly bold view seems to have been advocated later also in some of the Asian churches addressed in the book of Revelation, whose author condemns those whom he sees as promoting the eating of food sacrificed to idols. See Revelation 2:14-15, 20-25.

affirms the monotheistic premise that was used as justification by those Christians with a more bold view of their options. But he also urges these Christians to act in consideration of their fellow believers who may not share their outlook, lest the boldness of certain believers bring discouragement and confusion to others. That is, Paul reminds the Corinthian Christians that their fellow believers form a crucial social circle whose welfare they are to take as a matter of concern sufficient to shape their behavior in appropriate ways.

On the other hand, as to *eidōlolatria,* the actual worship of pagan deities, in 1 Corinthians 10:1-22, Paul makes it clear that participation in cultic activities in overt reverence to pagan deities is absolutely incompatible with Christian faith. There is no flexibility here. Paul characterizes pagan sacrifices as offered "to demons and not to God," and he insists that Christians who partake of the Christian sacred meal (the "Lord's Supper") must not also partake of meals devoted to these demons (10:19-22). So, we see here a firm stance against idolatry (i.e., direct participation in cultic reverence of the pagan deities), combined with a certain readiness to identify ways in which Gentile Christians could continue to function in their social settings.

Also, as Philip Harland's recent book has emphasized, in other ways as well, early Christians (as true of Roman-era Jews too) often understandably sought to limit the tension with their wider social circles in a variety of ways.[42] From Paul's general exhortation in 1 Corinthians 10:31-32 to seek to avoid being offensive "to Jews or to Greeks or to the church of God," the evidence extends to more specific instructions, especially in Christian writings from the later first and/or early second century. For example, in 1 Peter 2:11-17, Gentile Christians are not only urged to regard themselves as "aliens and exiles," abstaining from "desires of the flesh" that are incompatible with their faith, but also exhorted to "conduct yourselves honorably among the Gentiles, so that, though they malign you as evildoers, they may see your honorable deeds and glorify God when he comes to judge" (1 Pet. 2:11-12). Moreover, "for the Lord's [Jesus'] sake" they are urged to accept in principle the authority of human offices and institutions, such as the emperor and his appointed governors (1 Pet. 2:13-14). Along with their love of fellow believers, they are also to show rightful honor to all, includ-

---

42. See esp. Harland, *Associations, Synagogues, and Congregations,* 213-64. But on some points of detail I demur.

ing specifically the emperor (2:17). Although the intended readers are going through a "fiery ordeal" (4:12) that includes being "reviled for the name of Christ" (4:14), they are to make an extra effort to reply "with gentleness and reverence" and conduct themselves so that those who malign them may be put to shame (3:13-16).

In another New Testament text we may have further insight into how early Christians sought to honor rulers without violating their monotheistic scruples. The author of 1 Timothy urges "supplications, prayers, intercessions, and thanksgivings for everyone, for kings and all in high offices," with the hope that believers will then be able to lead "a quiet and peaceable life" (2:1-2). So, as was the practice in Second-Temple Jewish tradition as well, early Christians appear to have been ready to offer prayer and thanksgiving *for* the emperor and other governmental officials, though they characteristically refused to treat any such figure as a rightful *recipient* of prayer or worship.

In other passages as well, there are clear concerns to make as good an impression as possible with outsiders. Thus, those appointed to congregational leadership must meet clear personal standards and be well regarded by outsiders (1 Tim. 3:1-7). Also, slaves are urged to treat their masters honorably "so that the name of God and the teaching may not be blasphemed" (6:1).

Political Consequences

We turn now to consider briefly the "political" consequences of devotion to Jesus for early Christians. I have in mind specifically the consequences at the hands of rulers and those involved in related official capacities.[43] As with so many other matters, for this as well our earliest firsthand evidence is from Paul's letters. The earliest explicit reference to conflict with a political regime is in 2 Corinthians 11:32, where Paul refers to his escape from Damascus, evading seizure by an official of King Aretas.[44] Apparently, the

43. There is a great deal of scholarly literature on this whole subject. There is a very helpful collection of evidence from outside the New Testament in Peter Guyot and Richard Klein, *Das Frühe Christentum bis zum Ende der Verfolgungen: Eine Dokumentation,* 2 vols. (Darmstadt: Wissenschaftliche Buchgesellschaft, 1993). In English, there is the accessible collection of material in *A New Eusebius: Documents Illustrative of the History of the Church to A.D. 337,* ed. J. Stevenson (London: SPCK, 1974).

44. It is not entirely clear whether at this time Damascus was under the rule of Aretas,

preaching of the Christian gospel by the newly converted Paul generated this action against him by the Nabataean king.[45]

Moreover, as we have already noted, in the same context Paul also refers to being beaten with rods three times (2 Cor. 11:25), which must indicate arrests and punishment by civil authorities in some of the Roman cities where he proclaimed the gospel. As C. K. Barrett observes about this text, Paul's crime was likely creating "a public disturbance" during his activities.[46] In the Acts of the Apostles we have several dramatic incidents narrated where Paul is brought before city authorities, in one case resulting in a flogging with rods and imprisonment (e.g., Acts 16:19-40).

The Acts of the Apostles also relates other early incidents where Jewish Christians fell into the hands of political authorities on account of their visibility as leaders in the young Jesus movement. We noted earlier the stories of Jewish-Christian leaders in Jerusalem being arrested by the Temple authorities in Acts 4:1-22 and Acts 5:17-42. In Acts 12:1-5, we are told that King Herod (Agrippa I) took action against some members of the Jerusalem church, including James Zebedee (one of the twelve disciples of Jesus in the Gospels), whom Herod then executed with the sword, and Simon Peter, whom Herod imprisoned.

Returning to Paul's own direct testimony (and confining ourselves here to the letters commonly regarded by scholars as indisputably from his hand), he wrote the letter to the Philippians during his imprisonment (e.g., Phil. 1:7, 12-26), and he even raises the specter of his execution (2:17-18). The fascinating little letter to Philemon likewise comes from an imprisoned Paul. According to early Christian tradition, Paul and Peter as well were ultimately executed in Rome, probably under orders of the emperor Nero (I will comment a bit more on Nero's pogrom later).[47]

---

or if the "ethnarch" of Aretas was aiming to seize Paul when he left the city. See the curiously different account in Acts 9:23-25, which claims that Paul escaped a Jewish plot to kill him. For discussion of the historical issues, see commentaries — e.g., C. K. Barrett, *A Commentary on the Second Epistle to the Corinthians* (London: Adam & Charles Black, 1973), 303-4.

45. In Galatians 1:17, Paul says that after his conversion he went to "Arabia," and then at some point afterward returned to Damascus. For a full discussion of relevant matters, see esp. Martin Hengel and Anna Maria Schwemer, *Paul between Damascus and Antioch: The Unknown Years* (London: SCM Press; Louisville: Westminster John Knox Press, 1997).

46. Barrett, *A Commentary on the Second Epistle to the Corinthians*, 297.

47. Harry W. Tarja, *The Martyrdom of St. Paul: Historical and Judicial Context, Traditions, and Legends*, WUNT 2/67 (Tübingen: Mohr, 1994); Daniel W. O'Connor, *Peter in*

From another evidential quarter entirely, the Jewish writer Flavius
Josephus gives an account of the death of another James, the brother of Jesus, at the hands of the high priest Ananus, who is said to have acted during a short period between the death of the Roman governor and the arrival of his successor.[48] According to Josephus, Ananus convened a
"sanhedrin" before whom he denounced James as having transgressed the
Torah, and Ananus then had James executed by stoning.

But it would appear that, at least in the early decades of the Christian
movement, there was far less of a danger to ordinary believers of being
brought before political authorities. Paul's undisputed letters to Christian
congregations in various Roman cities, written from approximately 50-60
C.E., make no reference to the danger of being arrested or brought to trial
for their faith. The very real tensions, which occasionally might include the
threat of physical harm, seem largely to have been what I mean here by
"social" consequences rather than "political" ones involving civil or imperial authorities.

Nevertheless, even though they appear not to have been common, especially in the first several decades of the Christian movement, there were
other incidents in which "ordinary" believers found themselves the objects
of rather severe actions by political authorities. The most famous is the
short but violent pogrom against Roman Christians instigated by Nero, reported by the Roman writers Tacitus and Suetonius.[49] Tacitus gives the
fuller account, describing an arrest of all who admitted to being Christians,
"an immense multitude" who were convicted on the charge of "hatred of
the human race" *(odium humani generis)*. Their deaths were hideous: some
were torn apart by dogs, others nailed to crosses, still others burned alive.

As briefly indicated earlier in this discussion, some New Testament
texts written in the later decades of the first century, or perhaps somewhat
later, refer to the possibility of Christians being brought before the authorities (almost certainly local authorities) on account of their faith. In the
Gospel passages that we looked at earlier in considering tensions within
families and the wider social circles of Christians, we also find warnings

Rome: The Literary, Liturgical, and Archaeological Evidence (New York: Columbia University
Press, 1969); H. G. Thümmel, *Die Memorien für Petrus und Paulus in Rom: Die
archäologischen Denkmäler und die literarische Tradition*, Arbeiten zur Kirchengeschichte 76
(Berlin/New York: De Gruyter, 1999).

48. Josephus, *Jewish Antiquities*, 20.197-203.
49. Tacitus, *Annals*, 15.44; Suetonius, *Life of Nero*, 16.2.

about being handed over for trial before political authorities ("governors and kings," Mark 13:9-11, and see parallel passages in Matthew 10:17-20 and Luke 21:12-15). In these passages, Jesus is pictured as addressing his disciples, who are remembered as revered Christian leaders by the intended readers. In 1 Peter 3:13-17, however, ordinary Christians are unambiguously warned of the possibility of being brought to trial as believers in Jesus, and they are urged not to be intimidated but to use the trial as an opportunity to give an account of their faith (3:15-16).

But, among New Testament writings, the book of Revelation gives the starkest picture of what Christians might expect from the Roman political system.[50] The author, a Jewish Christian named John (Yohanan) who himself may have been sent to the mines on Patmos on account of his Christian activities (1:9), warns his intended readers that their future will be one of two terrible alternatives. They will be forced to choose between apostasy and death at the hands of the Roman imperial system. The bloody consequences lie almost entirely in the future for these readers, however, for it appears that at the time of the writing of the book, perhaps only one Christian in the churches addressed has actually suffered martyrdom (Antipas of the church of Pergamum; see Revelation 2:13). That is, Revelation is more of a direct indication of the anxieties of some Christians about where their relations with the government authorities would lead than it is evidence of actual consequences suffered by Christians at the time of the composition of the book.

But only a little more than a decade beyond the likely date of the composition of Revelation, we learn of further martyrdoms among Christians at the hands of the Roman authorities. About 112 C.E., the Roman governor of Bithynia (in modern-day Turkey) wrote to the emperor Trajan to report on his interrogation and punishment of those identified to him as Christians. He seems to have been ready to punish anyone, whether leaders or ordinary adherents, who identified themselves as Christians, either executing them or, in the case of Roman citizens, sending them to Rome for further trial. It is noteworthy that Pliny felt confident in letting go free those who denied that they had ever been Christians as well as those who claimed that they had once been Christians but were no longer, if they

---

50. Among the many studies of Revelation, see also Steven J. Friesen, *Imperial Cults and the Apocalypse of John: Reading Revelation in the Ruins* (Oxford/New York: Oxford University Press, 2001).

were willing to recite a prayer to the gods, make supplication with incense and wine to the emperor's cult image, and curse Christ, "things which (so it is said) those who are really Christians cannot be made to do."[51]

Pliny refers to Christian faith as "a perverse and extravagant superstition," phrasing similar to that used by other Roman critics of early Christianity. But he does not actually accuse Christians of any crime other than their refusal to recant their faith when he demanded them to do so. Yet, in fact, Pliny may give us a further indication of why Christians could stir up both social and political antagonism. He also reports that although this "superstition" had penetrated far into cities, villages, and the countryside, he was confident that the sort of vigorous action that he reported to Trajan in this letter could yet stop it, and that "the almost deserted temples" and their attendant ceremonies would be restored to popular favor. This, he says, would reinvigorate also the economic life associated with the temples, such as the sale of sacrificial victims and fodder for them.[52] In short, one of the reasons that the spread of Christian faith probably angered people and also brought the hostile attention of Roman authorities was that it could have an impact upon those economic activities associated with the deities whose worship Christians shunned completely out of exclusive devotion to the one God and his Christ.

Conclusion

Given the sorts of considerable negative consequences that could be suffered by becoming a Christian that we have surveyed here, we may wonder that the faith succeeded as it did. For Jewish Christians, there was the threat of disapproval and antagonism from fellow Jews, whether within the family or the larger Jewish community, which could even lead to community discipline. For Gentile Christians, the possibility of tensions appears to have been as great or even greater, for conversion to Christian faith meant a radical departure from their previous religious associations and practices, and these were central and pervasive features of social life in the Roman era.

51. Pliny (the Younger), *Epistles*, 10.96. See my discussion earlier (pp. 13-14), with further references.

52. See, e.g., Robert L. Wilken, *The Christians as the Romans Saw Them* (London/New Haven: Yale University Press, 1984).

Yet, clearly, those who embraced the early Christian faith felt that it was worth the negative consequences, whether these were social costs such as vilification and other expressions of antagonism, or — especially as the Christian movement came to the attention of Roman authorities — even political consequences. So, I think that we must assume that these early Christians found in their faith sufficient compensations to make up for the costs and consequences.

Part of what they obtained was (in sociological terms) a "fictive" family of meaningful intimacy. Fellow believers (both locally and wherever Christians were found) were their brothers and sisters; those older believers respected for their example and influence were their fathers and mothers. They exchanged with one another the "holy kiss," expressive of this intimate and committed relationship in their faith.[53] They were encouraged to care for one another also in practical terms, something remarked upon even by their pagan critics.

But behind this and other features of their corporate life as believers, there appears also to have been a powerful message and the nourishing experience of a religious devotion to the one God of the biblical tradition, and to Jesus, in whom they saw new and profound revelation of God's purposes.[54] I cite two eloquent examples. In a passage that still glows with the warmth of his fervor, although probably written not long before his own execution in Rome, the former Pharisee Paul exclaims that he regards as nothing all that he lost as a consequence of his faith in Jesus, and he professes himself still to have as his one great aim "to know him [Jesus] and the power of his resurrection and the sharing of his sufferings" (Phil. 3:10). My second example is that of Polycarp, a Gentile Christian of the second century. Offered freedom from a hideous execution by fire if he would "revile Christ," Polycarp's reported words are memorable: "For eighty-six years I have been his servant, and he has done me no wrong. How can I blaspheme my King who saved me?"[55] Though both passages are phrased for rhetorical effect, I contend that they also convey something of what devotion to Jesus meant for early Christians, and why they were ready to accept the social and political consequences of serving him in the Roman world.

---

53. See 1 Corinthians 16:20; 2 Corinthians 13:12; 1 Thessalonians 5:26; 1 Peter 5:14.
54. See, e.g., Hurtado, *At the Origins of Christian Worship*, 39-62.
55. *Martyrdom of Polycarp*, 9.3.

CHAPTER FOUR

A "Case Study" in Early Christian Devotion to Jesus: Philippians 2:6-11

Among New Testament passages expressive of early Christian devotion to Jesus, Philippians 2:6-11 holds a particular importance and has been the subject of considerable scholarly study. In the following discussion, my aims are to take stock of the passage and its remarkable religious stance, and to consider the occasion for these often-studied verses and their historical significance. That is, this will be a "case study" of a crucial passage that comprises a particularly revealing "window" upon early Christian belief and piety, especially with reference to the place of Jesus in early Christian faith and practice.[1]

Introductory Matters

Before we turn to the passage itself, it will be useful to take note of some major introductory questions and the most widely accepted answers to them. In the interest of having time to deal with the text itself, it is necessary to treat rather briefly issues to which in fact a huge body of scholarly publication has been devoted.[2]

---

1. I attempt here to build upon, and also to progress beyond, my own earlier studies of this passage: "Jesus as Lordly Example in Philippians 2:5-11," in *From Jesus to Paul: Studies in Honour of Francis Wright Beare,* ed. P. Richardson and J. C. Hurd (Waterloo: Wilfrid Laurier University Press, 1984), 113-26; and "Philippians 2:6-11," in *Prayer from Alexander to Constantine: A Critical Anthology,* ed. Mark Kiley (London/New York: Routledge, 1997), 235-39.

2. The most extensive analysis of scholarly investigation of the passage is Ralph P. Martin, *Carmen Christi: Philippians 2:5-11 in Recent Interpretation and in the Setting of Early*

A Hymn?

Although the idea does not seem to have occurred to anyone prior to the early twentieth century, it is now the dominant view of New Testament scholars that Philippians 2:6-11 preserves (or derives from) an early Christian "hymn" or "Christological ode" whose original provenance was in the setting of corporate worship.[3] In this view, Paul incorporated the words of this hymnic composition into his letter to the Philippian Christians, intending it as an inspiring narration of Jesus' humiliation and exaltation. The probable date of Paul's letter to the Philippians (ca. 60 C.E. if written during his imprisonment in Rome, which is the majority view; perhaps a few years earlier if written during a putative imprisonment in Ephesus, which some scholars propose) would make this passage the earliest extant example of a Christian hymnic composition. From other early texts we have references to the singing/chanting of "psalms" (probably the biblical psalms, at least some of which were understood with reference to Jesus in Christian circles) and of other compositions that were expressive of earliest Christian piety. We also hear of "hymns" and "spiritual songs" (Greek: *odai pneumatikai*), which were likely newly composed in early Christian circles.[4]

Prominent among the features widely thought to indicate the poetic nature of Philippians 2:6-11 are its highly compressed phrasing and its syntactical structure. There will be opportunities to illustrate these features when we look at the details of the passage shortly. Several other New Testament texts are also widely thought to be of a similar hymnic genre, but I repeat that this passage may be the earliest example that has survived from the very first few decades of the emergent Christian movement.[5]

Christian Worship, SNTSMS 4 (Cambridge: Cambridge University Press, 1967; rev. ed., Grand Rapids: Eerdmans, 1983; reprint, Downers Grove, Ill.: InterVarsity Press, 1997).

3. Among the few who dissent is G. D. Fee, *Paul's Letter to the Philippians* (Grand Rapids: Eerdmans, 1995), 192-97.

4. In 1 Corinthians 14:26, among the various verbal expressions that can form part of early Christian worship there is the "hymn," and in Colossians 3:16 and Ephesians 5:18-19, we have further references to such songs as part of corporate worship. For a full discussion of relevant matters, see Martin Hengel, "The Song about Christ in Earliest Worship," in *Studies in Early Christology* (Edinburgh: T&T Clark, 1995), 227-91. For a more introductory survey, see R. P. Martin, "Hymns, Hymn Fragments, Songs, Spiritual Songs," in *Dictionary of Paul and His Letters*, ed. G. F. Hawthorne and R. P. Martin (Downers Grove, Ill.: InterVarsity Press, 1993), 419-23.

5. Other New Testament passages often thought to embody early Christian odes/hymns

There have been numerous attempts to identify the specific poetic structure of this purported ode. Scholars have proposed two or three main "stanzas" and have even tried to discern poetic "strophes." The current printed editions of the Greek New Testament tend to reflect these efforts, setting out the passage in a poetic format. It is neither possible nor terribly important, however, to take further time here with these rather technical matters. I am more concerned here with the contents of the passage, and with what it signifies about the status of Jesus in earliest Christian religious devotion.

Clearly, the passage does not exhibit the formal features of Greek poetry, such as poetic meter. But we should expect this. In the hints and putative evidence within the New Testament about first-century Christian odes/hymns/songs used in worship, the clear impression is that in this period Christians imitated the style and structures of the biblical psalms. This is also exhibited in other compositions such as the extra-canonical Jewish collection of religious poetry known as the Psalms of Solomon (commonly dated sometime in the middle of the first century B.C.E.).[6] Moreover, earliest Christian "singing" was probably more like what we would call "chanting" rather than the more elaborate melodies that came to characterize Christian hymnody later. In the earliest period of Christianity, the use of meter and melody preferred in the wider culture was looked down upon by Christians as "pagan" elements that had no place in Christian worship.[7]

Original Language?

Likewise, it is not terribly worthwhile here to give much attention to the question of whether the Christological ode behind this passage was originally composed in Greek or Aramaic. It is in principle possible that there

---

include Colossians 1:15-20 and John 1:1-18. Curiously, many studies of New Testament hymns completely overlook the only passages that actually are clearly identified as hymns by the author: Revelation 4:8; 5:9-10; 15:3-4.

6. James H. Charlesworth, "Jewish Hymns, Odes, and Prayers (Ca. 167 B.C.E.–135 C.E.)," in *Early Judaism and Its Modern Interpreters,* ed. Robert A. Kraft and G. W. E. Nickelsburg (Atlanta: Scholars Press, 1986), 411-36.

7. See, e.g., Hengel, *Studies in Early Christology,* 249-62. For a wider-ranging survey, see James McKinnon, *Music in Early Christian Literature* (Cambridge: Cambridge University Press, 1987).

was an Aramaic "original," but there is no particular reason to think that this actually was the case.[8] If, as seems likely, Paul expected his readers to recognize the passage (or at least to recognize the ideas as expressed in the passage), then his Greek-speaking readers in Philippi must have been acquainted with the supposed ode (or with expressions like those of the passage) *in Greek*. Moreover, we should remind ourselves that from its earliest moments the young Christian movement (at least in Jerusalem and other urban settings) was a *bilingual* entity, comprising Greek-speaking and Aramaic-speaking believers, and a good many others who were effectively speakers of both languages. So, however early the Christological ode that may lie behind Philippians 2:6-11, it could have been composed from the outset in either language. But it survives in Greek, and our first duty is to take account of the text as we have it, to see what it may tell us about the piety that it reflects.

Hymns and Christology

As to content, it is patently clear that Philippians 2:6-11 is concerned with "Christology" (that is, with affirmations about the significance of Jesus). The clear thrust of the passage is an affirmation of Jesus' special significance. Indeed, virtually all of the earliest, sizeable, and significant Christological passages in the New Testament appear to be remnants of early Christian hymns, and it seems that such odes to and about Jesus may have been a crucial mode in which Jesus' exalted significance was articulated in the earliest years of Christianity. Under the impact of the religious fervor characteristic of earliest Christian circles, which they understood as the manifestation of God's Spirit, believers were moved to express their devotion to Jesus in composing and chanting odes that celebrated his deeds and high status.

With most previous studies of the passage, we are going to focus here on the *content* of this purported ode about Jesus, but it is also important to recognize the significance of the devotional *practice* of singing odes/songs about Jesus as a characteristic feature of worship. The singing/chanting of

8. See, e.g., J. A. Fitzmyer, "The Aramaic Background of Philippians 2:6-11," *Catholic Biblical Quarterly* 50 (1988): 470-83. Fitzmyer's "retro-translation" back into Aramaic illustrates the limits of our knowledge of first-century Aramaic. Moreover, merely making an Aramaic translation of the passage does not really comprise an argument that there ever was such an Aramaic version behind the present Greek text.

such odes is one of several phenomena that demonstrate the remarkable and innovative nature of early Christian worship, in which Jesus was programmatically included in the "devotional pattern" of early Christian circles along with God, and in ways otherwise reserved for God. I contend that this incorporation of Jesus into the devotional pattern as a subject and a recipient of corporate devotion is perhaps the most significant religious innovation that marks earliest Christian worship, especially in the context of Second-Temple Jewish religious tradition, which formed the immediate matrix out of which earliest Christianity developed.

Context and Purpose

I now turn to the passage itself, focusing first on the context and probable purpose. If what is now Philippians 2:6-11 originated as an early ode about Jesus, in its present context it forms part of a larger section of this epistle where Paul exhorts readers to humility and regard for others (esp. 2:1-5, 12-18). Although we are keenly interested in what the passage affirms about Jesus, it is important to note that Paul presents this material with no introduction or other indication that it needed an explanation for his readers. That is, although the passage is a particularly important expression of early Christian beliefs, the way it is used in Philippians practically requires us to think that Paul expected his readers to recognize and affirm either the passage (i.e., as an early ode/hymn known to them) or at least what the passage expresses *as reflective of what they already knew and affirmed about Jesus.*

This is very significant in historical terms. It means that the lofty things attributed to Jesus in this passage were already sufficiently familiar, at least in the early Christian circles in which Paul moved, that Paul felt no need to introduce or explain this remarkable, almost lyrical statement of Jesus' acts and standing. That is, Philippians 2:6-11 is strong evidence that what New Testament scholars call a "high" view of Jesus' significance and status had become reasonably widely shared within the short period between Jesus' death and the date of the epistle in which this passage appears. So, let us now turn to the passage to see more specifically what this "high" view of Jesus was as expressed in it.

Basic Approach

In view of the many publications on the passage, it is ironic that one of the most valuable studies, the Ph.D. of Takeshi Nagata, has never been published.[9] One of Nagata's valuable emphases is the importance of the interpretative standpoint from which we approach this passage. As I have noted already, the very compact mode of expression in Philippians 2:6-11 indicates that readers were expected to come to the passage acquainted with the convictions that it reflects and with the way that they are expressed. That is, these verses lay particular expectations or demands on readers. So a great deal of the scholarly discussion about the passage has been over what kind of conceptual scheme and standpoint it presupposes.

As Nagata shows, scholars have often approached Philippians 2:6-11 on the basis of this or that conceptual scheme and with presuppositions that are not developed inductively from the passage, and indeed that may do interpretative violence to it.[10] So, for example, one very influential interpreter, the German scholar Ernst Käsemann, presupposed a pre-Christian gnostic redeemer-myth as the background of the passage and its presentation of Jesus.[11] With the critical demise of this hypothesis, some scholars have proposed that the passage represents the adaptation of a supposedly pervasive Wisdom-myth, whereas other scholars have asserted a grand scheme of ancient Adam-speculation as the key background, these verses then seen as an expression of so-called Adam Christology, Jesus' obedience presented here in deliberate contrast with Adam's disobedience.[12]

In what follows, I shall take an approach that involves two major features. First, instead of presuming that the passage reflects the adaptation of

9. Takeshi Nagata, "Philippians 2:5-11: A Case Study in the Shaping of Early Christology," Ph.D. thesis, Princeton Theological Seminary, 1981, available from UMI Dissertation Services.

10. Nagata, "Philippians 2:5-11," esp. 9-95.

11. Ernst Käsemann, "Kritische Analyse von Phil. 2, 5-11," *Zeitschrift für Theologie und Kirche* 47 (1950): 313-60; the English translation can be found in *Journal for Theology and Church* 5 (New York: Harper & Row, 1968), 45-88. See also Robert Morgan, "Incarnation, Myth, and Theology: Ernst Käsemann's Interpretation of Philippians 2:5-11," in *Where Christology Began: Essays on Philippians 2,* ed. Ralph P. Martin and Brian J. Dodd (Louisville: Westminster John Knox Press, 1998), 43-73.

12. Perhaps the most well-known proponent of the Adam-Christology approach to this and many other New Testament passages is J. D. G. Dunn. See, e.g., his most recent defense of this approach: "Christ, Adam, and Pre-existence," in *Where Christology Began,* 74-83.

some pre-Christian conceptual scheme about this or that revealer or redeemer figure and then interpreting the statements through the lens of this scheme, I shall try a more inductive approach. I shall aim to build up a picture of what beliefs the passage presents and presupposes by close attention to the specifics of the passage itself. The second feature of my approach is perhaps the more novel one. Whereas most studies have focused more on the very difficult first few lines of the passage (vv. 6-8), I shall commence with the final verses (vv. 9-11) for reasons that I hope will become persuasive shortly.

Textual Analysis

I now turn to an more direct analysis. I wish to begin with an overview and more obvious observations, and then turn to more detailed matters. It may help to provide the Greek text and an English translation (my own).

Philippians 2:5-11

5 τοῦτο φρονεῖτε ἐν ὑμῖν ὃ καὶ	5 Maintain this attitude among yourselves,
ἐν Χριστῷ Ἰησοῦ,	which was also in Christ Jesus,
6 ὃς ἐν μορφῇ θεοῦ ὑπάρχων	6 who, being in the form of God,
οὐχ ἁρπαγμὸν ἡγήσατο	did not regard this being equal to God as
τὸ εἶναι ἴσα θεῷ,	something to be exploited,
7 ἀλλὰ ἑαυτὸν ἐκένωσεν	7 but instead he emptied himself,
μορφὴν δούλου λαβών,	taking[13] the form of a slave,
ἐν ὁμοιώματι ἀνθρώπων γενόμενος	and becoming in human likeness.
καὶ σχήματι εὑρεθεὶς ὡς ἄνθρωπος	And finding himself in human form
8 Ἐταπείνωσεν ἑαυτὸν	8 he humbled himself
γενόμενος ὑπήκοος μέχρι θανάτου,	becoming obedient to the point of death,
θανάτου δὲ σταυροῦ.	indeed, death on a cross.
9 διὸ καὶ ὁ θεὸς αὐτὸν ὑπερύψωσεν	9 Therefore, God also highly exalted him
καὶ ἐχαρίσατο αὐτῷ τὸ ὄνομα	and bestowed on him the name
τὸ ὑπὲρ πᾶν ὄνομα,	which is above every name,

---

13. I take the three Greek participles in vv. 7-8 as functioning to "unpack" the meaning of the main verbs ("emptied himself" and "humbled himself") with which they are linked. On this sort of use of the aorist participle, see, e.g., *A Greek Grammar of the New Testament*, ed. F. Blass, A. Debrunner, and R. W. Funk (Chicago: University of Chicago Press, 1961), 339.

10 ἵνα ἐν τῷ ὀνόματι Ἰησοῦ	10 so that in the name of Jesus
πᾶν γόνυ κάμψῃ	every knee should bow,
ἐπουρανίων καὶ ἐπιγείων	among heavenly and earthly
καὶ καταχθονίων	and nether-world spheres,
11 καὶ πᾶσα γλῶσσα ἐξομολογήσηται	11 and every tongue should acknowledge
ὅτι κύριος Ἰησοῦς Χριστὸς	that Jesus Christ is Lord[14]
εἰς δόξαν θεοῦ πατρός.	to the glory of God the Father.

Structure

We can begin by noting that the passage is a narrative, certain events and actions recited in a sequence. Note that there are two principal actors in this narrative. In vv. 6-8, Jesus is the subject of all the verbal forms and the key figure in view. In vv. 9-11, however, he is the object of all the verbs, and God is the figure whose actions direct all the events of these verses. So, as a very basic observation, the passage has two main parts, vv. 6-8 and vv. 9-11. Moreover, the actions in vv. 9-11 are presented not only as sequential to the actions in vv. 6-8 but also as in some direct way consequences of what is recited in these verses. The opening word of v. 9, "therefore" (Greek: διό), links what follows directly to what precedes. So the emphasis here is not primarily that God's exaltation reverses Jesus' humiliation (if that were the focus, we should expect to have a contrasting word such as ἀλλά, "but"). Instead, the "therefore" makes Jesus' humiliation in some way *a basis or grounds* for God's extraordinary exaltation of him. The humiliation and exaltation of Jesus, thus, are treated here as one connected set of actions, with one final outcome and purpose.

That outcome and purpose are set out in vv. 9-11, which means that these verses should be treated as the apex of the narrative, presenting the intended point of the whole drama. Yet, mainly because of the exhortation in 2:1-5 about humility and regard for others, which provides the immediate context for vv. 6-11, scholars have tended to focus much more on Jesus' actions in vv. 6-8, generally treating vv. 9-11 lightly, and sometimes even as an awkward bit difficult to incorporate into the concern about humility.[15] Moreover, vv. 6-8 bristle with exegetical difficulties that become apparent

14. The ὅτι in v. 11 could also be taken as functioning like quotation marks, and the words "Κύριος Ἰησοῦς Χριστός" could be read as the actual acclamation: "Lord Jesus Christ."

15. For review of scholarship on the matter, see esp. Larry J. Kreitzer, "When He at Last Is First!: Philippians 2:9-11 and the Exaltation of the Lord," in *Where Christology Began*, 111-27.

in attempting to determine the full sense of some very unusual expressions, such as "form of God," the statement about not regarding equality with God as something to be exploited, "emptied himself," "human likeness," and still others. Furthermore, the characteristic focus on Christological issues in Christian doctrinal reflection has been another reason why these fascinating statements about Jesus' actions and status have understandably drawn more attention than vv. 9-11.

But precisely because of the difficulties of vv. 6-8, there may be value in commencing with vv. 9-11. Also, because in the conceptual world presupposed in the text God is the ultimate authority, his actions and purposes giving meaning to all else, we have another good reason to focus on these verses where God is the key actor and where his purposes are, I submit, set forth rather transparently. I suggest that beginning with vv. 9-11 will more surely lead us to a correct understanding of the whole passage.

Acclamation of Jesus and Biblical Allusion

We may first note, as is fairly widely accepted, that in vv. 9-11 we have appropriations of biblical and Jewish tradition that readers are probably expected to recognize. This will give us a valuable pointer to the conceptual standpoint of the intended readers. The most obvious instance here is the appropriation and interpretative adaptation of wording from Isaiah 45:23 in vv. 10-11 to describe the obeisance to be given to Jesus by all spheres of creation. Isaiah 45:18-25 is unexcelled as a ringing declaration of the uniqueness of the God of biblical Israel. Three times we have the refrain that there is no other deity (vv. 18, 21, 22), and in 45:22-25 all the earth is summoned to join a universal submission to this one true God. It is nothing short of astonishing, therefore, to find phrasing from this passage appropriated to describe the acknowledgment of Jesus' universal supremacy. In what follows I will first translate from the Greek version of Isaiah (which is the likely form of Isaiah known among early Christian circles, whether Jewish or Gentile Christians of the time), and then I will note how the Isaiah passage is appropriated here in Philippians:

> Turn to me and be saved, those from the farthest part of the earth. I am God, and there is no other. By myself I have sworn; righteousness shall go forth from my mouth; my words shall not be turned aside. To me every knee shall bow and every tongue shall confess to God, [ἐμοὶ κάμψει

πᾶν γόνυ καὶ ἐξομολογήσεται πᾶσα γλῶσσα τῷ θεῷ] saying righteousness and glory shall be brought to him, and all who separate themselves shall be ashamed; from the LORD [ἀπὸ κυρίου] shall be vindicated, and in God [ἐν τῷ θεῷ] shall be glorified, all the seed of the sons of Israel.

In what may be thought of as a distinctively "Christological midrash" of this Isaiah passage, the universal acclamation of God is presented in Philippians 2:10-11 as taking the form of an acclamation of Jesus as "Lord" (Greek: *Kyrios*). Yet in the Philippians passage this obeisance to Jesus is ringed about, so to speak, by God himself. In v. 9 it is God who has exalted Jesus and has given him "the name above every name," and in the final (and, I contend, climactic) words of v. 11 it is the glory of God "the Father" that is ultimately served and expressed in the acclamation of Jesus' status.

Again, I wish to acknowledge Nagata's analysis, which seems to me to have captured very plausibly the specific nature of the early Christian exegetical move represented here.[16] He proposes that in Isaiah 45:23 the curious variation between the first-person pronoun ("to me") and the noun "God" (i.e., a third-person referent) may have provided a textual opening for some early Christian to discover in the passage two figures who are to be given reverence: Jesus, the "Lord" who speaks in first-person mode, and God. The same variation between "the Lord" and "God" appears elsewhere in the context as well — for example, in Isaiah 45:25.

So, having come to the passage with the prior conviction that God has exalted Jesus to heavenly prominence and has designated him as the "Lord" to whom all creation is to offer homage (a conviction that I think likely emerged through powerful religious experiences), some early Christian (or circle of Christians) found scriptural confirmation of this "binitarian" shape of the divine purpose portrayed in Isaiah 45:23. This creative understanding of the Isaiah passage must surely lie behind Philippians 2:9-11, and, indeed, this sort of "charismatic exegesis" of numerous biblical passages likely played a major part in earliest Christian efforts to understand the powerful religious events and experiences that prompted and shaped their faith.[17] Indeed, I suggest that it may have been

16. Nagata, "Philippians 2:5-11," 279-93, esp. 283.

17. David E. Aune, "Charismatic Exegesis in Early Judaism and Early Christianity," in *The Pseudepigrapha and Early Biblical Interpretation*, ed. James H. Charlesworth and Craig A. Evans (Sheffield: Sheffield Academic Press, 1993), 126-50.

particularly characteristic of *Jewish-Christian* circles, as they mined their traditional scriptures for insight into God's purposes in Jesus, and also sought to find scriptural justification for their convictions about his significance and status.

In addition to reading Isaiah 45:23 as referring to two figures, the "Lord" Jesus and God "the Father," the other adaptation of the passage is the midrashic-like specification of the universal acclamation of Jesus in Philippians 2:10. Jesus is to be given acclamation by all "heavenly, earthly, and nether-world [literally "under-earthly"] spheres/beings." This phrasing reflects, of course, an attested cosmology of the Roman era, reality understood as having both higher and lower dimensions beyond the earthly and mundane one. The worldwide supremacy of God in Isaiah 45:23 is expressed here as encompassing any and all dimensions of reality, however they may be understood.

Exaltation and the Supreme Name

That emphasis upon Jesus' high status has been struck already in v. 9, which relates the actions that represent God's response to Jesus' self-humbling. Following upon and responding to Jesus' humble obedience, even to death by crucifixion, God "highly exalted" Jesus. "Highly exalted" here translated the same Greek verb used in Psalm 96:9 (LXX; Psalm 97:9 in the Hebrew) to praise God's supremacy "far above all gods." God also gave to Jesus "the name above every name." Although we have no explicit reference to Jesus' resurrection here, it is most likely that God's exaltation of Jesus in Philippians 2:9 is implicitly linked to that event. In the New Testament, Jesus' resurrection was not simply a revivification of him; it also involved God's vindication and exaltation of him to a unique status — for example, "at the right hand" of God (the imagery and phrasing drawn from Psalm 110:1 [LXX 109:1], a key biblical text in earliest articulation of Jesus' status).[18]

---

18. It is commonly accepted that the many New Testament references to the resurrected Jesus being seated at God's "right hand" all reflect the early Christological interpretation of Psalm 110. New Testament references include Matthew 22:44/Mark 12:36/Luke 22:42; Mark 14:62; Acts 2:33; 5:31; 7:55-56; Romans 8:34; Ephesians 1:20; Colossians 3:1; Hebrews 1:3, 13; 8:1; 10:12; 1 Peter 3:21-22. For in-depth analysis, see, e.g., Martin Hengel, *Studies in Early Christology*, 119-225, and David M. Hay, *Glory at the Right Hand: Psalm 110 in Early Christianity* (Nashville: Abingdon Press, 1973).

Other early New Testament texts make similar claims about Jesus' exaltation by God. For instance, in Acts 2:29-36, we have claims about Jesus' resurrection (vv. 31-32) linked with God's exaltation of him (v. 33) and God's appointment of Jesus as "Lord and Christ/Messiah" (v. 36), all clearly complementary ways of referring to the same divine action. That is, Jesus' resurrection from death involved also his exaltation to heavenly glory and a unique status. In Romans 1:3-4, Paul refers to Jesus being designated as "Son of God in power . . . by his resurrection from the dead," phrasing that scholars commonly regard as reflecting an early faith-confession that Paul incorporated into his letter here. In the curious New Testament writing called "The Letter to the Hebrews," we have yet another reference to the idea that after his redemptive death Jesus was exalted to a unique heavenly status by God (1:3-4), and this is explicitly described as involving Jesus' superiority to angels and his obtaining a "name" that reflects his superiority. We may also note Ephesians 1:20-23, where again Jesus' resurrection is linked with his exaltation by God "far above every rule and authority and power and lordship and every name that is named, not only in this age but also in the coming age." In 1 Peter 3:21-22 there is a similar expression of faith.

To come back to our Philippians passage, in v. 9 particularly, the reference to Jesus being given "the name above every name" practically requires us to think of the traditional, devout Jewish estimation of the sacred name of God.[19] Moreover, we probably have here another echo of Isaiah 45:18-25. In the LXX of the Isaiah passage, *YHWH* is the *Kyrios* whose supremacy is to be manifest to all. So the acclamation in Philippians 2:11, *"Kyrios Iēsous Christos"* ("Jesus Christ/Messiah is [the] Lord"), specifies the exalted name now borne by Jesus.[20] As astonishing as it may be, Philippians 2:9 must be

19. See, e.g., Ephraim E. Urbach, "The Power of the Divine Name," in *The Sages: Their Concepts and Beliefs*, trans. Israel Abrahams (Cambridge: Harvard University Press, 1987), 124-34.

20. The Greek manuscript evidence indicating how the tetragrammaton was handled in pre-Christian Jewish Greek translations of biblical writings is very fragmentary. However, it appears that most often *YHWH* was not translated but written in some special and reverential manner (e.g., Hebrew characters). But equally strong evidence indicates that in reading Greek biblical manuscripts and in making oral references to the biblical God, devout Jews characteristically used a translation substitute, mainly *Kyrios*, just as the practice of substituting *Adonai* had begun to develop among devout readers of Hebrew biblical manuscripts. See, e.g., James R. Royse, "Philo, Kyrios, and the Tetragrammaton," *The Studia Philonica Annual* 3 (1991): 167-83.

taken as claiming that in some way God has given to Jesus (to share?) the divine name that was represented in Greek by *Kyrios* and represented in Hebrew by the tetragrammaton. As Nagata put it, "Vv. 10-11 make the exalted Jesus virtually God."[21] As we will see shortly, however, this does not mean that Jesus eclipses the God of biblical tradition. The exalted claims made about Jesus here represent a distinctive "mutation" in traditional Jewish monotheism, but certainly not an outright rejection of it.

In summary at this point, the description of God's action and purpose in Philippians 2:9-11 is adapted from, and makes deliberate allusion to, biblical and Jewish tradition. So, if there is a conceptual standpoint and an interpretative framework that readers are expected to bring to the passage, it appears to be this biblical/Jewish tradition, not some putatively pre-Christian gnostic redeemer-myth, or some other scheme such as Roman emperor-enthronement or the apotheosis of heroes. To be sure, what is done with biblical and Jewish tradition in Philippians 2:9-11 is novel and even astonishing. But one cannot really catch the full import of what is being asserted in these verses without recognizing the tradition that is drawn upon here to make these claims about God's actions and purposes with regard to Jesus. The obvious next question is what the circumstance was that may have led to the formation of these statements and this novel appropriation of biblical and Jewish tradition. I reserve this question for a bit later, after we have considered vv. 6-8.

Jesus' Self-humbling and Obedience

As we noted earlier in this discussion, most scholarship on Philippians 2:6-11 has been concerned primarily with vv. 6-8, where Jesus is the principal actor and the subject of all verbal forms. To probe these verses, we may commence at a basic syntactical level, and I ask readers who are not terribly fond of grammar to be patient as we do so. There are three indicative verbs that form the syntactical backbone of the passage. In v. 6, Jesus "did not regard" *(ouch hegēsato)* equality with God as an opportunity to exploit. Instead, he "emptied himself" (*heauton ekenōsen*, v. 7) and "humbled himself" (*etapeinōsen heauton,* v. 8).

The first of these main verbs forms part of an idiomatic phrase in Greek, the sense of which I accept as having been rightly identified by Roy

21. Nagata, "Philippians 2:5-11," 287.

Hoover.[22] The basic Greek idiomatic expression involves the verb *hēge-omai* (to consider/esteem/regard something), and the noun *harpagmos/harpagma* (advantage/opportunity), and the sort of expression used in Philippians 2:6 connotes regarding something as giving an opportunity to exploit for an advantage of some sort. In this case (v. 6), Jesus is pictured as having refused to regard "equality with God" in this way — that is, as something to exploit for his own advantage. Jesus' action of refusing to take advantage of his situation is clarified for us if we note that it is linked with the contrasting action of the next main verb in v. 7. Jesus did not exploit for himself being equal with God "*but* instead he emptied himself" (italics mine), and this action is explained further by the two participial phrases that immediately follow: "taking the form of a slave" *(morphēn doulou labōn)* and "being born in human likeness."[23]

So Jesus' self-emptying is portrayed here as having involved his taking a slave-form and being born in human likeness — that is, as a human. And this self-emptying is what Jesus *chose* for himself, instead of regarding equality with God as something to exploit for his own advantage. In short, v. 7 lays out the course of action Jesus took, in contrast to the possibility rejected in v. 6. But can we probe farther into what is portrayed in these verses?

In the first line of v. 6, Jesus is referred to as having "been/existed [*hyparchōn*] in the form of God [*en morphē theou*]." An enormous debate surrounds the meaning of this phrase, especially the connotation of the expression "in the form of God." But let us approach the phrase by bearing in mind its syntactically subordinate status in v. 6. That is, the syntax indicates that the emphasis here is on the two linked indicative verbs used in vv. 6 and 7 (which portray Jesus as choosing not to exploit "equality with God" and as having "emptied" himself). The participial phrase in the first line of v. 6, "being in the form of God," gives the setting, so to speak, for Jesus' choice not to regard equality with God as something to exploit for himself.

Although interpreters are understandably curious, even fascinated, about what "being in the form of God" might mean here, we should bear in mind that the phrasing gives little encouragement for metaphysical speculation. Whatever is ascribed to Jesus in the phrase, it is not the focus

22. Roy W. Hoover, "The Harpagmos Enigma: A Philological Solution," *Harvard Theological Review* 64 (1971): 95-119.

23. The aorist tense of the main verb, *ekenōsen*, and the participles of the dependent/modifying clauses, *labōn* and *genomenos*, mean that the actions are all in the past and are linked with each other.

and the key assertion, but is instead the context or setting for Jesus' self-humbling, which is the real focus in vv. 6-8. Moreover, it appears that the meaning of "being in the form of God" may have been presumed as apparent and known to the intended readers, for the text does virtually nothing to explain this interesting phrase.

But how are *we* to understand the function of this phrase? Is "being in the form of God" here to be taken as in some way heightening the significance of Jesus' decision? If so, should we then translate the phrase as "although being in the form of God, Jesus did not choose to exploit being equal with God, but instead emptied himself" (as, e.g., in the RSV, NRSV)? Or is this participial construction to be taken as simply setting the circumstance in which Jesus made his decision? That is, should we understand the phrase as something like "in the situation of being (already) in the form of God, he did not regard equality with God as something to exploit for himself"? Or, as C. F. D. Moule argues, are we to take this participial phrase as giving the basis or rationale for Jesus' decision: "Being in the form of God, he (therefore) did not regard equality with God as something to exploit for himself"?[24]

I am inclined toward what seems to me the simplest sense of the words among these options. I suggest that the most likely function of the opening participial phrase in v. 6 is simply to indicate Jesus' circumstance in which his decision took place. That is, in the situation of "being in the form of God," he chose not to exploit for his own advantage the equality with God that was involved. So Jesus' decision is to be seen here as made from a position in which he really had the opportunity to choose to do something else, something other than the self-humbling that he is pictured as having chosen in vv. 6-8.

"In the Form of God"

But what, more precisely, was Jesus' position or mode in which he was able to reject using equality with God as a selfish opportunity? What is meant by Jesus being "in the form of God"? This has generated such intense attention that we shall have to linger over the matter here as well, and this

---

24. C. F. D. Moule, "Further Reflections on Philippians 2:5-11," in *Apostolic History and the Gospel: Biblical and Historical Essays Presented to F. F. Bruce on His Sixtieth Birthday,* ed. W. Ward Gasque and Ralph P. Martin (Grand Rapids: Eerdmans, 1970), 264-76.

will require close attention to some further linguistic details. There are two main options proposed in current scholarship. One view that has gained some popularity in recent decades is that "form of God" *(morphē theou)* here is simply a fully synonymous expression for the "image of God" *(eikōn theou),* the phrase used to characterize Adam in the Genesis creation account (1:27). Those who advocate this view tend to see an intended and emphatic contrast here between Jesus and Adam, taking Philippians 2:6-8 as expressive of an "Adam Christology" that was supposedly well known in first-century Christian circles, and especially a feature of Paul's thought.[25] The other principal contender for the meaning of "form of God" is that it connotes some kind of divine-like status and mode of Jesus prior to his earthly life — that is, a heavenly "pre-existence." In this view, Jesus' choice to "empty" himself, which involved taking the "form of a slave" and "being born in human likeness" (v. 7), is to be understood as what in later Christian tradition is called the Incarnation, whereby he became the historic and genuinely human figure Jesus of Nazareth.

Those who propose an allusion to, and intended contrast with, Adam in vv. 6-8 also often question whether "being in the form of God" really connotes here Jesus' heavenly "pre-existence," urging instead that "form of God" was simply a way of referring to the Adam-like status of Jesus in his human/earthly existence. In this view, vv. 6-7 depict the decision of the human/earthly Jesus to take the path of humility and obedience to God, and Jesus' refusal to regard equality with God as something to exploit for himself is to be seen as an intended contrast to Adam's disobedient yielding to the temptation to be "like God/gods" (Gen. 3:5).[26]

One of the principal claims offered in support of this position is that the two Greek words, *morphē* and *eikōn,* are to be taken as synonymous terms in the same semantic field. This is, however, a dubious claim, at least as usually presented, for, as David Steenburg has shown, the two words in fact are used distinguishably.[27] Moreover, we must note that the semantic unit in question in Philippians 2:6 is not *morphē* but *morphē theou.* The question is not merely about the general scope of the Greek word for "form"; instead, the question is about the meaning of the specific Greek

25. See, e.g., Dunn, "Christ, Adam, and Pre-existence."

26. Cf. in Genesis 3:5 the LXX translation of the Hebrew *kelohim* as *hos theoi* ("like gods").

27. David Steenburg, "The Case against the Synonymity of *Morphe* and *Eikon,*" *Journal for the Study of the New Testament* 34 (1988): 77-86.

expression for "form of God." What we need to know is not whether the Greek words *morphē* and *eikōn* have some sort of general conceptual linkage, but whether the two words were *used* interchangeably, particularly in this sort of expression. Words often have a general set of possible meanings, but their particular meanings appear in *usage* and in syntactical relationship with other words, in phrases and sentences. So the more precise question before us is whether the expression "form of God" is likely to have been used here as a way of alluding to the description in Genesis of Adam as created "in the image of God."

As I have indicated in an earlier discussion of the matter, the answer is rather clearly negative.[28] In the Greek translation of relevant Genesis passages, the expression *eikōn theou* is consistently used to express the special status and significance of Adam and humankind (Gen. 1:26-27; 5:1; 9:6), and in subsequent allusions to this idea and to these texts in Greek writings of Jewish and early Christian provenance the same expression is likewise used consistently (e.g., Wisd. of Sol. 2:23; 7:26; Sirach 17:3; 1 Cor. 11:7; Col. 3:10). Furthermore, New Testament writers consistently use the term *eikōn* when they seem to appropriate the idea of divine "image" as a way of indicating Jesus' significance (2 Cor. 4:4; Col. 1:15), and when they make a clear linkage or contrast of Jesus with Adam (e.g., 1 Cor. 15:49; 2 Cor. 3:18). By contrast, *morphē* is never used elsewhere in any allusion to Adam in the New Testament, and *morphē theou* is not used at all in the Greek Tanach/ Old Testament or in any other Jewish or Christian text where we can identify an allusion to Adam.

So the alleged use of *morphē theou* to link Jesus with Adam in Philippians 2:6 would be a singular case without any analogy or precedent. As I have stated previously, such a way of making an allusion to Adam would also be "a particularly inept one as well."[29] For allusions to another text or oral tradition to work — that is, for intended readers/hearers to catch the allusion — one must use or adapt something from what one is alluding to that is sufficiently identifiable that the allusion can be noticed. In Philippians 2:6-8, however, there is not a single word from the Greek of the Genesis creation or temptation accounts, other than the word for "God." That hardly seems like an effective effort at allusion!

---

28. I draw here upon my discussion in *Lord Jesus Christ: Devotion to Jesus in Earliest Christianity* (Grand Rapids: Eerdmans, 2003), 121-23.

29. Hurtado, *Lord Jesus Christ*, 122.

The phrase used in Philippians 2:6 to describe what Jesus chose not to take advantage of, "being equal with/to God" *(to einai isa theō)*, appears to function here as another way of characterizing Jesus' status prior to his self-humbling, "being equal with God" paralleling the expression "in the form of God." The structure of the Greek here practically requires this, or at least links "being in the form of God" and "to be equal with God" rather closely.

It is worth noting, however, that "being equal to God" is likewise never used elsewhere in any identifiable allusion to Adam or his sin. In other writings of the ancient period, we do have references to people who sought to be equal with God/the gods, and in these references this is always treated negatively as foolish hubris.[30] So it would appear that in Philippians 2:6 we are to see Jesus' choice not to exploit being equal with God, a status that was his already, as a powerful contrast to the foolish efforts of humans to achieve such a status. In short, the allusion here is not particularly to Adam, but to a common expression of vain human hubris, Jesus' self-humbling to be seen as the opposite. And Jesus' action is presented as all the more impressive in that what he chose not to use for his own advantage is precisely what some arrogant humans were known to have sought in vain to obtain for themselves.

There is another problem in the claim that Philippians 2:6-8 makes an intended contrast with Adam that is strangely not often noticed. Neither in Genesis nor in references to Adam in other texts is Adam linked with the serpent's statement in Genesis 3:5 that eating of the fruit of the forbidden tree will make the humans "like God/gods." In the Genesis passage, of course, the serpent's insinuation is actually made to Eve, who is presented as drawn to eat the forbidden fruit because of what she judges to be its attractive qualities (Gen. 3:6). The references to Adam in subsequent writings make no point about him in particular as having sought to be "like God."[31] This motif just is not a part of the traditional ancient picture of

---

30. See, e.g., the Jewish accusation against Jesus in John 5:18, the lament of the dying Antiochus in 2 Maccabees 9:12, and Philo's scornful reference to the hubris of some rulers in *Legum allegoriae* 1.49.

31. To cite examples from the New Testament, Romans 5:12-21 simply refers to Adam's "transgression" (*parabasis*, v. 14, *paraptōma*, vv. 15, 17, 18), "disobedience" (*parakoēs*, v. 19), and to him as having sinned (*hamartēsantos*, v. 16). In 1 Timothy 2:14, Eve is specified as the one deceived by the serpent. In 2 Esdras (3:7, 21, 26; 7:11, 116, 117), Adam is said to have transgressed or sinned, but the specific nature of his act is not explicit.

Adam as transgressor. So, once again, if in Philippians 2:6 we are expected to see an allusion to Adam in the reference to Jesus' choice not to take advantage of equality with God, this would be without precedent or analogy.

There is yet one further observation that I think is relevant and has not been given sufficient attention. Remember from our preceding analysis of vv. 9-11 that we have there rather clear appropriation of, and allusion to, biblical and Jewish traditions. We can judge these to be so because they are signaled by the use of phrasing that can easily be identified with a biblical passage (as in the appropriation of Isaiah 45:23 in vv. 10-11, and probably an allusion to Psalm 97:9 in v. 9), or phrasing that readily connotes a traditional concept (as in v. 9, "the name above every name"). So we must ask why an author (whether Paul or some anonymous composer of an ode that Paul incorporated) who readily knew how to make allusions by the use of such verbal devices would have failed so completely to use any such device in vv. 6-7, if in fact he sought there to make an allusion to and contrast with Adam. Thus, in vv. 6-7, the more likely conclusion is that no allusion or direct contrast with Adam was intended.[32]

So, for a variety of reasons it seems more likely that vv. 6-7 refer to Jesus as being in some way "divine" in status or mode, and then becoming a human being.[33] We know that this sort of view of Jesus appeared early and is rather explicitly expressed in the Gospel of John, especially in John 1:1-18. Note also John 17:5, where, with his death looming, Jesus is pictured as praying "Father, glorify me in your own presence with the glory that I had in your presence before the world existed." The Gospel of John is usually dated sometime near 80-90 C.E., so, by then, this sort of idea was clearly circulating in at least some Christian circles. But can we really imagine that already by the date of Paul's letter to the Philippians, twenty to thirty years earlier than the Gospel of John, this notion was formed? In light of the preceding analysis of Philippians 2:6-7, it seems so. Indeed, in these verses the use of compact phrasing without explanation (e.g., "in the form of God") suggests that readers were expected to recognize what was being referred to, which would mean that well before this epistle the idea of Jesus' "preexistence" had become a part of Christian belief.

---

32. Nagata judged that, in comparison with Romans 5:12-21, "the motif of Adam-Christ is completely lacking in the hymn" ("Philippians 2:5-11," 258).

33. So also, e.g., Nagata, who took *morphē theou* in v. 6 as meaning that "Christ was clothed in the divine form" and "was a divine figure" ("Philippians 2:5-11," 208-10).

As I have indicated in an earlier publication, there is sufficient evidence that in pre-Christian Jewish tradition "there was a freedom, a tendency perhaps, to link particular characters of exceptional importance to the heavenly and pretemporal state."[34] Especially in ancient Jewish and Christian apocalyptic thought, figures of great eschatological significance could be thought of as in some way having a heavenly "pre-existence." So, given the strong conviction that Jesus is *the* eschatological redeemer, it would perhaps have been a logical move to think that he must also be ascribed a prior, heavenly status or existence, however that was understood.[35]

As for corroborating evidence from early New Testament writings, most scholars see Paul's reference to Jesus as the one "through whom are all things and through whom we exist" (1 Cor. 8:6) as reflecting the conviction that in some way Jesus was the agent of creation as well as the agent of redemption. Most scholars also see a more figurative reference to the idea of Jesus' pre-existence and "incarnation" in 2 Corinthians 8:9, where Paul tells his intended readers that Jesus "made himself poor, though he was rich, so that you might become rich through his poverty."

In Philippians 2:6, Jesus "being in the form of God" is clearly intended as in some way a contrast/comparison with his then "taking the form of a slave" in v. 7. If the latter represents his status and mode as a historical, earthly, human figure, then "being in the form of God" is surely best taken to represent a different and prior status or mode of being much higher than being human, which he chose not to exploit for his own advantage. This too suggests that we must imagine some notion of Jesus' heavenly "pre-existence" behind the opening words of v. 6.

Jesus' Obedience

The last of the three main verbs used in Philippians 2:6-8 to describe Jesus' actions is in v. 8, which tells us that Jesus "*humbled himself,* becoming obedient to the point of [his] death, indeed, death on a cross." One obvious question is how this action is to be understood in relation to the actions portrayed in vv. 6-7. For example, are we intended to take Jesus' self-

34. Hurtado, "Pre-existence," in *Dictionary of Paul and His Letters,* 744 (743-46), with citations of texts there.

35. For the "logic" involved, see esp. N. A. Dahl, "Christ, Creation, and the Church," in *The Background of the New Testament and Its Eschatology,* ed. W. D. Davies and D. Daube (Cambridge: Cambridge University Press, 1964), 422-43.

humbling in v. 8 as essentially a parallel description of Jesus' "self-emptying" in v. 7? Or do vv. 6-7 recount Jesus' movement from "being in the form of God" (and thus able to consider and reject exploiting for his own advantage equality with God) downward, so to speak, to take the "form of a slave" and become/be born "in human likeness," whereas v. 8 recounts a connected but distinguishable and subsequent action of self-humbling?

The latter option seems to do better justice to the Greek syntax of vv. 7-8, particularly if we take the last line of v. 7, "and finding himself in human form", as giving the circumstance in which Jesus "humbled himself, becoming obedient to the point of [his] death" (v. 8).[36] That is, the self-humbling and obedience in v. 8 are probably to be taken as referring to the readiness of the human Jesus to take the path of service (and this must be taken as obedience to God), even at the cost of his life through the violence of crucifixion.

Summary

Philippians 2:6-11 represents a two-part narrative recounting Jesus' self-abnegation, followed by God's consequent exaltation of him, and a presentation of God's aim in doing so. We began with vv. 9-11, where the stress is on God's exaltation of Jesus, noting in these verses the rather easily detectable allusion to Jewish and biblical traditions. We noted also the astonishing claims expressed in these allusions. The statement of God's exaltation of Jesus in the first line of v. 9 employs a verb that is used to celebrate God's own superiority over all divine/heavenly beings in Psalm 97:9 (96:9 LXX). In the same verse, Jesus is then portrayed as given God's own unique name, alluding to traditional Jewish reverence for the tetragrammaton. In vv. 10-11, the phrasing of Isaiah 45:23 is adapted to portray the divinely intended and universal acclamation of Jesus as "Lord." Yet this universal acclamation of Jesus is in fact also intended to serve "the glory of God the Father." Verses 9-11 give the ultimate outcome of the actions narrated in the entire passage. This outcome is determined by God, yet it involves the breathtaking inclusion of Jesus at the center of things, as the "Lord" by God's own appointment, and the one to whom cosmic acclamation is due.

---

36. Again, we have an aorist participial phrase in v. 7, καὶ σχήματι εὑρεθεὶς ὡς ἄνθρωπος, connected with an aorist verb, ἐταπείνωσεν. In such a construction, the participle indicates a prior circumstance for the action portrayed in the main verb.

This incomparable exaltation of Jesus by God is presented here as God's answer to Jesus' actions, as they are recounted in vv. 6-8. In these verses Jesus is the sole actor, and his deeds tend entirely in the direction of self-abnegation, service, and obedience, even to the point of a cruel death. The full extent of Jesus' self-abnegation probably includes an incarnation in which he moved in some way from previously "being in the form of God" and able to consider as his own "equality with God" (v. 6), instead "emptying" himself and taking the place and form of a slave, being born as a human (v. 7). In this situation/condition of being a man, he then humbled himself in an obedience that must be understood as offered to God (v. 8), his death by crucifixion thus to be seen as the deepest expression of his readiness to take the path of obedience.

The Occasion for This Ode

In its present immediate context, Philippians 2:6-11 seems to be intended to inspire the humility and consideration of others that Paul exhorts his readers to strive for in 2:1-5. Yet it is clear that 2:6-11 does not simply present Jesus as an example to be imitated, for the passage recounts actions that are not really feasible for the readers. For instance, if our estimate of the meaning of vv. 6-8 is correct, and Jesus is portrayed here as being in a divine status or mode, in which situation he chose freely to take on human existence, this is obviously not a choice that mere mortals can replicate! Likewise, although Philippian Christians are certainly encouraged to submit themselves to God in the hope of divine vindication, including a resurrection (3:20-21), the vindication and exaltation of Jesus portrayed in 2:9-11 is categorically unique. We have no reason to think that the intended readers were expected to aspire to an equivalent exaltation for themselves, with the entire cosmos acclaiming them as divine "Lord."

Moreover, to draw attention to another important point, in the description of Jesus' self-abnegation in vv. 6-8, there is no direct indication of his doing this for the sake of others. *The redemptive efficacy of his actions is not in view* in these verses. Had Paul composed the passage in the process of writing this letter to Philippi, I suggest that we would expect him to have described Jesus' self-humbling with more explicit reference to it as done for others. But, within the limits of 2:6-11, the focus is entirely on Jesus' self-humbling, God's answering exaltation of him, and the intended outcome of all this, with no direct reference to any benefit to others. Furthermore, the real apex of the actions recited in the passage is in vv. 9-11, where Jesus' incomparable exaltation and its ultimate purpose are portrayed.

Also, although the passage certainly presents us with some compact expressions that seem more to presuppose major beliefs and concepts than to explicate them, 2:6-11 does form a whole line of thought on its own. That is, readers are expected to bring to the passage some previous acquaintance with the faith stance that it reflects. With such an acquaintance, the "story line" in these verses is reasonably complete, even if the passage is read apart from its context. Answering the radically "downward" movement of Jesus that eventuated in his crucifixion, there is the radically "upward" movement of vv. 9-11, where God exalts him to a status far above all else. This recitation of Jesus' self-abnegation and God's exaltation of him is a "story" that is complete in itself and has an explicit point: the glory of God.

All of these considerations combine to support the suggestion that 2:6-11 was likely not composed by Paul while he was writing this letter to Philippi. Instead, as most New Testament scholars now think probable, this passage was originally composed in some other circumstance, and was then incorporated by Paul into this letter, where it presents Jesus as the "Lordly example" for believers.[37] In what follows, I want to consider briefly the possible setting in which these fascinating lines may first have been created. We have to ask what sort of concern might have prompted some early Christian to compose these famous verses. I suggest, again, that the focus and the contents of this ode give us our best hints.

Let us begin by reiterating that, where we can identify allusions, they are entirely to Jewish and biblical texts and traditions. Thus, for example, that which Jesus refused to take advantage of for his own benefit (being equal to God) is precisely what Jewish writers of the time condemned as representing the most benighted type of foolish human hubris (especially exhibited by human rulers who sought to be treated as divine). Likewise, the positive statements in the passage concerning Jesus' self-humbling and obedience and God's exaltation of him make recognizable general allusions to biblical texts and Jewish traditions (e.g., the righteous sufferer vindicated by God). I propose, therefore, that the most plausible originating context for this ode was a concern to express and defend devotion to Jesus

---

37. I allude here to the title and argument of my essay entitled "Jesus as Lordly Example in Philippians 2:5-11."

for those whose religious outlook and world of reference were shaped by Jewish and biblical traditions. That is, the ode appears to have been composed initially to portray in inspiring ways the earthly career of Jesus, including his hideous death, precisely as the expression of his exemplary, obedient service to God, and also to assert a unique exaltation of him as God's response to Jesus' life and violent death.[38] Moreover, the ode also implicitly justifies (for others?) the Christian cultic veneration of Jesus as "Lord," for in offering this devotion, believers respond to God's exaltation of him and its purpose, and they anticipate the universal acclamation that is presented here as eventually involving all spheres of reality.

This is, however, an ode, not an apologetic discourse. The passage is primarily a *celebration* of the actions of Jesus and God that are recounted in it, presenting in lyrical (though also dense and compact) phrasing notions that could require pages to explicate in ordinary prose. The passage still glows with the heat of the religious devotion that generated it in the first place. The impetus is clearly the convictions that it expresses, and the originating purpose was likely "doxological" — to affirm and praise Jesus and God.

More specifically, however, I suggest that the ode may reflect the desire to emphasize that the earthly events of Jesus' life are to be seen as the career of the uniquely obedient one, that the outcome of that career was God's unique exaltation and vindication of him, and that all this in turn both manifests and serves the glory of God. That is, while asserting an astonishing "binitarian" view, in which Jesus is linked with God and with divine purposes in an unprecedented way, the passage also reflects a concern to emphasize that Jesus' career and his subsequent exaltation as well do not really represent a threat to the one God of biblical tradition. Jesus' exaltation, in fact, has its basis and its ultimate meaning in the glory of the one God.

So perhaps (we can scarcely be any more confident of any suggestion)

---

38. I do not find persuasive the proposals that the phrases "indeed, death on a cross" *(thanatou de staurou)* in v. 8, and "to the glory of God the Father" *(eis doxan theou patros)* in v. 11 are not an original part of the ode but were added by Paul. Such proposals all seem to rest on misguided assumptions that the ode would have followed Greek poetic conventions about meter, even line length, etc. Moreover, the need to account for Jesus' crucifixion and the view that his high status was really the grandest expression of God's own purpose were hardly peculiar to Paul. It is an entirely reasonable idea, and a more economical one as well, to assume that the composer of this ode would have included these ideas and phrasing.

this ode originated, at least in part, to articulate a worshipful celebration and understanding of the earthly and exalted Jesus, particularly among and for Jewish Christians, or at least believers for whom this kind of "binitarian monotheism," presented with allusions to biblical and Jewish traditions, would have been especially meaningful. In the words of Nagata, "The theological issue is Jewish . . ."[39] In particular, the creative adaptation and interpretation of Isaiah 45:23 reflected in Philippians 2:10-11 represents an effort to present the exalted place of Jesus in Christian devotion as valid and defensible, and precisely in terms of the biblical passage that was unsurpassed as an expression of God's uniqueness. In short, this memorable articulation of Christian faith in Philippians 2:6-11 may preserve for us one remarkable instance of earliest Christians discovering Jesus in the sacred scriptures of Second-Temple Judaism under the impact of powerful religious experiences of revelation and inspiration.

---

39. Nagata, "Philippians 2:5-11," 363; cf. also 337. Nagata rightly judges that the effort to legitimate reverence for Jesus seems primarily intended for people linked to Jewish religious concerns, and would not have been so effective for those not acquainted with such concerns or with the biblical texts drawn upon in this passage.

PART II

DEFINITIONS AND DEFENSE

CHAPTER FIVE

First-Century Jewish Monotheism

In recent years a number of scholars have given attention to the question of "monotheism" in first-century Jewish religion, especially (but not exclusively) scholars interested in the emergence of "high Christology" and the reverence given to Jesus as divine in early Christian groups. In my book *One God, One Lord: Early Christian Devotion and Ancient Jewish Monotheism,* I urge that first-century Jewish religious commitment to the uniqueness of God is the crucial context in which to approach early Christian devotion to Christ.[1] More specifically, I emphasize two characteristics of ancient Jewish religiousness: (1) a remarkable ability to combine a genuine concern for God's uniqueness with an interest in other figures with transcendent attributes which are described in the most exalted terms and which we may call "principal agent" figures who are even likened to God in some cases; and (2) an exhibition of monotheistic scruples, particularly and most distinctively in public cultic/liturgical behavior.

The readiness of ancient Jews to include exalted figures, especially "principal agent" figures, in their conceptual schemes of God's sovereignty provides us with useful (though limited) analogies and valuable background for the early Christian conceptual accommodation of the risen/ex-

---

1. Larry W. Hurtado, *One God, One Lord: Early Christian Devotion and Ancient Jewish Monotheism* (Philadelphia: Fortress Press, 1988).

The original version of this chapter appeared in *Journal for the Study of the New Testament* 71 (1998): 3-26. Reprinted by permission of Sage Publications Ltd. My thanks to the editor and the publisher for permission to reuse the essay. I have made some small editorial changes for this book.

alted Jesus as God's designated plenipotentiary. On the other hand, ancient Jewish reluctance to offer public, corporate worship to principal-agent figures also makes the early Christian pattern of "binitarian" worship genuinely innovative and striking.

Recently a number of other scholars as well have explicitly made monotheism a crucial contextual feature of the Jewish religious matrix of earliest Christian belief and worship, including A. E. Harvey, J. D. G. Dunn, P. M. Casey, R. Bauckham, and N. T. Wright.[2] There are interesting disagreements among us about the development of devotion to Christ, but we all attribute to Greco-Roman Jewish religion a monotheistic stance, and we all find it a significant aspect of the historical context of earliest Christianity.[3] Moreover, we all agree that the worship of the glorified Jesus as divine marks a major and singular development in the context of Jewish monotheism.[4]

On the other hand, a few other scholars have argued that Jewish religion in the Greco-Roman period was not really monotheistic but was instead very much ready to acknowledge and reverence more than one divine being. Thus, these scholars contend, the early Christian cultic reverence of Christ is to be seen as merely a particular manifestation or extension of what they allege to have been a wider Jewish "ditheistic" (two deities) tendency.[5]

---

2. A. E. Harvey, *Jesus and the Constraints of History* (Philadelphia: Westminster Press, 1982); P. M. Casey, *From Jewish Prophet to Gentile God: The Origins and Development of New Testament Christology* (Louisville: Westminster John Knox Press; Cambridge: James Clarke & Co., 1991); J. D. G. Dunn, "Was Christianity a Monotheistic Faith from the Beginning?" *Scottish Journal of Theology* 35 (1982): 303-36; Dunn, "Foreword to the Second Edition," *Christology in the Making*, 2d ed. (London: SCM Press, 1989), where Dunn explicitly indicates how his views developed in the years after the first edition of this book in 1980; Dunn, *The Partings of the Ways between Christianity and Judaism and Their Significance for the Character of Christianity* (London: SCM Press, 1991), esp. chaps. 9-11; R. Bauckham, "The Worship of Jesus," in *The Climax of Prophecy* (Edinburgh: T&T Clark, 1993), 118-49; N. T. Wright, *The New Testament and the People of God* (Minneapolis: Fortress Press; London: SPCK, 1992), 248-59.

3. E.g., note the critique of Casey by Dunn, "The Making of Christology — Evolution or Unfolding?" in *Jesus of Nazareth, Lord and Christ: Essays on the Historical Jesus and New Testament Christology*, ed. J. B. Green and Max Turner (Carlisle: Paternoster Press; Grand Rapids: Eerdmans, 1994), 437-52.

4. I use the word "worship" here to designate open, formal, public, and intentional actions of invocation, adoration, appeal, praise, and communion that characterized the corporate cultic gatherings of early Christian groups and that were clearly patterned after the sort of cultic devotional actions otherwise reserved for God in scrupulous Jewish monotheistic circles.

5. See in particular Peter Hayman, "Monotheism — A Misused Word in Jewish

That informed scholars can disagree about whether Greco-Roman Jewish religion was in fact monotheistic indicates the need for further improvement in our approach to the question. In this discussion, I wish to strengthen and elaborate my own earlier argument that first-century Jewish religion characteristically exhibited a strongly monotheistic scruple, and I also offer some refinements in method and clarifications of key matters that I hope can assist us all in characterizing more accurately the religious setting of the origins of Christ-devotion. I begin with some methodological matters, after which I offer an analysis of the specific nature of first-century Jewish monotheism.

Methodological Matters

The first methodological point to emphasize is the importance of proceeding inductively in forming and using analytical categories such as "monotheism." On both sides of the issue (to varying degrees among the individual studies) there has been a tendency to proceed deductively from a priori presumptions of what "monotheism" must mean, instead of building up a view inductively from the evidence of the thought and practice of ancient Jews (and earliest Christians). It is mistaken to assume that we can evaluate ancient Jewish texts and beliefs in terms of whether or how closely they meet our own preconceived idea of "pure" monotheism.[6]

Studies?" *Journal of Jewish Studies* 42 (1991): 1-15; and Margaret Barker, *The Great Angel: A Study of Israel's Second God* (London: SPCK, 1992). Both of them argue that Greco-Roman Jewish religion manifests what amounts to a ditheistic tendency. Christopher Rowland claims that in Second-Temple Jewish tradition there developed a speculation about a bifurcation of the divine involving God and his personified glory; see "The Vision of the Risen Christ in Rev. i.13ff: The Debt of an Early Christology to an Aspect of Jewish Angelology," *Journal of Theological Studies* 31 (1980): 1-11; and *The Open Heaven* (London: SPCK; New York: Crossroad, 1982), 94-113. Traditions about the divine glory (and the divine name) are certainly important, but I do not find Rowland's case for a bifurcation of God convincing. See my discussion of his view in *One God, One Lord*, 85-90. On the divine glory, see esp. Carey C. Newman, *Paul's Glory-Christology: Tradition and Rhetoric*, NovTSup, 69 (Leiden: E. J. Brill, 1992); and cf. J. E. Fossum, *The Image of the Invisible God* (Göttingen: Vandenhoeck & Ruprecht; Freiburg: Universitätsverlag, 1995), 13-14.

6. E.g., early in his essay Hayman says, "I do not intend to proceed here by setting up a model definition of monotheism and then assessing the Jewish tradition against this yardstick." But unfortunately, he then proceeds to do so, in my judgment, by imposing such

Unless we proceed inductively, we almost unavoidably import a definition from the sphere of theological polemics in an attempt to do historical analysis. Protestants, for example, might find some forms of Roman
Catholic or Orthodox piety involving the saints and the Virgin problematic forms of monotheism, and this might constitute a fully valid *theological* issue to be explored. But scholars interested in historical analysis, I suggest, should take the various Protestant, Roman Catholic, and Orthodox
traditions as representing varying forms of Christian monotheism. If we
are to avoid a priori definitions and the imposition of our own theological
judgments, we have no choice but to accept as monotheism the religion of
those who profess to be monotheists, however much their religion varies
and may seem "complicated" with other beings in addition to the one God.
For historical investigation, our policy should be to take people as monotheistic if that is what they profess to be, in spite of what we might be inclined to regard at first as anomalies in their beliefs and religious practices.
Such "anomalies," I suggest, are extremely valuable data in shaping out of
the actual beliefs of real people and traditions our understanding of the
limits, flexibility, and varieties of monotheism.

To cite one important matter, there seems to be an implicit assumption on both sides that more than one transcendent being of any significance complicates or constitutes a weakening of or threat to monotheism.
Those who see first-century Jewish religion as monotheistic tend, therefore, to minimize the significance and attributes given by ancient Jews to
any transcendent beings other than God. But it is fairly clear that such figures as principal angels are to be understood as distinct beings that can
sometimes be described as exhibiting and bearing divine attributes and
powers. The descriptions of such beings are not simply rhetorical exer-
cises; they indicate in varying ways the participation of these beings in the
operation of divine purposes.

Those who question whether Greco-Roman Jewish religion was
monotheistic tend to emphasize the honorific ways in which transcendent
beings other than God are described and the prominent positions they oc-
cupy in the religious conceptions reflected in ancient Jewish texts. It is
clear that ancient Jews often envisioned a host of heavenly beings, includ-

---

things as a doctrine of *creatio ex nihilo* as a requirement of true monotheism ("Monotheism," 3-4), and by making the question turn on whether ancient Jews were "truly monistic"
(2) — that is, whether they believed in a plurality of heavenly beings.

ing powerful figures likened to God and closely associated with God. But does this plurality of heavenly beings indicate that Greco-Roman Jewish religion was not monotheistic, or does it rather indicate that historical expressions of monotheistic commitment may have been fully compatible with acknowledging important heavenly beings complementary in some way to, but also distinguished from, the "one God"? Only an inductive investigation of the religious professions and practices of particular groups and traditions can answer this question properly.

The evidence indicates interesting flexibility and variety in the expressions of monotheistic religiousness chronologically relevant for first-century Jewish and Christian groups. In previous work I have emphasized how early Christians such as Paul were able to refer to their beliefs in monotheistic language while accommodating devotion to Christ in terms and actions characteristically deemed by them as otherwise reserved for God (e.g., 1 Cor. 8:4-6). Though I have not found another fully analogous example of quite such a robust and programmatic binitarian monotheistic devotion in first-century Jewish tradition, with other scholars I have illustrated the sometimes astonishingly exalted ways that divine agents can be described in Jewish texts that exhibit a strong monotheistic orientation.[7] In particular, we should note the cases where a principal angel is given God's name (e.g., Yahoel) and is visually described in theophanic language, sometimes causing the human who encounters the angel to confuse the being initially with God.[8] These data illustrate the variety and flexibility in ancient Jewish monotheistic tradition, especially the ability to accommodate "divine" figures in addition to the God of Israel in the belief structure and religious outlook.

My second methodological point is that in addition to variety, we should allow for change and development across time periods. In his proposal that Jewish monotheism may have undergone some significant changes and developments in the late first and early second century, whether or not one finds his proposal persuasive in all specifics, Dunn seems commendably to allow for a more flexible and dynamic Jewish monotheism than is sometimes reflected in other studies.[9] It is possible,

7. Hurtado, *One God, One Lord,* esp. chaps. 2-4.

8. Hurtado, *One God, One Lord,* chap. 4. See Bauckham's study of this motif of confusing angels with God: "The Worship of Jesus," esp. 120-32; and L. T. Stuckenbruck, *Angel Veneration and Christology,* WUNT, 2/70 (Tübingen: J. C. B. Mohr [Paul Siebeck], 1995), 75-103.

9. See, e.g., Dunn, "Was Christianity a Monotheistic Faith?" 321-22.

for example, that in reaction to Jewish-Christian reverence for Jesus (and the exalted status of other divine agent figures in other Jewish circles, such as the "Elect One" of the *Similitudes of Enoch*), some rabbinic authorities may have advocated a less tolerant attitude toward the veneration of heavenly figures than may have characterized the earlier decades of the first century.[10] Or it may be that Jewish authorities sought to identify more explicitly acceptable and unacceptable kinds of reverence. In light of these possibilities, a careful and inductive approach sensitive to the dating of evidence and the possibility of change and development within religious traditions is essential.

As a third methodological point, I wish to emphasize the importance of giving attention to religious practices, especially cultic and liturgical practices and related behavior in forming our understanding of religious groups. In dealing with ancient religious traditions there is an understandable tendency for scholars to focus on questions about concepts and doctrines, and to exegete texts without paying sufficient attention to the larger context of religious practice of the people who produced and used the texts.

Thus, for example, scholars argue largely about whether ancient Jews conceived of more than one figure as divine, and they seek to answer the question almost entirely on the basis of semantic arguments about the meaning of honorific titles or phrases, without always studying adequately how ancient Jews practiced their faith. But in the same way that modern principles of linguistics persuasively teach us that the particular meaning of a word in any given occurrence is shaped crucially by the sentence in which it is used, and just as it is a basic principle of exegesis to understand the meaning of phrases and statements in the larger context of a passage or even a whole document, so it should be recognized as a basic principle in the analysis of religious traditions that the real meaning of words, phrases, and statements is always connected with the practice(s) of the religious tradition.

For ancient Jews, Christians, and pagans, the primary exhibitions of what we would call their religiousness were in cultic and liturgical behavior (e.g., sacrifice and equivalent phenomena), and Jewish and Christian

10. But it has to be noted that strong interest in exalted heavenly beings alongside God continues in post-Yavneh Jewish circles for a considerable period, as reflected, for e.g., in 3 Enoch. For a discussion of date, provenance, and religious significance, see P. Alexander, "3 (Hebrew Apocalypse of) Enoch," in *Old Testament Pseudepigrapha*, 2 vols., ed. J. H. Charlesworth (Garden City, N.Y.: Doubleday, 1983-85), 1:225-53.

monotheistic commitment was exhibited most explicitly and sharply in scruples about such worship behavior (as I shall argue more extensively later in this chapter). Consequently, if we wish to understand ancient Jewish and Christian monotheism, if we wish to measure its intensity, if we wish to know how it operated and what it meant "on the ground" (so to speak) in the lives of adherents, we should pay considerable attention to the way that their commitment to the uniqueness of one God was exhibited in their practice with regard to granting *cultic* veneration to other beings or figures.

Conscientious Jews (and Christians) not only refused to offer worship to other gods. As I have argued in *One God, One Lord,* and as I shall reiterate again below, it is precisely with reference to worship that ancient Jewish religious tradition also most clearly distinguished the unique one God from those other heavenly beings such as principal angels, which they clothed with god-like attributes and referred to as participating prominently in God's entourage. This is what makes the early readiness of monotheistic Christians to participate in the public cultic veneration of Jesus the most striking evidence that Christian devotion quickly constituted a significant innovation in Jewish exclusivist monotheism.

Jewish Monotheistic Profession

In light of the methodological points that I have urged in the preceding pages, let us now consider the question of whether first-century Jewish religion can really be considered meaningfully as monotheistic. The first thing to note is the strongly monotheistic profession characteristic of Jewish religiousness of this period. We are fortunate to have available studies by several other scholars, and so I shall restrict my discussion here to a few illustrations of ancient Jewish monotheistic rhetoric and point the reader to the studies in question for fuller presentations of the evidence.

In a lengthy article from 1955, Samuel Cohon surveys references in both ancient Jewish and non-Jewish texts illustrating Jewish self-affirmation and their identification by others in clearly monotheistic rhetoric.[11] Of non-

11. Samuel S. Cohon, "The Unity of God: A Study in Hellenistic and Rabbinic Theology," *Hebrew Union College Annual* 26 (1955): 425-79.

Jewish writers, we may note Tacitus as an example: "The Jews acknowledge one God only, and conceive of Him by the mind alone,"[12] reflecting Jewish monotheism and rejection of cultic images. Among non-rabbinic texts of Jewish provenance, Cohon surveys affirmations of God's uniqueness in *Sibylline Oracles* (3.11-12, 545-61; cf. 4.27-32; 5.172-76, 493-500), *Letter of Aristeas* (132-38), Wisdom of Solomon (13-15), and references in Philo (e.g., *Quaest. in Gen.* 4.8; *Vit. Mos.* 1.75; *Dec.* 52-81; *Spec. Leg.* 1.1-52; *Leg. All.* 3.97-99, 436-38) and Josephus (e.g., *Ant.* 2.12.4; *Apion* 2.33-198).[13]

We may also cite Ralph Marcus's frequently overlooked but very valuable compilation of theological vocabulary from Jewish Hellenistic texts (excluding Josephus and with only illustrative citations from Philo).[14] Marcus's main point was to indicate the degree to which Greek-speaking Jews maintained traditional expressions for God and the degree to which they adopted religious and philosophical vocabulary of Greek literature. Marcus listed about 470 expressions, attributing about 25 percent as borrowed from Greek literary tradition, the remaining, overwhelming majority coming from the Greek Bible.[15] His summary of the theological themes reflected in these expressions shows the strongly monotheistic nature of the concept of God they reflect: "God is variously represented as one and unique, as creator, ruler and king, residing in heaven, all-powerful, all-seeing, omniscient, as father of Israel, as saviour, as judge, as righteous, terrible, merciful, benevolent and forbearing."[16]

Marcus left Josephus out of his study because Adolf Schlatter had earlier devoted two publications to an in-depth analysis of Josephus's language and conception of God, showing Josephus's indebtedness and fidelity to the Jewish emphases on the uniqueness and sovereignty of the God of Israel.[17] Schlatter's studies were supplemented by R. J. H. Shutt in an article investigating whether Josephus's ways of referring to and describing God "show any appreciable influence of Greek language and cul-

12. Tacitus, *Histories* 5.3, cited in Cohon, "The Unity of God," 429.
13. Cohon, "The Unity of God," esp. 428-38.
14. Ralph Marcus, "Divine Names and Attributes in Hellenistic Jewish Literature," *Proceedings of the American Academy for Jewish Research 1931-32*, 43-120.
15. Marcus, "Divine Names and Attributes in Hellenistic Jewish Literature," esp. 47-48.
16. Marcus, "Divine Names and Attributes in Hellenistic Jewish Literature," 48.
17. Adolf Schlatter, *Wie sprach Josephus von Gott?* BFCT, 1/14 (Gütersloh: Bertelsmann, 1910), and *Die Theologie des Judentums nach dem Bericht des Josephus*, BFCT, 2/26 (Gütersloh: Bertelsmann, 1932).

ture."[18] Though he concedes that Josephus's expressions show the influence upon him of non-Jewish terms and ideas (e.g., references to "Fate" and "Fortune"), Shutt concludes that "fundamental theological principles of Judaism remained dominant in Josephus's writings, including the belief in the sovereignty of the one God of Israel over all."[19]

H. J. Wicks conducted a still valuable study covering Jewish apocryphal and apocalyptic literature of the Second-Temple period, analyzing the language and doctrine of God reflected therein. He gives persuasive evidence of strong monotheistic beliefs throughout the period and of a lively religious sense of God's sovereignty and accessibility.[20]

Surely the most wide-ranging analysis of Second-Temple Jewish monotheistic rhetoric, however, is in the Ph.D. dissertation of Paul Rainbow.[21] Working from a database of 200 passages where he finds monotheistic expressions (including about 25 passages from the New Testament), Rainbow offers some sophisticated linguistic analysis of the ten "forms of explicit monotheistic speech" characteristic of Greco-Roman Jewish texts.[22] These are as follows:

1. phrases linking a divine title with adjectives such as "one," "only," "sole," "alone," and the like;
2. God pictured as monarch over all;
3. a divine title linked with "living" and/or "true";
4. positive confessional formulas — "Yahweh is God" and the like;
5. explicit denials of other gods;
6. God's glory defined as not transferable;
7. God described as without rival;

18. R. J. H. Shutt, "The Concept of God in the Works of Flavius Josephus," *Journal of Jewish Studies* 31 (1980): 171-87. The quotation is from 172.

19. Shutt, "The Concept of God in the Works of Flavius Josephus," 185-86.

20. Henry J. Wicks, *The Doctrine of God in the Jewish Apocryphal and Apocalyptic Literature* (London: Hunter & Longhurst, 1915).

21. Paul A. Rainbow, "Monotheism and Christology in 1 Corinthians 8:4-6," Ph.D. dissertation, Oxford, 1987. See also Rainbow, "Jewish Monotheism as the Matrix for New Testament Christology: A Review Article," *Novum Testamentum* 33 (1991): 78-91, esp. 81-83 for an abbreviated citation of evidence from his dissertation.

22. Rainbow, "Monotheism and Christology in 1 Corinthians 8:4-6," esp. chap. 4. The 200 passages are listed in Appendix 1 (228-86). They include some passages from the Old Testament and the New Testament, but are mainly drawn from extra-canonical Jewish documents, with only token citations of Philo and Josephus.

8. God referred to as incomparable;
9. scriptural passages used as expressions of monotheism, e.g., the Shema; and
10. restrictions of worship to the one God.[23]

As the studies I have summarized here lay out the data in considerable detail and can be consulted, it would be tedious to burden this discussion with a host of additional references to the primary texts. I submit that the religious rhetoric of Greco-Roman Jewish texts indicates that Jews saw themselves as monotheists. If their willingness to include other heavenly beings in their beliefs may cause problems for some modern expectations that "pure" monotheism should entertain no such beings (as Peter Hayman and Margaret Barker complain), the real problem is in imposing such expectations. If we follow the principle that I advocate of taking as monotheists those who proclaim such a commitment, then ancient Jews must be seen characteristically as monotheists.

There are two major themes or concerns that seem to come through in this monotheistic rhetoric.[24] First, there is a concern to assert God's universal *sovereignty*. This is reflected with particular frequency in statements insisting that the one God created everything and rules over all, even nations that do not acknowledge this God. Even where spiritual powers of evil are pictured as opposing God, as is often the case in apocalyptic writings, their opposition is characteristically described as temporary and ultimately futile. Satan/Beliel/Mastema figures are rebellious servants of God whose attempts to thwart God's will only serve it by exposing the wicked

23. Of course, "one/only god" formulae can be found in "pagan" sources of the Greco-Roman period as well, as Erik Peterson has shown in *Heis Theos: Epigraphische, formgeschichtliche und religionsgeschichtliche Untersuchungen*, FRLANT, 24 (Göttingen: Vandenhoeck & Ruprecht, 1926). Note also Morton Smith, "The Common Theology of the Ancient Near East," *Journal of Biblical Literature* 71 (1952): 135-47. But in pagan religious practice, these formulae were fully compatible with the recognition and worship of all the gods, either as all valid manifestations of one common divine essence or as valid second-order gods under a high (often unknowable) god.

24. E. P. Sanders, *Judaism: Practice and Belief, 63 B.C.E.–66 C.E.* (London: SCM Press; Philadelphia: Trinity Press International, 1992), esp. 241-51; Yehoshua Amir, "Die Begegnung des biblischen und des philosophischen Monotheismus als Grundthema des jüdischen Hellenismus," *Evangelische Theologie* 38 (1978): 2-19; Amir, "Der jüdische Eingottglaube als Stein des Anstosses in der hellenistisch-römischen Welt," *Jahrbuch für biblische Theologie* 2 (1987): 58-75.

(who cooperate with evil) and by testing and proving the righteous (who oppose evil and remain true to God).

Second, there is a concern to assert God's *uniqueness*, which is characteristically expressed by contrasting God with the other deities familiar to ancient Jews in the larger religious environment. The classic ridicule of other gods and of the practice of worshipping images in Deutero-Isaiah (e.g., 40:18-20; 41:21-24; 45:20-21; 46:5-7) is echoed in texts of the Hellenistic and Roman periods (e.g., Wis. 13-15). We may take Philo's comment in his discussion of the First Commandment as representative of conscientious Jews of his time: "Let us, then, engrave deep in our hearts this as the first and most sacred of commandments; to acknowledge and honour one God who is above all, and let the idea that gods are many never even reach the ears of the man whose rule of life is to seek for truth in purity and guilelessness" (*Dec.* 65).

It is important to note that this concern for God's uniqueness also comes to expression in a contrast or distinction between God and his loyal heavenly retinue, the angels.[25] For example, angels, as created beings, can be distinguished from God, who is uncreated. In general, God is distinguished from the angels rhetorically with the emphasis that he is superior to them and is their master. Even when we have a principal angel such as Yahoel, who bears the divine name within him and in some sense may be taken thereby as "divine," as a special vehicle of God's attributes (*Apoc. Abr.* 10.3-4, 8-17), the angel acts at the pleasure of God, and is finally a minister of God, an extension of the sovereignty of the one God.

Worship Practice

The monotheistic profession evidenced in Greco-Roman Jewish religion is particularly exhibited in religious practice, especially devotional actions connected with the cultic setting.[26] Before we examine the evidence, it may be helpful to clarify the terms and distinctions that I shall use.

25. See Michael Mach, *Entwicklungsstadien des jüdischen Engelglaubens in vorrabinischer Zeit*, TSAJ, 34 (Tübingen: J. C. B. Mohr [Paul Siebeck], 1992) for an analysis of material from biblical texts through Josephus and other Greco-Roman evidence. In *A Thousand Thousands Served Him: Exegesis and the Naming of Angels in Ancient Judaism*, TSAJ, 36 (Tübingen: J. C. B. Mohr [Paul Siebeck], 1993), Saul M. Olyan emphasizes the Jewish creative exegetical use of the Old Testament as a source for naming and ranking God's angelic entourage.

26. This point is made persuasively by Amir, "Die Begegnung des biblischen und des

We may speak of various kinds and levels of veneration or reverence that members of a religious group or tradition may give to various beings and figures. As indicated already, ancient Jews (and Christians) were quite clearly able to accord honored places to angels and other exalted figures (e.g., Moses, Enoch, the Messiah) in their religious thought and life. We may refer to the sum of the overtly religious practices and actions of a person or group as a "pattern of devotion" or "devotional pattern." Within the spectrum of the devotional actions of a person or group, we may identify "cultic" actions or behavior, that is, prescribed and characteristic actions set within the sacred place or liturgical occasion, explicitly functioning as components of a person's or group's religious identity, and intended to effect, represent, maintain, and enhance the relationship between the devotee(s) and the deity/deities affirmed by the person or group. For example, ritual sacrifices are formal cultic actions for ancient Jews, as is formal and corporate or liturgical prayer. These specifically cultic devotional actions we may refer to as the "worship" practice(s) of a person or group. Not necessarily every venerative action or gesture may be intended or seen by the devotee(s) as "worship" in this specific sense of the term. We will see that Greco-Roman Jewish religion exhibits strong scruples about the legitimate objects of formal cultic or liturgical devotion and can be described as reserving "worship" for the one God, although the wider devotional activities may include other forms of reverence expressed for other figures.

We may begin our examination of devotional practices by pointing to an obvious datum about which I assume there will be no controversy: at least in the Greek and Roman eras, Jerusalem Temple sacrifice was offered exclusively to the one God of Israel. In other words, this central Jewish religious institution by its cultic practice reflects a strongly monotheistic ori-

---

philosophischen Monotheismus als Grundthema des jüdischen Hellenismus": "I would insist that monolatry was not only, as is usually thought, the preliminary stage, but actually the religious core of biblical monotheism" (4; trans. mine). On Jewish devotional practice in general, see Sanders, *Judaism,* esp. 95-209. Older studies include Adolf Büchler, *Types of Jewish-Palestinian Piety from 70 B.C.E. to 70 C.E.: The Ancient Pious Men,* Jews College Publications, 8 (London: Jews College, 1922), whose rather uncritical handling of rabbinic traditions will now be questioned, but whose study is still worth noting, especially for his discussion of the piety of the Psalms of Solomon (128-95). Schlatter, *Die Theologie des Judentums nach dem Bericht des Josephus,* includes a lengthy chapter (96-158) on the piety reflected in Josephus.

entation.[27] For all the lofty ways patriarchs and angels were described in contemporary Jewish texts, there was no cultus to them, no evidence of them receiving liturgical honors in the Temple services.

The Qumran texts show an apparent dissent from the administration of the Jerusalem Temple, but reflect no different orientation of religious devotion. The hymns (1QH) are sung to the one God. The prayers are offered to the one God. The *Songs of the Sabbath Sacrifice* show an interest in the worship offered by the heavenly court, with the angels' worship as a pattern and an inspiration for the earthly elect, but the angels are not objects of worship.[28]

As to the nature of synagogue services, though recent studies caution us about reading too much of later material into the pre-70 C.E. period and suggest greater variety and flexibility than was later the case, nevertheless all available evidence points to synagogue religious devotion focused on the one God and his Torah.[29] The Nash Papyrus (second century B.C.E.) gives evidence of the Decalogue and the *Shema*, key traditional expressions of God's uniqueness, being used for instructional and/or liturgical purposes.[30] Other texts suggest daily recitations of the *Shema* by at least some pious Jews of the Greco-Roman period, and there are wider indications of the impact of this classic monotheistic text on the devotional practices of Jews as shown in the use of *tefillin* and *mezuzot* and the custom of daily prayers (e.g., Josephus, *Ant.* 4.212).[31]

---

27. As I have pointed out elsewhere, whatever the pattern of cultic devotion at Elephantine, the material is hardly characteristic of the Jewish population of the Greco-Roman period and is, in any case, too early to be of direct relevance. See my *One God, One Lord*, 144 n. 83.

28. Carol Newsom, *Songs of the Sabbath Sacrifice: A Critical Edition*, HSS, 27 (Atlanta: Scholars Press, 1985). And see my comments and references to additional literature in *One God, One Lord*, 84-85.

29. For a helpful review of recent scholarship on the early synagogue service, see Paul Bradshaw, *The Search for the Origins of Christian Worship* (London: SPCK, 1992), 1-29.

30. See W. F. Albright, "A Biblical Fragment of the Maccabaean Age: The Nash Papyrus," *Journal of Biblical Literature* 56 (1937): 145-76. But cf. V. A. Tcherikover and A. Fuks, *Corpus Papyrorum Judaicarum*, 3 vols. (Cambridge: Harvard University Press, 1957-64), 1.107-8 (n. 48), who argue that the Nash Papyrus may date from the first or second century C.E. and may reflect a revival of Hebrew among Alexandrian Jews in this period.

31. See Sanders, *Judaism*, 196-97. Qumran phylacteries containing the *Shema* e.g., 4Q128-30, 4Q135, 4Q140, 4Q150, 4Q151 — are printed in R. De Vaux and J. T. Milik, *Qumran Grotte 4*, DJD, 6 (Oxford: Clarendon Press, 1977), 49-82.

We have a good deal of material with which to form impressions of the patterns of Jewish prayer in the Second-Temple period, as J. H. Charlesworth and David Flusser have shown in helpful inventories of the evidence.[32] Though the prayers recorded in the surviving texts may well be more rhetorically sophisticated than most spontaneous prayers of ordinary Jews of the time, it is likely that the basic pattern and themes are representative.

In his study of the doctrine of God in non-canonical Second-Temple texts cited earlier, Wicks included special attention to the prayers of these writings. Somewhat later, N. B. Johnson devoted a monograph to the prayers in these texts. Both demonstrated that all the prayers in these writings are offered to the God of Israel alone. Though angels may serve as bearers of prayers and as intercessors for humans (e.g., Tob. 12:11-15), God is the object of prayers by humans and angels alike.[33] As I have pointed out elsewhere, in those texts where angels figure prominently in the operation of God's sovereignty, God is the recipient of worship and the object of the prayers.[34] We may also note Bauckham's study of apocalyptic passages in which a human recipient of a revelation initially mistakes for God the angel who delivers it and starts to offer the being worship, but is forbidden by the angel to proceed.[35]

In the 1992 meeting of the Society of Biblical Literature, Clinton Arnold presented a study of epigraphical evidence in an effort to determine the pattern of Jewish piety reflected in it, especially concerned with the role of angels.[36] He grants that angels "figure prominently in the belief sys-

---

32. J. H. Charlesworth, "A Prolegomena to a New Study of the Jewish Background of the Hymns and Prayers in the New Testament," *Journal of Jewish Studies* 33 (1982): 265-85; Charlesworth, "Jewish Hymns, Odes, and Prayers (ca. 167 B.C.E.–135 C.E.)," in *Early Judaism and Its Modern Interpreters*, ed. R. A. Kraft and G. W. E. Nickelsburg (Atlanta: Scholars Press, 1986), 411-36; David Flusser, "Psalms, Hymns and Prayers," in *Jewish Writings of the Second Temple Period*, ed. M. E. Stone (Assen: Van Gorcum; Philadelphia: Fortress Press, 1984), 551-77.

33. Wicks, *The Doctrine of God in the Jewish Apocryphal and Apocalyptic Literature*, esp. 122-29; N. B. Johnson, *Prayer in the Apocrypha and Pseudepigrapha: A Study of the Jewish Concept of God*, SBLMS, 2 (Philadelphia: Society of Biblical Literature, 1948). More recently, see Agneta Enermalm-Ogawa, *Un langage de prière juif en grec: Le témoignage des deux premiers livres des Maccabées*, ConBNT, 17 (Uppsala: Almquist & Wiksell, 1987).

34. *One God, One Lord*, esp. 24-27.

35. Bauckham, "The Worship of Jesus." The key texts are *Apoc. Zeph.* 6.15; *Asc. Isa.* 7.21-22; Rev. 19:10; 22:8-9.

36. C. E. Arnold, "Mediator Figures in Asia Minor: Epigraphic Evidence," unpublished

tem" of the Jewish individuals or circles from which the inscriptions derive, and that angels are invoked for protection in an apotropaic manner. But he emphasizes that the evidence does not indicate any organized devotional pattern in which Jews "gather regularly to adore, pray to, and worship angels."[37] Subsequently, Arnold reaffirmed these points more extensively.[38] In another study, Loren Stuckenbruck likewise concludes that Jewish venerative language and practices involving angels (including invocations for assistance) were not intended to infringe on traditional Jewish monotheistic commitment and did not in fact amount to cultic worship of angels.[39] The inclusion of angels in rabbinic lists of prohibited objects of worship may be directed in part against such apotropaic invocations and against Jewish syncretistic dabbling in magical practices, as Michael Mach suggests.[40] These prohibitions, however, hardly reflect an actual Jewish angel cultus in operation.[41] The syncretistic behavior of some Jews is, of course, important to note as an indication that monotheistic scruples were not always shared or not always observed among all. Moreover, other devout and scrupulous Jews may well have seen such things as wearing and using amulets that invoke angels as compatible with affirming the uniqueness of God, and they likely distinguished between this and what we may call formal "worship."

---

paper presented at the SBL Consultation on Jewish and Christian Mediator Figures in Greco-Roman Antiquity, San Francisco, November 1992.

37. Arnold, "Mediator Figures in Asia Minor," 21; see also his conclusions, 26-27. Cf. also L. H. Kant, "Jewish Inscriptions in Greek and Latin," *Aufstieg und Niedergang der römischen Welt*, 2.20/2, 671-713, for further evidence of variation in the practices of Greco-Roman Jews. But this data has to be analyzed carefully. For example, the appearance of "DM" *(Dis Manibis)* on a gravestone does not necessarily indicate the religious beliefs of the deceased or those who buried him/her. Gravestones were often pre-inscribed with such conventional expressions, the names and particulars of the individual deceased being added later, so anyone purchasing a gravestone from a shop might well have had no choice but to use one with "DM" inscribed.

38. C. E. Arnold, *The Colossian Syncretism*, WUNT, 2/77 (Tübingen: J. C. B. Mohr, 1995), 8-102, esp. 59-60, 82-83.

39. Stuckenbruck, *Angel Veneration and Christology*, esp. the summary, 200-203.

40. Mach, *Entwicklungsstadien des jüdischen Engelglaubens in vorrabinischer Zeit*, 291-300.

41. See my discussion of these prohibitions in *One God, One Lord*, 31-32. Whatever one makes of the rabbinic passages, their late date makes them questionable evidence for first-century Jewish religion. Cf. the carefully nuanced analysis by Stuckenbruck, *Angel Veneration and Christology*, 51-75.

In references to *One God, One Lord,* several scholars demurred from my position that there is no evidence of organized devotion to angels or other figures among groups of devout Jews. Andrew Chester alluded to the *Life of Adam and Eve* (13-16) and *Joseph and Aseneth* (15.11-12) as possible references to such practices.[42] But I find neither text persuasive. The scene in *Adam and Eve* is surely laden with theological meaning, specifically the idea that humans are God's most favored creature, superior to the angels (cf. 1 Cor. 6.3), and that Satan's hostility to humans is rebellion against God. But this aetiological story of God's demand that the angels acknowledge the superior honor of the human creature as God's "image" hardly constitutes evidence that Jews actually met to offer worship to Adam.[43] Chester's allusion to *Joseph and Aseneth* seems to ignore my observation that the mysterious angel who appears to Aseneth in fact refuses to cooperate with her desire to offer him worship, which suggests that her request is to be taken as a misguided pagan response corrected by the angel.[44]

Paul Rainbow pointed to *Pseudo-Philo* 13.6 (where God says, "The feast of Trumpets will be an offering for your watchers") as a possible hint of angel worship, but this is not the more plausible way to take the passage, as the translator in the Charlesworth edition indicates.[45] Moreover, 34.2 makes it clear that the author regards sacrificing to (disobedient) angels as a forbidden practice of Gentile magicians.[46] Nor is there in fact any cogent evidence from Philo of prayer or worship being offered to figures other than God.[47] More recently, Rainbow has proposed that the LXX reading in

---

42. Andrew Chester, "Jewish Messianic Expectations and Mediatorial Figures and Pauline Christology," in *Paulus und das antike Judentum,* ed. M. Hengel and U. Heckel, WUNT, 58 (Tübingen: J. C. B. Mohr [Paul Siebeck], 1991), 17-89, esp. 64. Chester does not give the exact passages, but I presume these are the ones that he intended.

43. Cf. David Steenburg, "The Worship of Adam and Christ as the Image of God," *Journal for the Study of the New Testament* 39 (1990): 77-93.

44. See *One God, One Lord,* 81, 84.

45. Rainbow, "Jewish Monotheism as the Matrix for New Testament Christology," 83. Cf. D. J. Harrington's comment in Charlesworth, *Old Testament Pseudepigrapha,* 2.321 n. "e," at *Ps.-Philo* 13.6.

46. The Midianite magician works miracles by the aid of fallen angels "for he had been sacrificing to them for a long time" (*Ps.-Philo* 34.2). This tells us how the author explained the feats of Gentile magicians, but it is hardly evidence of a Jewish devotion to angels.

47. Cf. F. G. Downing's curious claim that in *Somn.* 1.163-64 "Philo clearly takes [Abraham's appeal in Gen. 28:21] as 'prayer,' addressed to the Word. . . ." This has no basis in this passage (cf. "Ontological Asymmetry in Philo and Christological Realism in Paul, Hebrews,

Daniel 7:13-14 (ὡς παλαιὸς ἡμερῶν ["as ancient of days"]; cf. ἕως τοῦ παλαιοῦ τῶν ἡμερῶν ["unto the ancient of days," Theodotion) produces a passage in which a "Son of Man" figure is identified with/as God and receives worship.[48] But it is not clear that the LXX of Daniel 7:13-14 is to be preferred over the Theodotion text as reflecting pre-Christian Jewish Greek translation of the passage, nor is it clear that Rainbow's proposed translation and exegesis are to be preferred. The reverence offered in LXX of Daniel 7:14 may be directed to a "Son of Man" figure, but it seems to be scarcely more than the sort of gestures of submission to and acknowledgment of a victor that characterizes ancient cultures. Even if the LXX reading is taken as describing a heavenly or eschatological "worship" (in the cultic sense) of a Son of Man, there is certainly no indication that historical Jewish groups met to address such cultic devotion to some heavenly "Son of Man" figure. For historical analysis, we must always ask about actual religious practices.

In short, the data largely represent faithful Jews expressing their scruples about worship and prayer to figures other than God.[49] We may have

---

and John," *Journal of Theological Studies* 41 [1990]: 423-40 [440 n. 281]). The Logos is not even mentioned here. Philo takes Abraham as requesting God to be to him "bestower of kindness" and not merely "ruler." Philo's deliberately rhetorical invocation of the "Sacred Guide" (ἱεροφάντα) in *Somn.* 164 is not addressed to the Logos but may allude to Moses in his role as great teacher of true religion who works through his sacred writings. Downing's citations of *Abr.* 127 and *Gig.* 54 are likewise puzzling. Neither in fact offers any historical evidence for worship directed to any being but God. Philo merely makes distinctions between inferior and superior understandings of the nature of God and, in somewhat elitist-sounding language, claims that few of humankind achieve a higher perception of God.

48. Paul Rainbow, "One God and His Anointed in Early Judaism," seminar presentation notes sent to me by Rainbow in private correspondence. Rainbow reads the LXX of Daniel 7:14 as showing all the nations of the earth giving glory (καὶ πᾶσα δόξα αὐτῷ λατεύουσα) to this "son of man" figure, who is likened to "the ancient of days."

49. Sanders (*Judaism*, 245-46) discusses Josephus's reference to Essene prayer practices connected with the rising sun (*War* 2.128, 148), concluding that "the Essenes really offered prayer to the sun." Solar symbolism was certainly widespread in both non-Jewish and Jewish religion, but I doubt that Josephus is to be taken as Sanders does. But cf. Marc Philonenko, "Prière au soleil et liturgie angélique," in *La littérature intertestamentaire, Colloque de Strasbourg,* 17-19 Octobre 1983, Bibliotheque des centres d'étude supérieures spécialisés (Paris: Presses universitaire de France, 1985): 221-28. (I thank W. Horbury for this reference.) On Christian appropriation of solar symbolism, see the classic study by Franz J. Dölger, *Sol Salutis: Gebet und Gesang im christlichen Altertum, mit besonderer Rücksicht auf die Ostung in Gebet und Liturgie* (Münster: Aschendorff, 1925). On the use of solar images

hints here and there of a concern that some Jews were not sufficiently faithful in maintaining a sharp distinction between the unique God of Israel and other figures, whether pagan gods or servants of the true God (a concern explicitly expressed in rabbinic criticism of "two powers" heretics).[50] We certainly have evidence of faithful Jews attempting to maintain and strengthen a distinction between their monotheistic devotional pattern and the polytheistic pattern of the larger Greco-Roman world. But we hardly have evidence of Jewish religious groups in which cultic or liturgical devotion to angels or patriarchs formed part of their corporate religious practice and was intended as offering to these beings the sort of cultic devotion otherwise reserved for God.

Jews were even willing to imagine beings who bear the divine name within them and can be referred to by one or more of God's titles (e.g., Yahoel or Melchizedek as *elohim* or, later, Metatron as *yahweh hakaton*), beings so endowed with divine attributes as to make it difficult to distinguish them descriptively from God, beings who are very direct personal

---

(and other motifs) in ancient Jewish synagogues, see Elias Bickerman, "Symbolism in the Dura Synagogue," in Bickerman, *Studies in Jewish and Christian History: Part Three* (Leiden: E. J. Brill, 1986), 225-44 (critical of Goodenough's interpretation); Rachel Hachlili, *Ancient Jewish Art and Archaeology in the Land of Israel,* Handbuch der Orientalistik (Leiden: E. J. Brill, 1988); and J. H. Charlesworth, "Jewish Interest in Astrology during the Hellenistic and Roman Period," in *Aufstieg und Niedergang der römischen Welt*, 2.20/2, 926-50.

50. On the rabbinic "two powers" theme and its background, see Alan F. Segal, *Two Powers in Heaven: Early Rabbinic Reports about Christianity and Gnosticism*, SJLA, 25 (Leiden: E. J. Brill, 1977). J. H. Tigay, "A Second Temple Parallel to the Blessings from Kuntillet Ajrud," *Israel Exploration Journal* 40 (1990): 218, cites *m. Suk.* 4.5 and *t. Suk.* 3.1, in which there are invocations addressed to "Yah and to you, O Altar," and he concludes that "the address itself shows that people who were unquestionably monotheistic did not hesitate to address YHWH and a personified cult object in a way which seems to give comparable status to each." Clearly, however, homage is given to the Jerusalem Temple altar solely because it is the only revered place where valid sacrifice can be offered to the one God. Roy Kotansky, "Two Inscribed Jewish Aramaic Amulets from Syria," *Israel Exploration Journal* 41 (1991): 267-81, discusses protective amulets cataloging angels in incantations, which illustrate the sort of practices an unknown number of ancient Jews may have combined with a profession of monotheism. I offer two comments: (1) such incantations/invocations of angels addressed beings that were seen as servants of the one God, and so the practice may not have been intended in any way as diminishing God's uniqueness; and (2) such invocations seem not to have been made a part of corporate, public Jewish worship, and this suggests that a scruple about God's uniqueness operated to keep such practices within certain limits as far as more formal Jewish worship was concerned.

extensions of God's powers and sovereignty. About this, there is clear evidence. This clothing of servants of God with God's attributes and even his name will perhaps seem to us "theologically very confusing" if we go looking for a "strict monotheism" of relatively modern distinctions of "ontological status" between God and these figures, and expect such distinctions to be expressed in terms of "attributes and functions." By such definitions of the term, Greco-Roman Jews seem to have been quite ready to accommodate various divine beings.[51] The evidence that we have surveyed here, however, shows that it is in fact in the area of worship that we find "the decisive criterion" by which Jews maintained the uniqueness of God over against both idols and God's own deputies. I may also add that the characteristic willingness of Greco-Roman Jews to endure the opprobrium of non-Jews over their refusal to worship the other deities, even to the point of martyrdom, seems to me to reflect a fairly "strict monotheism" expressed in fairly powerful measures.

The Religious Outlook

We may understand this ancient Jewish religious outlook as constituting a distinctive version of the commonly attested belief structure described by M. P. Nilsson as involving a "high god" who presides over other deities.[52] The God of Israel presides over a court of heavenly beings who are in some measure likened to him (as is reflected in, for example, the Old Testament term for them, "sons of God"). In pagan versions, too, the high god can be described as father and source of the other divine beings, and as utterly superior to them.[53] In this sense, Jewish (and Christian) monotheism, what-

51. In this paragraph, I lift phrasing from Chester, "Jewish Messianic Expectations and Mediatorial Figures and Pauline Christology," 64-65, whose otherwise very helpful essay shows here a failure to appreciate these points adequately. Part of the problem in estimating what Jews made of heavenly beings other than God "ontologically" is that scholars tend to employ distinctions and assumptions formed by Christian theological/philosophical tradition. For a helpful critique of such anachronism and an illustration of the much wider and more complex semantic field represented by "divine" and "god" in ancient Greek, see S. R. F. Price, "Gods and Emperors: The Greek Language of the Roman Imperial Cult," *Journal of Hellenic Studies* 104 (1984): 79-95.

52. M. P. Nilsson, "The High God and the Mediator," *Harvard Theological Review* 56 (1963): 101-20.

53. Smith, "The Common Theology of the Ancient Near East."

ever its distinctives, shows its historical links with the larger religious environment of the ancient world.

There are distinctives of the Jewish version (inherited and adapted by early Christians), however, both in beliefs and, even more emphatically, in religious practice. As Nilsson has shown, in pagan versions often the high god is posited but not really known. Indeed, in some cases (particularly in Greek philosophical traditions) it is emphasized that the high god cannot be known. Accordingly, often one does not expect to relate directly to the high god or to address this deity directly in worship or petition.[54] In Greco-Roman Jewish belief, however, the high god is known as the God of Israel, whose ways and nature are revealed in the Scriptures of Israel. Also, as the evidence of Jewish prayer and cultic practice surveyed above shows, Jews characteristically expected — indeed, felt obliged — to address their high God directly in prayer and worship.

Moreover, in pagan versions, beliefs about a high god were not characteristically taken as demanding or justifying a cultic neglect of the other divine/heavenly beings. In Jewish religious practice, however, cultic reverence ("worship" — for example, sacrifice) characteristically is restricted to the high God alone. This is not simply a religious preference; it is taken as an obligation, and failure to observe this obligation is idolatry. Philo, for example, urges his readers to avoid confusing the "satraps" with "the Great King" (Dec. 61-65) when it comes to worship.

These constitute chief distinctives of the ancient Jewish understanding of the nature of the divine. In basic structure, their view involved a principal deity distinguished from all other divine/heavenly beings but characteristically accompanied by them, a "high-god" or "monarchical" theology not completely unlike other high-god beliefs of the ancient world. But in the identification of the high god specifically as the God revealed in the Bible, and, even more emphatically, in their characteristic reservation of worship to this one God, their religion demonstrates what we can call "exclusivist monotheism." Both in theology and in practice, Greco-Roman Jews demonstrate concerns for God's supremacy and uniqueness with an intensity and a solidarity that seem to go far beyond anything else previously known in the Greco-Roman world.

Quite a lot could be accommodated in Jewish speculations about God's retinue of heavenly beings, provided that God's sovereignty and

54. Nilsson, "The High God and the Mediator," 110-11, 115-16.

uniqueness were maintained, especially in cultic actions. I think that we may take it as likely that the glorious beings such as principal angels who attend God in ancient Jewish apocalyptic and mystical texts were intended by the authors very much as indicating God's splendor and majesty, and not as threatening or diminishing God in any way. The greater and more glorious the high king, the greater and more glorious his ministers, particularly those charged with administering his kingdom.

God's sovereignty was expressed and protected by portraying all spheres of creation and all the heavenly beings, even those temporarily "disobedient" (Satan/Beliel, demons, fallen angels), as inferior and subservient to God, ultimately within God's power. God's uniqueness was characteristically manifested and protected in religious practice, by directing prayer (especially in the cultic/liturgical setting) and worship to God alone, withholding such devotion from any other heavenly being, including God's closest ministers and agents.

In his study of rabbinic criticisms of "two powers" heresies, Alan Segal has identified two types of heresies attacked, and he has suggested that one type was Jewish-Christian reverence of Jesus, and the other (which Segal dates a bit later) was Gnostic speculation about a demiurge creator-god.[55] I think that Segal is correct, and that the two developments in question were considered heretical because they were seen to challenge the two fundamental concerns of Jewish monotheism. Gnostic speculations attributing the creation to a divine being other than the high god were likely taken as constituting a severe diminishing of the universal sovereignty of God, removing from God's purposes and control the sensory world and human history. Jewish-Christian cultic reverence of the exalted Jesus in terms and actions characteristically reserved for God, as described in *One God, One Lord*,[56] though it was initially a development ("mutation") within Jewish monotheistic tradition, was a sufficiently distinctive variant form to have been seen by many non-Christian Jews as compromising the uniqueness of God in the important sphere of cultic action. Whether there were other variant forms that constituted equally innovative forms of monotheism that developed within the Jewish monotheistic tradition of the late first or early second century remains an intriguing but thus far debatable possibility.

55. Segal, *Two Powers in Heaven.*
56. *One God, One Lord,* esp. chap. 5, "The Early Christian Mutation."

The reactions against the known "heresies" the rabbis had in mind — Jewish Christianity and Gnostic groups — may well have produced a hardening of rabbinic monotheism in the direction away from a more flexible and monarchical monotheism and toward a more stringently "monistic" stance, as Dunn and Wright have suggested.[57] But, as already noted above, the flexibility in speculations about figures associated with God — such as angels, the Messiah, and patriarchs — even in the pre-70 C.E. period seems not to have involved cultic devotion (worship) given to these figures in their own name, and openly as a feature of liturgical practice. It is in the explicit and programmatic inclusion of Christ with God in the prayer and worship practices of early Christianity that we see an apparent and major innovation in previous Jewish monotheistic religious practice.[58]

Moreover, as Michael Mach has recently argued, we should probably also allow for other (e.g., political) factors in accounting for rabbinic unease with angel speculations.[59] We should also recognize that interest in angels, including principal angels likened to God and closely associated with God, may have declined in some circles and in some periods, but remained in some devout Jewish circles after the first century, as evidenced in 3 *Enoch* and other texts.

There were reactions against Christian and Gnostic developments, but it is not clear that these reactions produced a significantly and widely embraced modification of the fundamental shape of Jewish monotheistic belief and practice. It does seem a very cogent possibility, however, that reaction against the Jewish-Christian form of binitarian monotheism (devotion to God and to the exalted Christ) may have had the effect of making any other such programmatic binitarian development unacceptable thereafter.

---

57. E.g., Wright, *The New Testament and the People of God*, 259. E. E. Ellis has claimed also that rabbinic leaders of the second century and later "brought into final definition the unitarian monotheism of talmudic Judaism." See *The Old Testament in Early Christianity* (Grand Rapids: Baker, 1992), 115-16.

58. Rainbow ("Jewish Monotheism as the Matrix for New Testament Christology," 88n.22) seems to me to overestimate the ease with which cultic devotion to a divine-agent figure could be seen as logical and acceptable in the Greco-Roman Jewish tradition.

59. Mach, *Entwicklungsstadien des jüdischen Engelglaubens in vorrabinischer Zeit*, esp. 300-332.

Conclusion

In addressing the question of whether or how Greco-Roman Jewish religion can be regarded as "monotheistic," it is advisable to take an inductive approach. Such an approach must (1) take seriously the religious professions and self-understanding of the people/groups studied, (2) allow for variety and development in the kinds and expressions of monotheistic religiousness, and (3) recognize the crucial importance of religious practice(s), particularly cultic (worship) practice(s) in understanding a religious group or tradition.

When we follow this inductive approach, we find clear evidence that devout Jews proclaimed their faith in monotheistic professions which emphasized the universal sovereignty and uniqueness of the one God of Israel, and which manifested a devotional pattern involving the reservation of cultic devotion (formal/liturgical "worship") for this one God, and a refusal to offer these cultic honors to other gods or even to the divine agents of God that often figure so prominently in ancient Jewish conceptions of the heavenly world and the exercise and outworking of God's will. The plurality of heavenly beings in first-century Jewish tradition is not in itself reason to question the appropriateness of calling these traditions monotheistic, particularly if we give due weight to the distinctions that devout Jews made between the levels of reverence appropriate for divine-agent figures and the full cultic reverence (worship) due the one God. This more precise and inductively formed view of Greco-Roman Jewish religion also gives us a firmer basis for understanding the historical significance of cultic devotion or worship offered to the exalted Jesus in early Christian circles that professed a monotheistic stance.

CHAPTER SIX

Homage to the Historical Jesus
and Early Christian Devotion

In previous publications, I have spent a good deal of effort on historical inquiry into the devotional practice of earliest Christianity, focusing on the "binitarian" shape of earliest Christian devotion in which Jesus figures with God as recipient of worship.[1] Joining in a line of researchers that goes back to the early *religionsgeschichtliche Schule* (history of religions school), I have focused on questions about the nature and origins of Christian devotion in the first two centuries after Jesus (although, with a number of more recent scholars, I have been led to revise heavily the influential analysis that emerged from the *religionsgeschichtliche Schule*).[2] In this chapter, I

---

1. Most recently, Larry W. Hurtado, *Lord Jesus Christ: Devotion to Jesus in Earliest Christianity* (Grand Rapids: Eerdmans, 2003). Among my relevant previous publications, see esp. "The Binitarian Shape of Early Christian Worship," in *The Jewish Roots of Christological Monotheism*, ed. C. C. Newman, J. R. Davila, and G. S. Lewis, JSJSup 63 (Leiden: E. J. Brill, 1999), 187-213; *At the Origins of Christian Worship: The Context and Character of Earliest Christian Devotion* (Carlisle, U.K.: Paternoster Press, 1999; Grand Rapids: Eerdmans, 2000), esp. 63-97; and *One God, One Lord: Early Christian Devotion and Ancient Jewish Monotheism* (Philadelphia: Fortress Press, 1988; 2d ed., Edinburgh: T&T Clark, 1998). In the following paragraphs I summarize results presented and defended more fully in these publications.

2. The classic expression of the *religionsgeschichtliche Schule* on devotion to Jesus was, of course, Wilhelm Bousset's influential volume *Kyrios Christos: Geschichte des Christusglaubens von den Anfängen des Christentums bis Irenaeus*, FRLANT, 4 (Göttingen: Vanden-

---

This chapter is a slightly edited version of my essay that appeared in *Journal for the Study of the Historical Jesus* 1.2 (2003): 131-46. Reprinted by permission of Sage Publications Ltd. Thanks to the editor and publisher for permission to republish the essay here.

wish to turn to the question of what historical connection, if any, there may have been between this "post-Easter" devotional pattern and the "historical Jesus." More precisely, how is the extraordinary reverence that was accorded to Jesus as the "Lord" so quickly in the earliest Christian decades related to the respectful attitudes and gestures toward Jesus that characterized the period of Jesus' ministry, prior to his execution and the eruption of the conviction that God had vindicated him and exalted him to heavenly glory? To address this question, we must first determine what we can say, and with what warrants, about the kinds of reverence that might have been accorded to the "historical" Jesus.

Definitions

But, before we proceed to the data that I will focus on in this discussion, in the interests of clarity and avoiding misunderstanding, it may be helpful to define a few important terms and to say just a bit more about early Christian reverence of Jesus in the early decades after his ministry.

First, I use the term "devotion" as a *portmanteau* term for the honorific beliefs and reverential actions that express the religious stance of early Christians toward God and Jesus. More frequently, scholars have focused on the "Christology" of this or that text or early Christian leader/writer, the beliefs about Jesus (e.g., his redemptive death, resurrection, preexistence) and the linguistic terms (e.g., the well-known Christological "titles") and conceptual categories involved. I regard "Christology" in this sense as a subset of phenomena expressive of the religious "devotion" of early Christians, the other key subset of phenomena being their "devotional practices."

Among the devotional practices of earliest Christian circles reflected in extant sources were such things as invoking Jesus' name in healing and exorcism (e.g., Acts 3:6; 16:18), in baptism (e.g., Acts 2:38), and in other actions intended to execute divine power (e.g., the judgment of the man accused of an incestuous union in 1 Cor. 5:3-5).[3] In these and other actions

---

hoeck & Ruprecht, 1913, 1921). The English translation in 1970 both indicated and furthered the continuing influence of his study: *Kyrios Christos: A History of the Belief in Christ from the Beginnings of Christianity to Irenaeus,* trans. J. E. Steely (Nashville: Abingdon Press, 1970).

3. In 1 Corinthians 5:4, whether the phrase "in the name of the/our Lord Jesus" is taken

that I have discussed elsewhere, we have a remarkable feature of early Christian devotional practice, which was that Jesus was apparently given the sort of place that was otherwise reserved for God alone.[4] That is, Jesus was treated as a recipient of "cultic" reverence that was given in the setting of corporate worship, this reverence of Jesus comprising a central characteristic of early Christian corporate worship practice. Also among the constellation of specific devotional actions involved were songs/hymns concerning Jesus (and in some cases sung to him) that formed a characteristic feature of early Christian corporate worship, the well-known passages commonly thought to be "Christological hymns" and, thus, the earliest extant artifacts of this particular practice.[5]

To gain a full appreciation of the historical significance of this devotion to Jesus, it is important to remember that earliest Christians, both Jewish and Gentile believers, seem characteristically to have practiced a rather strict "monotheistic" worship, rejecting all the deities of the wider religious environment as bogus and even demonic forces unworthy of reverence (e.g., 1 Cor. 10:14-22), and worshipping only the one God of the Jewish scriptures as the "living and true God" (1 Thess. 1:9-10). In this stance, they were affirming for themselves the well-known exclusivist monotheism of Roman-era Jewish tradition, and, of course, were significantly marking themselves off in matters of worship from the more inclusive attitudes and practices of the Roman world.[6] This exclusivist behavior of ear-

---

as referring to Paul's personal judgment about the matter or to the gathering of the Corinthian congregation, the phrase clearly links ritual use of Jesus' name with the exercise of spiritual power that Paul calls for here. See, e.g., Gordon D. Fee, *The First Epistle to the Corinthians* (Grand Rapids: Eerdmans, 1987), 206-8. On the ritual use of Jesus' name, the classic study is Wilhelm Heitmüller, *"Im Namen Jesu": Eine sprach-und-religionsgeschichtliche Untersuchung zum Neuen Testament, speziell zur altchristlichen Taufe*, FRLANT, 1.2 (Göttingen: Vandenhoeck & Ruprecht, 1903). See also Adelheid Ruck-Schröder, *Der Name Gottes und der Name Jesu: Eine neutestamentliche Studie*, WMANT, 80 (Neukirchen-Vluyn: Neukirchener-Verlag, 1999); and Lars Hartman, *"Into the Name of the Lord Jesus": Baptism in the Early Church* (Edinburgh: T&T Clark, 1997).

4. Again, I refer readers to the publications listed in n. 1 for further discussion of the evidence concerning the specific actions that manifest the treatment of Jesus as recipient of devotion: (1) the place of Jesus in early Christian prayer, (2) cultic invocation of Jesus and confession of him/his name, (3) baptism in his name, (4) the "Lord's Supper," (5) hymns sung about and to Jesus, and (6) prophecy given in his name and as his "voice."

5. See esp. Martin Hengel, "The Song about Christ in Earliest Worship," in Hengel, *Studies in Early Christology* (Edinburgh: T&T Clark, 1995), 227-93.

6. Robert M. Grant, *The Gods and the One God* (Philadelphia: Westminster Press, 1986);

liest Christian circles makes all the more striking the programmatic inclusion of the glorified Jesus as recipient of corporate liturgical praise and appeal along with God and, indeed, as the unique figure through whom the one God now was validly to be worshipped.

This programmatic inclusion of Jesus as recipient of such reverence gave to early Christian devotional practice what I have termed a "binitarian shape," in which corporate liturgical reverence was directed to God and to (or through) Jesus. Furthermore, insofar as the place of Jesus in early Christian devotional practice was (a) unparalleled in comparison to the ways that "divine agent" figures were treated in devout Jewish circles of the day, and (b) was analogous only to the kind of devotion otherwise reserved for God, it is appropriate to refer to early Christian "worship" of Jesus along with God.

To be sure, in the early Christian sources that reflect and affirm this worship pattern (which include our earliest extant Christian writings that take us back to devotional practice of the first couple of decades), Jesus is presented as entitled to such reverence precisely because God ("the Father") has exalted him to unique glory and status as the "Lord" (e.g., Phil. 2:9-11). Consequently, cultic acclamation of Jesus as "Lord" and exalted "Son" redounds also to the glory of God. Indeed, to refuse to give such honor to Jesus is to fail to honor God aright (John 5:23). That is, although remarkable and even unparalleled, the worship of Jesus in earliest Christianity was practiced not as in any way detracting from the worship of God "the Father," but instead as the distinctively Christian way of offering worship to the one true God. The exalted Jesus was worshipped as the "image" of God who reflects God's glory, the "Son" of God who uniquely represents and executes God's will, and the "Lord" who has been exalted to a unique status that is defined solely with reference to God (e.g., "at God's right hand"). Nevertheless, to repeat a point for emphasis, although Jesus is defined with reference to, and reverenced as unique agent of, God "the Father," the constellation of devotional actions that characterized early Christian practice is justifiably described as reflecting the "worship" of Jesus in the cultic sense of that word.

Insofar as the preceding summary-discussion is essentially correct, major historical questions are obvious.[7] In particular, how are we to ac-

---

Larry W. Hurtado, "First-Century Jewish Monotheism," *Journal for the Study of the New Testament* 71 (1998): 3-26 (Chapter Five of the present book).

7. The phenomena to which I point, and the dates of the texts in which they are re-

count for Christian circles of the first few decades, which were either in or shaped by the rather strictly monotheistic ethos of Roman-era Jewish religious tradition, so quickly and so strikingly affirming this binitarian devotional pattern? More specifically, how are we to account for Jesus becoming the recipient of the sort of devotion that is attested from our earliest extant Christian writings onward? One of the important aims in my own research on this matter has been to identify historical forces and factors that might account for this development. One of the factors/forces that I invoke is the ministry of Jesus, particularly his polarizing impact. It is not possible here to go further into that discussion.[8] Instead, as indicated already, in this chapter I wish to explore a cognate question about how much the "post-Easter" devotion to Jesus was either continuous or discontinuous with phenomena of the "historical" Jesus.

Reverence for Jesus in the Gospels

Any reader of the intra-canonical Gospels will note that they frequently portray people making reverential/respectful gestures toward Jesus.[9] But,

---

flected, are hardly in dispute. Because J. D. G. Dunn and Maurice Casey see Jesus reaching fully divine status in early Christianity only toward the end of the first century (both emphasizing Johannine Christianity as the setting, though they invoke conflicting explanations), they demur from characterizing the reverence given to Jesus as "worship" prior to those later decades, although they grant that it amounts to a notable development. In Chapter One of this book, I have indicated why I do not find their views persuasive.

8. I have identified four major forces/factors that interacted in driving and shaping earliest Christian devotion as a novel variant-form ("mutation") in Jewish monotheism: (1) Jewish religious tradition, esp. its exclusivist monotheistic commitment and the role of figures portrayed as God's "principal agent"; (2) the effects of Jesus' ministry, most importantly the polarization of opinion about him reflected in the following that he collected and the mortal opposition that he generated; (3) religious experiences taken by recipients as revelatory; and (4) interaction with the larger religious environment. For elaboration, see esp. Chapter 1 of my book *Lord Jesus Christ*.

9. I focus here on the four intra-canonical Gospels for several reasons. First, with most scholars, I take these texts to be earlier than the extra-canonical gospels. The latter (e.g., *Gospel of Thomas*) may well draw upon some Jesus-tradition as early as that reflected in the intra-canonical Gospels, but *as literary products* I judge them to be later. Second, the literary relationships of the intra-canonical Gospels (in whatever scheme of priority and dependence) along with their commonalities and individual emphases show that these texts reflect a certain diversity of first-century Christians who nevertheless also shared a considerable

as with many other things that these Gospels narrate, the question is what we are to make of these scenes as evidence of the actual behavior of people in relationship to the historical Jesus. That is, prior to the question of what continuity there may have been between any reverential gestures toward the historical Jesus and the devotional practice of earliest Christianity, there is the question of what sort(s) of gesture(s) of respect or homage people might have offered to Jesus in the time of his ministry. As a first step toward answering this question, let us take careful note of the terms used in the Gospels to describe the gestures of those whom the narratives portray as giving Jesus homage.

The Gospels' Language of Homage

There are six expressions to consider, some of them used in combination: προσκυνέω, πίπτω, προσπίπτω, προσπίπτω ταῖς γόνασιν, γονυπετέω, and τίθημι τὰ γόνατα. We can also note the use of these expressions in other New Testament writings, which will help us form a better sense of what they connoted in first-century Christian usage.[10] The first thing to note is that they all describe the same or very similar physical gestures of falling down before someone (on the knees or fully prostrate). Moreover, it is important to observe that all of these terms fit within the vocabulary of homage and respect of the time, and they describe the actual gestures widely used in various traditional cultures to express homage, respect, and reverence toward a figure deemed one's superior (whether human or divine), and/or any figure from whom one seeks an important favor or benefit in a circumstance of great need.[11]

---

amount of tradition and beliefs. Finally, for various reasons (including their early usage and emergence as preferred accounts of Jesus), the intra-canonical Gospels seem to reflect Christian circles that were concerned with narrative traditions about Jesus. Consequently, it is more appropriate to test the relationship between their devotional practice and the descriptions of reverence/homage given to Jesus in the intra-canonical accounts.

10. Though not used in the Gospels to describe homage to Jesus, the expression κάπτω γόνυ/τὰ γόνατα also appears in the cultic vocabulary in other first-century Christian texts (Rom. 11:4; 14:11; Eph. 3:14), including also Philippians 2:10, where it forms part of the description of universal homage and acclamation of Jesus as κύριος (πᾶν γόνυ κάμψῃ ... Καὶ πᾶσα γλῶσσα ἐξομολογήσηται).

11. Note, e.g., the following entries in the *Exegetical Dictionary of the New Testament*, ed. H. Balz and G. Schneider, 3 vols. (Grand Rapids: Eerdmans, 1990-93): E. Palzkill, "πίπτω," 3.90-91; J. M. Nützel, "προσκυνέω," 3.173-75; idem, "γόνυ," 1.257-58 (all with further bibliography).

The term γονυπετέω (to "fall on the knees/fall down before") is used only a few times in Matthew and Mark, and nowhere else in the New Testament.[12] In Matthew it describes the gesture of the man who begs Jesus to deliver his afflicted son (17:14), and it appears in the Markan account of the man who approaches Jesus to ask about how to inherit eternal life (10:17). Also, in the textually uncertain Mark 1:40, some textual witnesses attribute this action to the leper who asks Jesus to heal him. Finally, Matthew uses the term in his description of the abusive mockery of Jesus by Pilate's soldiers (27:29), in preference to Mark's portrayal of them as τιθέντες τὰ γόνατα προσεκύνουν αὐτῷ ("kneeling down to him," 15:19), illustrative of relevant terminological variations among the Evangelists to which I return below. In Luke 5:8 we have a somewhat synonymous expression used to describe Peter's posture in beseeching Jesus after the miraculous catch of fish (προσέπεσεν τοῖς γόνασιν, "he fell to his knees").

In fact, both πίπτω and the compound form προσπίπτω mean "to fall (down)," and are used several times to describe reverential gestures toward Jesus in Mark and Luke, the two verb-forms seeming to function almost interchangeably. Thus the variant expressions πίπτω/προσπίπτω αὐτῷ ("fall down to/before him") and πίπτω/προσπίπτω πρὸς/παρὰ τοὺς πόδας αὐτοῦ ("fall at his feet") describe the gestures made by demoniacs (Mark 3:11/Luke 8:28) and others who seek some favor from Jesus or wish to show respect (the healed woman of Mark 5:33/Luke 8:47, the Syrophoenician woman of Mark 7:25, and Jairus in Mark 5:22/Luke 8:41). The expression πίπτω ἐπὶ πρόσωπον (to "fall upon [one's] face") appears in the description of the leper's supplication of Jesus in Luke 5:12; and in Luke 17:16 we have the rather pleonastic description of the Samaritan leper's gesture of gratitude to Jesus for his healing, ἔπεσεν ἐπὶ πρόσωπον παρὰ τοὺς πόδος αὐτοῦ εὐχαριστῶν ("he fell on his face at his feet, thanking him"). In Matthew 17:6, the disciples "fell on their faces" (ἔπεσαν ἐπὶ πρόσωπον αὐτῶν) at Jesus' transfiguration, but here it is not entirely clear whether this posture is reverence for Jesus or simply part of their frightened response to the divine voice from heaven in 17:5. The one Johannine usage of πίπτω to describe reverence to Jesus is in 11:32, where the grieving Mary falls at Jesus' feet (ἔπεσεν αὐτοῦ πρὸς τοὺς πόδας).

As indicated earlier, these expressions all refer to the sort of reverential

12. Also, the word is not used in the LXX.

gestures that were deemed appropriate in that ancient Near Eastern culture, and the gestures do not necessarily signal that the person to whom
such homage is offered is treated as divine. To be sure, prostration and falling to one's knees can also feature in supplication to gods. For example, in
Luke 22:41, Jesus goes to his knees to pray in Gethsemane (θεὶς τὰ γόνατα;
cf. ἔπιπτεν ἐπὶ τῆς γῆς, "he fell down on the ground," Mark 14:35; ἔπεσεν
ἐπὶ πρόσωπον αὐτοῦ, "he fell down on his face," Matt. 26:39). In addition,
we have several uses of forms of τίθημι τὰ γόνατα ("kneel down") in Acts
to describe the posture adopted for supplicative prayer (7:60; 9:40; 20:36;
21:5). Note also the description of the imploring postures (using either
πίπτω or προσπίπτω) of the Philippian jailor toward Paul and Silas in Acts
16:29, and of the indebted servant in Matthew 18:29. We have a different
use of the expression in Acts 5:10, where it describes Ananias's wife collaps-
ing and dying upon having been confronted with the financial deception
in which she was a party with her husband.

However, the most important term, with the most interesting variation in usage among the Evangelists, is προσκυνέω ("make obeisance, do
reverence to, worship").[13] In the LXX and the New Testament this verb also
can be used to designate the reverence given, for example, by servants to
their masters (Matt. 18:26), or by others who demonstrate by the gesture
the superiority of another person (e.g., Gen. 27:29; 37:10; 49:8; Acts 10:25).
More characteristically, however, in the LXX (e.g., Exod. 20:5; Deut. 4:19;
Josh. 23:19) and also in the New Testament (e.g., 1 Cor. 14:5; Matt. 4:9-10;
Luke 4:7-8), it is used to refer to the gesture of reverence given to a deity
and intended specifically to register what we mean by the term "worship."[14] Indeed, an interesting feature of Jewish and early Christian usage
is the absolute form of προσκυνέω (i.e., without an accusative or a dative

---

13. Note esp. the thoroughgoing study by Johannes Horst, *Proskynein: Zur Anbetung im
Urchristentum nach ihrer religionsgeschichtlichen Eigenart*, NTF, 3.2 (Gütersloh:
C. Bertelsmann Verlag, 1932), who discusses both philological data and visual representa-
tions of the action. More summary treatments appear in the *Theological Dictionary of the
New Testament*, ed. G. Kittel and G. Friedrich, 10 vols. (Grand Rapids: Eerdmans, 1964-76),
6:758-66 (H. Greeven); and the *Exegetical Dictionary of the New Testament*, 3:173-75 (J. M.
Nützel).

14. According to Greeven (*Theological Dictionary of the New Testament*, 6:760 n. 23), of
the 171 instances of השתחוה (hithpalel form of שחה) in the Hebrew Bible, 164 are translated
by προσκυνέω in the LXX. Moreover, προσκυνέω is used in the LXX almost exclusively to
render *this* Hebrew expression.

noun as object) as the designation of what is involved in "worship" (e.g., 1 Sam. 1:13; John 4:20; 12:20; Acts 8:27; 24:11).

The importance of the term is reflected in the pattern of its usages in the New Testament, which are concentrated heavily in Matthew, John, and Revelation. It appears with particular frequency in passages about worship of divine beings. In the Johannine account of Jesus' conversation with the Samaritan woman about the proper place and mode of valid worship, forms of προσκυνέω are used consistently (eight times in 4:20-24, plus the cognate noun προσκυνηταί, "worshippers," in 4:23). The largest number of uses is in Revelation (twenty-four), indicative of the major emphasis of this writing on contrasting worship of the true God with the invalid worship of the "Beast" and its image.[15]

Προσκυνέω in the Gospels

It is especially interesting, therefore, to take account of the use of this term in the Gospels. The first thing to note is the variation in frequency of usage: it appears twice in Mark, three times in Luke (in two passages), eight times in John (in three passages), and thirteen times in Matthew (in nine distinguishable passages). Clearly, "Matthew" had a special fondness for the word, and it will be important, therefore, to inquire why. But, as we shall see, for all four of the Evangelists there seems to be a special connotation of the term when it is used to refer to the reverence given to Jesus by figures in their narratives.

---

15. Even in Revelation, however, we see an instance where προσκυνέω represents homage rightly given to human figures in 3:9, where Jesus promises that he will cause those of "the synagogue of Satan" to come and give obeisance before the Philadelphian Christians (προσκυνήσουσιν ἐνώπιον τῶν ποδῶν σου), who are thereby acknowledged as those whom Jesus loves. The phrasing is similar to that used in Revelation 15:4 to describe the homage to be given to God by all nations. It is arguable, however, that in Revelation 3:9 the homage given to the elect constitutes indirectly worship of God, the vindicated elect thus manifesting the future triumph of God and Christ over those who now oppose them. Moreover, Jesus' promise in Revelation 3:9 echoes Old Testament passages where God promises Israel such obeisance from foreigners (e.g., Isa. 49:23; 60:14). Elsewhere in Revelation, however, the term refers to the direct worship of God and the "Lamb" (4:10; 5:14; 7:11; 11:1, 16; 14:7; 15:4; 19:4, 10; 22:9) or its unholy opposite, worship of demons (9:20), the Dragon (13:4), and the Beast and its image (13:4, 8, 12, 15; 14:9, 11; 16:2; 19:20; 20:4). This strong usage of the verb is also reflected in the two passages where the seer mistakenly starts to offer worship to the angel who accompanies the visions but is forbidden from doing so by the angel, who urges the seer to "worship God" instead (19:10; 22:8-9).

Other than in the temptation narrative (Luke 4:1-13), where Satan urges Jesus to worship him and Jesus refuses by citing the command in Deuteronomy 6:13 to worship the Lord God only (Luke 4:7-8), Luke's only other use of προσκυνέω is in 22:52, where he portrays Jesus' disciples worshipping the risen Jesus (προσκυνήσαντες αὐτόν) and then joyfully returning to Jerusalem. As noted earlier, Luke elsewhere uses other terms that do not have the same association with the worship of deities to describe the respectful postures of people who come to Jesus in supplication or thankfulness (πίπτω ἐπὶ πρόσωπον/παρὰ τοὺς πόδας, 5:12; 8:41; 17:16; προσπίπτω αὐτῷ, 8:28, 47; προσπίπτω ταῖς γόνασιν, 5:8). That is, the only Lukan use of the term προσκυνέω to describe reverence given to Jesus is with reference to the *risen* Jesus, in the narratives of the appearances of the resurrected Jesus that are so commonly recognized as intended to prefigure the worship of early Christian circles. Thus Luke somewhat carefully "periodizes" reverence given to Jesus, distinguishing between the period of Jesus' ministry and the "post-Easter" period in the language that he uses to portray people's actions.

The one case where John uses προσκυνέω with Jesus as the recipient is in 9:38, where, upon Jesus' identification of himself as the one who healed him, the former blind man declares "I believe, Lord," and bows in reverence. Like the Lukan narrative of the appearances of the risen Jesus, this story in John 9 is also commonly recognized as metaphorical of the readers for whom the Evangelist wrote.[16] Here, the healing of the blind man anticipates the illumination of all those who recognize Jesus' unique significance and reverence him with the same honor that they give to God "the Father" (5:23). That is, the readers were to see their own rescue from the darkness of ignorance and unbelief in the account of the healing of the man born blind, and in his dramatic gesture of adoring reverence they were sure to recognize their own devotional practice registered. In short, John also portrays Jesus receiving divine-like honor only once, in this deliberately styled story that was particularly shaped to connect to the religious stance of the readers.

The two uses of προσκυνέω in Mark likewise appear to be selective and significant. But they also reflect Mark's penchant for irony.[17] The ex-

---

16. E.g., J. Louis Martyn, *History and Theology in the Fourth Gospel* (Nashville: Abingdon Press, 1979), 24-62.

17. Jerry Camery-Hoggatt, *Irony in Mark's Gospel: Text and Subtext*, SNTSMS, 72 (Cambridge: Cambridge University Press, 1992).

tent and detailed nature of the account of the man possessed by a multitude of demons in Mark 5:1-20 indicates the narrative importance of this story of Jesus triumphing over spiritual forces in dramatic fashion.[18] It is, therefore, noteworthy that this account features one of the two Markan uses of προσκυνέω (5:6). Having seen Jesus, the demonized man rushes to him, reverencing him with the physical gesture of approach to a deity (προσκύνησεν αὐτῷ), and the collective demonic voice acclaims Jesus as "Son of the most high God," entreating him not to torment them. It is almost inescapable that readers were intended to see in this dramatic scene a transparent anticipation of their own deliverance from evil, and in the uncanny recognition of Jesus' true status a prefiguring and confirmation of their own confessional claim and their devotional practice. I submit that in this respect the Markan story in 5:1-20 functions similarly to the Johannine account of the man born blind, and that this selective use of προσκυνέω is, like the use in John 9, a deliberate anachronism by the Evangelist.

But in this account of the demonized man we probably have a distinctively Markan note of irony too. As is well known, over against the misconstrual of Jesus' significance by his enemies and disciples, Mark has the demons alone confess correctly his transcendent status (e.g., 1:24, 34; 3:11). Similarly, in the account of the man possessed by the Legion of evil in 5:1-20, the longest and most detailed of all the Markan exorcism stories, Mark uses προσκυνέω to portray the demonic powers as *worshipping* Jesus, in an intensification of this ironic Markan motif of demonic recognition of him.

The other Markan scene where προσκυνέω appears is of a different type, but I propose that this use, too, was a deliberate editorial move by the Evangelist. In 15:17-19, Mark gives a detailed account of how Pilate's soldiers ridiculed and abused Jesus, the purple clothing, the thorny crown, the taunting acclamation, and the gestures of reverence all clearly a mockery of a ritual of coronation of Jesus as "king of the Jews" (the importance of the title in the Markan passion narrative is indicated by its repeated use: 15:2, 9, 12, 18, 26). The final, and probably climactic, description of their mockery of Jesus has the soldiers kneeling and reverencing him (καὶ τιθέντες τὰ γόνατα προσεκύνουν αὐτῷ, 15:19).

18. Earl S. Johnson, "Mark 5:1-20: The Other Side," *Irish Bible Studies* 20 (1998): 50-74, has shown the likely references in the story to Roman religious and political power.

In considering this use of προσκυνέω, it is important to note that the whole of the Markan account of Jesus' trial before Pilate and the subsequent crucifixion has been shown to be richly ironical.[19] So, Mark's Christian readers were probably expected to see the soldiers' cynical reverence of Jesus as unwitting expression of Jesus' true status as Messiah and Son of God. Though intended by the soldiers as cruel taunting, their gesture of worship in fact correctly accords with what the readers know to be the right response to Jesus' true significance. That is, in the use of προσκυνέω here, Mark portrays the soldiers as ignorantly acting out the valid worshipful reverence of Jesus that characterized the devotional practice of those for whom the text was originally written.

In sum, except for the few passages quickly noted here, where the Evangelists seem to use deliberately the more cultically "loaded" term προσκυνέω, Mark, Luke, and John all prefer to describe the reverential actions of people toward Jesus in less intensive language that was used to denote the bodily gestures used in ancient Near Eastern culture to supplicate for an important favor or to give thanks for one. In the main, the kind of reverence that they portray as given to Jesus seems perfectly plausible as phenomena of the "historical Jesus." Although Mark, Luke, and John likely intended these gestures of homage as broadly serving their aim to present Jesus favorably, they do not programmatically read back into the ministry of Jesus the devotional stance of the "post-Easter" circles of Christians, except for the particular instances noted. I propose, however, that these Evangelists do selectively use the particular instances discussed here to prefigure and "echo" more obviously the devotional stance and practice of their Christian readers, and that this is signaled for readers in the use of the term προσκυνέω, with its more frequent connotation of heightened reverence given to a divine being.

The Worship of Jesus in Matthew

When we come to Matthew, however, there is a very different verbal pattern.[20] But I submit further that Matthew's distinguishable use of language in scenes where people give homage to Jesus both confirms our observa-

---

19. Donald Juel, *Messiah and Temple,* SBLDS, 31 (Missoula, Mont.: Scholars Press, 1977).

20. This has been noted by previous scholars: e.g., Günther Bornkamm, Gerhard Barth, and Heinz Joachim Held, *Tradition and Interpretation in Matthew,* NTL (Philadelphia: Westminster Press, 1963), 229-30; and Horst, *Proskynein,* 204-37.

tions about the other Evangelists and signals his own very particular editorial intention. As noted already, the term προσκυνέω is a recurrent feature of Matthew's narrative vocabulary, with thirteen occurrences, a frequency exceeded only by the twenty-four uses in Revelation among the New Testament writings.[21] Moreover, ten of these Matthean occurrences describe homage offered to Jesus, which makes it Matthew's favorite word to designate the reverence given to Jesus by people.[22] Of these ten uses, eight are in scenes where the earthly Jesus is given reverence (the remaining two uses in scenes where disciples reverence the risen Jesus, 28:9, 17).

Matthew's preference for προσκυνέω to characterize reverence given to Jesus is most clearly seen in his handling of incidents narrated also by the other Evangelists. Whereas Mark describes the leper of 1:40-45 as beseeching Jesus (παρακαλῶν) and (depending on one's decision about the textual variant here) perhaps kneeling (γονυπετῶν), and Luke (5:12) has the man fall on his face (πεσὼν ἐπὶ πρόσωπον), Matthew prefers προσκυνέω to characterize the leper's reverence (8:2). Whereas in Mark 5:22-23, Jairus falls at Jesus' feet (πίπτει πρὸς τοὺς πόδας αὐτοῦ), and Luke (8:41) uses a similar expression (πεσὼν παρὰ τοὺς πόδας 'Ιησοῦ), Matthew again prefers the stronger term, προσεκύνει (9:18). In Mark 7:25, the Syrophoenician woman likewise falls at Jesus' feet (προσέπεσεν πρὸς τοὺς πόδας αὐτοῦ), whereas in Matthew 15:25 προσεκύνει designates the woman's reverential gesture. This pattern of preference for προσκυνέω, with its strong associations with cultic worship, suggests that Matthew has chosen to make these scenes all function as foreshadowings of the exalted reverence of Jesus familiar to his Christian readers in their collective worship.[23]

This conviction that Matthew's use of προσκυνέω is selective and in-

21. Cf. the total number of uses in other New Testament writings: Mark (2), Luke (3, of which two refer to worship of God), John (10, all but one of which refer to the worship of God), Acts (4, three of which designate worship of God), 1 Corinthians (1), Hebrews (2).

22. The three remaining uses of προσκυνέω are in Matthew 4:9-10, where Satan tempts Jesus to give him reverence and Jesus recites the command to worship God alone; and Matthew 18:26, where the indebted servant of the parable dramatically begs his master for mercy. Bornkamm, Barth, and Held propose that in this last instance the use of προσκυνέω signals that readers are to understand the parable allegorically, the master in the parable read as God (*Tradition and Interpretation in Matthew*, 229 n. 3). This may be so, or the passage may simply be the one case where the author uses the verb in its wider possible meaning.

23. Note also the insertion of gestures of reverence in the Matthean account of the transfiguration (ἔπεσαν ἐπὶ πρόσωπον αὐτῶν, Matt. 17:6; cf. Mark 9:8; Luke 9:36), and the story of the demoniac boy that follows (γονυπετῶν αὐτόν, 17:14; cf. Mark 9:17; Luke 9:38).

tentional is confirmed by noting that he omits the word from the two places where it was used in Mark (I am assuming, with most scholars, that Mark served "Matthew" as his principal narrative source and precedent). In place of Mark's use of προσκυνέω in 5:6, Matthew prefers the more bland description of the two demoniacs in his version of the story as "meeting" Jesus (ὑπήντησαν αὐτῷ, Matt. 8:28; cf. Luke 8:28, προσέπεσεν αὐτῷ, "fell down to him"). Likewise, in place of προσκυνέω in the Markan description of the mockery of Jesus by Pilate's soldiers (15:19) noted earlier, Matthew describes them simply as kneeling before Jesus (γονυπετήσαντες ἔμπροσθεν αὐτοῦ, 27:29).

The net effect of Matthew's numerous omissions and insertions of προσκυνέω in cases where Jesus is the recipient of homage is a consistent pattern. It is not simply a matter of preference of one somewhat synonymous word for others. Matthew reserves the word προσκυνέω for the reverence of Jesus given by disciples and those who are presented as sincerely intending to give him homage. As Günther Bornkamm, Gerhard Barth, and Heinz Joachim Held concluded from their analysis of scenes where Jesus is the recipient of the gesture in Matthew, προσκυνέω is used "only in the sense of genuine worship of Jesus."[24]

But surely the most blatant of such differences between incidents in Matthew and the other Evangelists is in the accounts of the story of Jesus walking to the disciples on the waves in Mark 6:45-52 and Matthew 14:22-33 (a story also recounted in John 6:16-21). In keeping with the dominant view of the Gospels today, I propose that each account reflects the editorial emphases of the respective Evangelist. Whereas in Mark 6:52 the disciples' response is uncomprehending astonishment, described with allusions backward and forward to other Markan scenes concerning "the loaves" of the two bread miracles, in Matthew 14:33 the disciples offer Jesus adoring reverence (προσεκύνησαν αὐτῷ) and acclaim him as Son of God, the key confessional title for Matthew.[25]

---

24. Bornkamm, Barth, and Held, *Tradition and Interpretation in Matthew*, 229. I agree with them, against Horst (*Proskynein*, 217-18), who claimed that in Matthew 8:2; 9:18; and 15:25, προσκυνέω registers something less exalted than in 2:11; 14:33; and 28:9, 17.

25. On the importance of the confession of Jesus' divine sonship in Matthew, see, e.g., Jack Dean Kingsbury, *Matthew: Structure, Christology, Kingdom* (Philadelphia: Fortress Press, 1975). The allusions in Mark 6:52 are to Mark 8:14-21 in particular, where Jesus quizzes the disciples about the numbers of baskets of leftovers of the feeding miracles in Mark 6:35-44 and 8:1-9.

As previous scholarship has noted, one of Matthew's concerns in his use of miracle stories in general, and this story in particular, was to move the intended readers to regard Jesus as ready and able to respond to their own petitions for the exercise of his mighty power on their behalf.[26] In Matthew, the readers are to identify with the two stories of Jesus and the disciples in the boat (8:23-27; 14:22-33), seeing Jesus "the helper of his disciples in their trouble" as encouragement for their own situation. Especially in the second sea story, in 14:22-33, it is clear that, instead of a narrative merely about a past miracle, Matthew "lays before the eyes of the [Christian] congregation her present possibility of meeting with the miracle-working Lord."[27] Both the Christian confession that Matthew ascribes to the disciples and his characterization of their reverence with the verb προσκυνέω combine to make the scene in 14:33 "an image of the congregation of the risen Lord."[28]

So, whereas Mark uses the term προσκυνέω solely in two ironic scenes where Jesus is reverenced by demons and his tormentors, and Luke uses the term solely to characterize the reverence given to the risen Jesus, Matthew repeatedly employs προσκυνέω to describe the homage given by disciples and supplicants (and by them alone) to the earthly Jesus. But, in this programmatic use of the verb, "Matthew" was not simply slipping accidentally into anachronism. Instead, whether used to portray the "adoring petition" of supplicants (8:2; 9:18; 15:25; 20:20) or the worshipful acclamation by the Magi (2:2-11) and disciples (14:33), προσκυνέω manifests the Evangelist's aim to make these accounts "accessible to the believing congregation," the characteristic setting in which the original readers themselves would have reverenced the risen Jesus as Lord.[29]

Reverence of the Historical Jesus and Early Christian Devotion

To return now to the core question that prompts this study, what can we conclude about the relationship of early Christian devotional practice and the homage that was probably given to the historical Jesus?

26. See esp. Bornkamm, Barth, and Held, *Tradition and Interpretation in Matthew*, 265-70, "The Lord and His Congregation in the Miracle Stories."

27. Bornkamm, Barth, and Held, *Tradition and Interpretation in Matthew*, 265.

28. Bornkamm, Barth, and Held, *Tradition and Interpretation in Matthew*, 266.

29. Bornkamm, Barth, and Held, *Tradition and Interpretation in Matthew*, 229.

To state something that hardly requires argumentation, in the setting of first-century Jewish society, the profound commitment to the exclusive worship of the one God and an equally profound antipathy toward deification of humans make it most improbable that either Jesus' followers or those Jews who approached him for help offered what they would have intended as "worship" of him as divine. Though Gentiles may have been more comfortable with reverencing human figures as divine, any who might have offered such reverence to Jesus in supplicating him for his healing and exorcistic powers would have been regarded by Jews as misguided. To be sure, in Jesus' cultural setting, it would have been fully appropriate to make reverential gestures toward someone regarded as a respected teacher or a source of desperately needed help. But the far more intense devotion to Jesus that characterized early Christian circles so amazingly early was not simply the continuation of the pattern of homage given to the historical Jesus, and it cannot be accounted for adequately by reference to Jesus' ministry.[30]

The "binitarian" pattern of devotion that we see already taken for granted in Paul's letters and affirmed throughout the New Testament initially amounted to a major and apparently novel "mutation" in, or variant form of, Jewish monotheistic practice. Among first-century Christian circles, in spite of the rapid acceptance of the view that Jesus rightly shares in divine glory and status, such a conviction represented a further, major development beyond the impact of the earthly ministry of Jesus. Just as it is inaccurate to restrict the belief that the risen Jesus shares in divine glory to circles of a supposedly distinctive "Christ cult" (*à la* Wilhelm Bousset and others subsequently in his train), so it would be simplistic to see this exalted a view of Jesus as having arisen in the time of his earthly ministry.

What we have seen in this study is that the collective evidence of the intra-canonical Gospels, which provide us our best access to early narrative traditions, in fact reinforces this position. Each in his own way, the Evangelists distinguish between the level of recognition of Jesus' status that characterized the time of his ministry and that which came to be expressed in the post-Easter period. In Mark this distinction is perhaps thematized most forcefully, all human characters in this account portrayed

---

30. Cf. R. T. France, "The Worship of Jesus: A Neglected Factor in Christological Debate?" in *Christ the Lord: Studies in Christology Presented to Donald Guthrie*, ed. H. H. Rowdon (Leicester, U.K.: Inter-Varsity Press, 1982), 17-36.

as woefully failing to perceive Jesus' true significance and calling, and the term προσκυνέω used only in ironic descriptions of acclamation of Jesus.[31] As in Mark, so also in Luke the homage offered to Jesus by his disciples and those who supplicate him is described in language expressive of the sorts of reverence for a social superior deemed appropriate in Jesus' cultural setting. Only after Jesus' resurrection does Luke portray the reverence given by Jesus' disciples as validly what seems to be "worship." Even in John, with its more explicit presentation of Jesus' person from the standpoint of "post-Easter" faith, except for the paradigmatic story of the healing of the blind man in chapter 9, the author does not generally read back into his account the Christian devotional practice of the time for which he wrote.

In Matthew, however, we see a clear programmatic effort to heighten the homage given by people to the earthly Jesus. Granted, in Matthew 28:18 it is the risen Jesus who claims to have been given "all authority in heaven and upon earth," which shows that Matthew also operated with a certain distinction between the earthly and the resurrected Jesus. Nevertheless, this Evangelist rather consistently portrays Jesus' disciples and those who approached him for favors as offering him reverence that was almost certainly to be seen by readers as prefiguring their own "post-Easter" devotional practice. This is particularly obvious in Matthew's repeated use of προσκυνέω, over against the language preferred by the other Evangelists. In the scenes where "Matthew" uses this term, we have what can only be taken as his deliberate editorial efforts. But, to reiterate the point, Matthew's aim was not simple historical distortion. Instead, this Evangelist sought to encourage his Christian readers to identify themselves with the actions in these scenes, his heightening of descriptions of people's reverence of Jesus intended to enhance this engagement with them.

But therefore, of course, we should not mistake these scenes as evidence of direct continuity between the homage that people gave to the his-

31. I include the centurion of 15:39. I take the statement of the centurion to be another instance of Markan irony, the words of this executioner expressing what the readers know to be Jesus' true significance, whatever sense Mark intended us to attribute to the centurion as a character in the scene. See my discussion in Larry W. Hurtado, *Mark: New International Biblical Commentary* (Peabody, Mass.: Hendrickson, 1989), 269. Cf. Jack Dean Kingsbury, *The Christology of Mark's Gospel* (Philadelphia: Fortress Press, 1983), 129-33, who takes the centurion's statement as indicative that he functions as "the first human being in Mark's story truly to penetrate the secret of Jesus' identity" (133). But the Markan narrative here functions more to excite knowing readers than to accredit the centurion.

torical Jesus and the worship of post-Easter Christian circles. The latter represents a notable development beyond the time of Jesus' ministry, and this development can be accounted for historically only by invoking additional factors, including powerful experiences of new "revelation" that helped to generate the remarkable "binitarian pattern" of devotion characteristic of earliest Christianity and the unprecedented association of Jesus with God that was so central in its beliefs.[32]

---

32. Larry W. Hurtado, "Religious Experience and Religious Innovation in the New Testament," *Journal of Religion* 80 (2000): 183-205 (Chapter Eight of this book).

CHAPTER SEVEN

Early Jewish Opposition to Jesus-Devotion

B y the end of the first century, among the matters in dispute between Christians (Jewish and Gentile) and Jewish religious authorities, Christian devotion to Jesus had become prominent.[1] In particular, it is commonly recognized today that the Gospel of John (ca. 90-100 C.E.) gives us evidence of sharp conflict in the late first century between Johannine Christians and Jewish authorities over Christological claims, although this conflict appears in John's narrative as one between "the Jews" and Jesus over claims he makes for himself. Perhaps especially in light of J. L. Martyn's influential study, scholars today commonly see John's Gospel as reflecting a bitter polemic between Jewish synagogues and Johannine Jewish Christians that led (at some point) to the expulsion of Johannine Jew-

---

1. The separation of "Christianity" and "Judaism" has received considerable attention especially in recent years. See, e.g., A. F. Segal, *Rebecca's Children: Judaism and Christianity in the Roman World* (Cambridge: Harvard University Press, 1986); *Jews and Christians: The Parting of the Ways A.D. 70 to 135*, ed. J. D. G. Dunn (Tübingen: J. C. B. Mohr [Paul Siebeck], 1992); Dunn, *The Partings of the Ways: Between Judaism and Christianity and Their Significance for the Character of Christianity* (London: SCM Press; Philadelphia: Trinity Press, 1991); and S. G. Wilson, *Related Strangers: Jews and Christians, 70-170 C.E.* (Minneapolis: Fortress Press, 1995). Scholarship has tended to focus on Christian developments, but see C. J. Setzer, *Jewish Responses to Early Christians: History and Polemics, 30-150 C.E.* (Minneapolis: Fortress Press, 1994). See also Setzer, "'You Invent a Christ!': Christological Claims as Points of Jewish-Christian Dispute," *Union Seminary Quarterly Review* 44 (1991): 315-28.

This chapter was published as an article in the *Journal of Theological Studies* 50 (1999): 35-58, and reprinted by permission of Oxford University Press. I thank the editor and publishers for permission to reproduce the essay here, slightly edited.

ish Christians from these synagogues (which I take to mean expulsion of these Jewish Christians from their Jewish communities).[2]

But when did "non-Christian" Jews first begin to suspect that Christian reverence of Jesus was blasphemous and incompatible with Jewish (monotheistic) commitment to the uniqueness of God, and not simply peculiar, annoying, ridiculous, or disturbing?[3] This is the question we focus on in this chapter, a question sharpened in recent debate.[4]

Focusing upon the Synoptic Gospels (Matthew, Mark, and Luke) and Paul (working chronologically backward to progressively earlier texts), I will argue that there is evidence pointing to, and evidence from, the decades earlier than the Gospel of John (hereafter GJohn), indicating sharp conflicts between Jewish Christians and other devout Jews over devotion to Jesus. This in turn indicates that in these early decades Jesus-devotion was already being taken by at least some Jews as an objectionable "mutation" in Jewish monotheistic devotional practice.

2. J. L. Martyn, *History and Theology in the Fourth Gospel*, rev. ed. (1967; Nashville: Abingdon Press, 1979). R. E. Brown advances a basically similar view. See, e.g., *The Gospel According to John*, 2 vols., Anchor Bible Commentary (Garden City, N.Y.: Doubleday, 1966-70), and *The Community of the Beloved Disciple* (New York: Paulist Press, 1979).

3. Setzer's *Jewish Responses to Early Christians* is heavily concerned with the question of whether Jews saw Jewish Christians as part of the Jewish community in the period 30-150 C.E. At several points, however, she discusses Jewish-Christian claims for Jesus (e.g., 137, 139, 140-42, 178-82) as matters of serious contention from the earliest days of the Christian movement (e.g., 42). See also Setzer, "'You Invent a Christ!'"

4. There is debate over how early in the first century Christ-devotion was perceived by Jews as amounting to a serious variation from traditional patterns of Jewish monotheistic commitment. Cf. Larry W. Hurtado, *One God, One Lord: Early Christian Devotion and Ancient Jewish Monotheism* (Philadelphia: Fortress Press, 1988), esp. 93-124, arguing for an emergence of noticeable "mutation" in the first few decades. But cf. J. D. G. Dunn, "Foreward to Second Edition," *Christology in the Making* (London: SCM Press, 1989), esp. xxviii-xxxi, xxxviii-xxxix; Dunn, *The Partings of the Ways*, 183-229; Dunn, "How Controversial Was Paul's Christology?" in *From Jesus to John: Essays on Jesus and New Testament Christology in Honor of Marinus de Jonge*, ed. M. C. De Boer, JSNTSup 84 (Sheffield: JSOT Press, 1993), 148-67, esp. 162-65; and Maurice Casey, *From Jewish Prophet to Gentile God: The Origins and Development of New Testament Christology* (Cambridge: James Clarke & Co., 1991), esp. chaps. 3, 8-9; and Casey, "The Deification of Jesus," in *Society of Biblical Literature Seminar Papers* 33 (1994): 97-114. Both Dunn and Casey (but for different reasons) contend that it is only with the Gospel of John that we see evidence of Jesus being treated as a fully divine figure. Space here does not permit an adequate critique of their arguments. Instead, I limit myself to presenting the evidence for my own view of the matter.

Blasphemy in the Synoptics

If the accusations of blasphemy against Jesus in GJohn are significant indicators of Jewish responses to the Jesus-devotion of the Johannine Christians, it is important to note that Jewish authorities accuse Jesus of blasphemy in the Synoptics as well. It is widely accepted among scholars that the Gospels' accounts of Jewish authorities accusing Jesus of blasphemy are at least partially shaped by, and are reflections of, Jewish responses to (Jewish) Christian Christological claims and devotional practice. Thus, Jewish accusations of blasphemy in the Synoptics must mean that the (Jewish) Christian experiences of being accused of blasphemy were not restricted to the Johannine Christian "community" and were earlier than the commonly accepted dating of GJohn.[5]

In GJohn, the Jewish accusation of blasphemy is directed against Jesus in a scene of dialogue and debate between Jesus and "the Jews," and is connected with Jesus' claim to be "Son of God" (10:36), which the Jewish leaders construe as Jesus making an outrageous claim to divinity ("You, though a man, make yourself a god/God," 10:33). In 19:7 "the Jews" claim that Jesus is guilty of a capital violation of the Torah in making himself "Son of God."[6] In the Synoptics, the blasphemy charge appears in two scenes: (1) the forgiveness/healing of the paralytic (Mark 2:7; Matt. 9:3; Luke 5:21), and (2) Jesus' arraignment before the Jewish authorities in the passion account (Mark 14:64; Matt. 26:65). In the first of these Synoptics scenes, the scribes' rationale is that Jesus takes unto himself an exclusive prerogative of God (explicit in Mark 2:7; Luke 5:21). This is very close to the reason for the blasphemy charge in GJohn. In these Matthean and Markan trial narratives, thus, the Jewish leaders are presented as outraged because Jesus' claims transgress the bounds of proper respect for

---

5. On the use of the term *blasphēmia* and its cognates in the New Testament, see H. W. Beyer, *Theological Dictionary of the New Testament,* ed. G. Kittel and G. Friedrich, 10 vols. (Grand Rapids: Eerdmans, 1964-76), 1:621-25; O. Hofius, *Exegetical Dictionary of the New Testament,* ed. H. Balz and G. Schneider, 3 vols. (Grand Rapids: Eerdmans, 1990-93), 1:219-21; H. Wärisch and C. Brown, *New International Dictionary of New Testament Theology,* ed. Colin Brown, 3 vols. (Grand Rapids: Zondervan, 1975-78), 3:340-45.

6. Most textual witnesses support *theon* without the definite article in 10:33, but the original hand of P66 has *ton theon.* In 19:7, *huion theou* is anarthrous, but is probably to be taken as referring to the Johannine Christological connotation of the Son of God title. Note also 5:18 for a similar charge against Jesus on the lips of "the Jews."

God's unique honor.[7] Moreover, in their narratives of Jesus' "trial" before the Jewish authorities, the same basic Christological claims, messiahship and divine sonship, are highlighted as blasphemous, just as in GJohn (Matt. 26:63/Mark 14:61).[8] In short, both Synoptic and Johannine accounts of the accusations of blasphemy hurled against Jesus link the charge to offensive Christological claims that form a key component of the devotional pattern of the Christians whose experience is reflected in these accounts.[9]

Jesus-Devotion and Jewish Opposition in Matthew

It may be asked, however, whether the offense taken in the Synoptics is in response merely to Jesus' followers attributing messiahship to him, rather than to a more radical level of Jesus-devotion. Let us survey a bit further the Synoptic evidence of Jewish opposition to Jesus-devotion.[10] I contend that the Synoptics manifest a full pattern of exalted Christological claims and accompanying devotional practices that amount to something considerably more than merely claiming royal-messianic status for Jesus.

To expedite our consideration of the evidence from GMatthew, we can make use of D. R. A. Hare's study of the theme of Jewish persecution in this Gospel. Hare concludes that GMatthew reflects the experiences of opposition from Jewish authorities directed against Jewish Christians' Jesus-devotion: "The Christological titles applied to Jesus by Christians must have been early regarded as a challenge to Jewish monotheism, and Chris-

---

7. In the Lukan account of the Jewish trial, the blasphemy charge does not appear explicitly. Instead, after Jesus' responses to the questions about whether he claims to be the Messiah and the Son of God, the assembled Jewish leaders take offense and hand Jesus over to Pilate (22:66-71). On the other hand, Luke is much more explicit in the political charges preferred against Jesus in the hearing before Pilate (23:1-5).

8. In John 10:31-36, divine sonship is the problematic claim. But elsewhere confessing Jesus as Christ is portrayed as the cause of strong Jewish reaction (9:22; cf. 12:42). In GJohn the various Christological titles and claims cross-interpret one another, and so the true "Christ/Messiah" is the divine Jesus.

9. On the Synoptics' trial narratives and the blasphemy charge, see R. E. Brown, *The Death of the Messiah*, 2 vols. (New York: Doubleday, 1994), 1:520-27.

10. See also G. Theissen, *The Gospels in Context: Social and Political History in the Synoptic Tradition*, trans. L. M. Maloney (Minneapolis: Fortress Press, 1991).

tian adoration of their risen Lord must have provoked cries of 'idolatry!' from many fellow Jews."[11]

Hare urges as "most probable" the view that Christological claims and associated devotional actions were for GMatthew "the central point at issue in the conflict between the church and Judaism."[12] He takes the blasphemy charge in Matthew 9:3 as provoked by Jewish Christians proclaiming in their meetings "Jesus' unique relation to God in terms of the authority to remit sins."[13] Hare points to Matthew 9:34 and 12:22-34 as evidence of early Christian exorcism and healing in Jesus' name, and as reflecting also the Jewish counterclaim that Jesus "was simply a magician." Hare judges that the Sabbath controversy in Matthew 12:1-14 echoes the "intense hostility" aroused by "the Christian declaration that Jesus was Lord of the Sabbath."[14]

Hare also reasons that the appearance of the blasphemy accusation in the Matthean narrative of Jesus' interrogation by the Jewish leaders (26:63-66) is to be understood as "a reflection of the Jewish rejection of the claims made on behalf of Jesus by his followers in their mission to the Jews," Matthew 26:64 echoing the proclamation of Jesus as "a divine being at the right hand of God," which was doubtless regarded as "blasphemous in the non-technical sense."[15] In light of the growing separation of Christian groups and Jewish communities after the Jewish revolt of 66-70 C.E., Hare argues that the Jewish persecution alluded to in Matthew 23:29-39 more plausibly reflects the pre-revolt period, a view supported by other scholars as well.[16]

11. D. R. A. Hare, *The Theme of Jewish Persecution of Christians in the Gospel according to St. Matthew*, SNTSMS 6 (Cambridge: Cambridge University Press, 1967), 17.

12. Hare, *The Theme of Jewish Persecution of Christians in the Gospel according to St. Matthew*, 133.

13. Hare, *The Theme of Jewish Persecution of Christians in the Gospel according to St. Matthew*, 135.

14. Hare, *The Theme of Jewish Persecution of Christians in the Gospel according to St. Matthew*, 135.

15. Hare, *The Theme of Jewish Persecution of Christians in the Gospel according to St. Matthew*, 25, 136. By "non-technical sense," Hare means that many Jews would have regarded these Christological claims as violations of God's honor, even if the technical/legal definition of blasphemy might have been much more narrow, along the lines of *M. Sanh.* 7:5, where the crime is confined to improper utterance of the divine name.

16. Hare, *The Theme of Jewish Persecution of Christians in the Gospel according to St. Matthew*, 127. He also argues that the harrying of Jewish-Christian missionaries, including

The causes of this Jewish persecution are not specified in Matthew 23:29-39. But in Matthew 10:16-25, Jesus' followers are warned of punishments inflicted by councils and synagogues as well as by governors and kings "because of me" (v. 18) and "because of my name" (v. 22). These phrases explicitly connect the persecutions predicted here from Jewish and Gentile authorities with Jewish-Christian devotion to Jesus, which was manifested in their Christological claims and in such religious practices as healings and exorcisms performed through Jesus' name.[17] In Matthew 7:22, we have reference to prophecy, exorcism, and healing in Jesus' name as features of the devotional practice familiar to the readers. These practices reflect a view of Jesus as possessing transcendent authority that can be mediated through his name, which thus functioned in a way similar to a divine name.[18]

To be sure, the conflict evidenced in GMatthew between Jesus' followers and the Jewish leadership involved disputes over a number of matters, including Torah observance, which seem to lie behind such passages as Matthew 5:17-48 and 23:1-36. Moreover, in a very general sense, these disputes can be likened to other conflicts between Jewish groups of the Second-Temple period (e.g., the Qumran group). But, for the Jewish followers of Jesus and for their Jewish opponents reflected in GMatthew, the central issue was what to make of Jesus. Disputes over Halakhah and other matters were corollaries of the more fundamental difference over the significance and authority of Jesus. In GMatthew the opponents of Jesus' followers do not merely claim that he is wrong or inferior in his Halakhic views;

---

synagogue floggings (Matt. 23:34), more probably took place in pre-revolt Diaspora settings rather than in Palestine. H. D. Betz, *The Sermon on the Mount,* Hermeneia (Minneapolis: Fortress Press, 1995), 149-50, concludes that Matthew 5:10-11 suggests persecution of Jewish Christians by a larger Jewish community that must be placed prior to 70 c.e. G. N. Stanton has argued that the Matthean community was still making missionizing overtures among Jews as well as non-Jews, and that the Jewish opposition/persecution mentioned in Matthew was continuing at the time GMatthew was written. See *A Gospel for a New People: Studies in Matthew* (Edinburgh: T&T Clark, 1992), 159-60; see also 113-45. Even so, this persecution has its beginnings much earlier.

17. The narratives in Acts 3–4; 5:12-42; and 6:8-15 all portray Jewish opposition to Jewish-Christian Christological claims and to the theurgic use of Jesus' name. Whatever one thinks of the specific historicity of these narratives, it seems reasonable to view them as reflecting at least in general terms real experiences of Jewish Christians of the pre-70 c.e. period.

18. Cf. Betz, *The Sermon on the Mount,* 554-55.

they utterly condemn Jesus as a sorcerer in league with the devil (9:34; 10:25; 12:24, 27), a deceiver (27:63, reflecting Deut. 13), and a blasphemer (9:3; 26:65).[19] If, as scholars commonly think, these charges more directly reflect the reaction of Jewish authorities to Jewish-Christian devotion to Jesus in the period after his execution, the intensity and the severity of these charges in GMatthew suggest Christological claims and devotional practices focused on Jesus that were intolerable to the Jewish authorities.

In fact, it is not difficult to see what could have outraged Jewish opponents. In GMatthew, not only is Jesus the ultimately authoritative spokesman for God, whose teachings supervene any other religious authority; he is also the Son of God who combines full messianic significance and transcendent, divine-like status as well. This exalted quality is particularly conveyed in the Matthean emphasis upon Jesus receiving worship, something surprisingly little-discussed in many studies of GMatthew's Christology but very significant for the issue before us.[20] The Matthean theme of worship of Jesus shows that the Jesus-devotion he affirms and to which he presents Jewish outrage amounts to treating Jesus as divine.

The Greek verb *proskyneō* appears frequently in GMatthew, and ten of its thirteen uses are in Christologically significant scenes.[21] In itself, the gesture represented by the verb can connote a variety of degrees of reverence given to earthly superiors or to gods, and it is likely that any who so reverenced Jesus during his ministry meant merely to offer respect to a holy man or prophet from whom they sought a favor. But Matthew seems

19. See esp. Stanton, *A Gospel for a New People,* 171-91 and 237-46, on the Jewish accusations against Jesus.

20. Cf. M. A. Powell, "A Typology of Worship in the Gospel of Matthew," *Journal for the Study of the New Testament* 57 (1995): 3-17, who rather cursorily handles GMatthew's use of the Greek word *proskyneō* and theme of worship. Cf. my discussion in Chapter Six of this book.

21. The term *proskyneō* is clearly a Matthean favorite. The ten Christologically significant uses are 2:2, 8, 11; 8:2; 9:18; 14:33; 15:25; 20:20; 28:9, 17. The three other Matthean uses of the term are in 4:9-10 (where Jesus is tempted to worship Satan and insists upon worship of God alone) and 15:25 (where a slave throws himself upon his master's mercy). Cf. Mark's two uses of the term: 5:6 (a key "epiphanic" scene where Jesus' divine sonship is confessed by the demonized man), and 15:19 (where the mocking worship is probably to be taken ironically as unwittingly correct, as seems to be so with other features of the Markan passion account). Cf. also Luke's three uses: 4:7-8 (the Lukan version of the temptation account), and 24:52 (where disciples worship the risen and ascended Christ). *Proskyneō* is also a important term in Revelation (24 uses), where cultic reverence is such a major emphasis.

to have intended his readers to see the incidents he narrates as anticipations and reflections of the cultic reverence of the exalted Jesus in early Christian circles.

In addition to the magi's reverence of the infant Jesus in the Nativity account (commonly recognized as laden with Christological significance),[22] the obeisance of those who seek miracles, and the mother seeking eschatological preferment for her sons, there are two other Matthean settings of even more transparent significance. One of these is the account of Jesus walking on the water in 14:22-33. Both this version of the story and its Markan parallel (6:45-52) are commonly recognized as epiphanic scenes, where Jesus' power is displayed (with subtle allusions to Old Testament references to God's power over the sea — e.g., Ps. 77:19; Isa. 43:16). In both the Matthean and the Markan accounts, Jesus' expression *"egō eimi"* (Matt. 14:27/Mark 6:50) is probably to be taken as an epiphanic utterance, using the divine revelation-formula from the Greek translation of Isaiah (LXX 43:10; 45:18; 46:4; 48:12; 51:12). In GMatthew, the epiphanic significance of the story is dramatically made explicit in its conclusion, where the disciples offer reverence to Jesus complete with the acclamation "Truly, you are the Son of God," giving a scene probably intended to prefigure the liturgical practices of the Matthean readers.[23]

The resurrected Jesus receives similar obeisance both from the women at the tomb (28:9) and, even more dramatically, from the eleven disciples in the final scene of GMatthew (28:16-20). This latter passage is thick with indications that Jesus is now to be regarded as holding divine-like significance and status, and that the obeisance pictured here is to be taken as cultic devotion offered to a divine figure. Jesus has been given universal authority (v. 18), and now orders a worldwide mission, summoning all nations to follow all his teachings and to become his own disciples through a baptismal initiation rite in which the name of the Father, Son, and Holy Spirit are invoked and identify both the rite and its recipients (vv. 19-20).

Mere differences in Halakhic opinion and practice seem inadequate to account for the apparent frequency and severity of the opposition reflected

22. On the didactic function of the birth narrative, see R. E. Brown, *The Birth of the Messiah* (Garden City, N.Y.: Doubleday, 1977), 177-83.

23. Comparing the Matthean and Markan conclusions to the accounts, J. Kingsbury notes that the acclamation in Matthew 14:33 shows that the *egō eimi* of 14:27 is a "divine revelation-formula." See *Matthew: Structure, Christology, Kingdom* (Minneapolis: Fortress Press, 1975), 66.

in GMatthew, as has been concluded by several other scholars as well.[24] In the pre-70 C.E. period especially, all indications point to wide diversity among Jews in their Halakhic application of the Torah. Even over such matters as the terms on which to relate to Gentiles, there appears to have been diversity.[25] Also, we have no examples of Halakhic differences that provoked against other groups the sort of aggressive disciplinary measures directed against Jewish Christians.[26] I submit that only a veneration of Jesus deeply offensive to "non-Christian" Jewish sensibilities in the prior history of the Jewish Christians behind the GMatthew would account for the kind of opposition referred to in this writing.[27]

Jesus-Devotion and Jewish Opposition in Luke-Acts

This view of things is supported by references in Luke-Acts as well. In the Acts accounts of Jewish-Christian developments and Jewish opposition, there are striking indications of the centrality of devotion directed to Jesus.[28] The Jerusalem disciples are warned to cease speaking in Jesus' name (4:17-18; 5:40), which they are pictured as proclaiming as the sole basis of salvation (4:12). Philip's preaching in Samaria concerns both "the kingdom

24. Hare, *The Theme of Jewish Persecution of Christians in the Gospel according to St. Matthew*, 5; also C. C. Hill, *Hellenists and Hebrews: Reappraising Division within the Earliest Church* (Minneapolis: Fortress Press, 1992), 195; A. J. Hultgren, "Paul's Pre-Christian Persecutions of the Church: Their Purpose, Locale, and Nature," *Journal of Biblical Literature* 95 (1976): 97-111, 102; and T. L. Donaldson, "Zealot and Convert: The Origin of Paul's Christ-Torah Antithesis," *Catholic Biblical Quarterly* 51 (1989): 655-82, esp. 672-75.

25. See Hill's critique of Esler's claim that there was a widely agreed-upon Jewish concern not to share any meals with Gentiles. See Hill, *Hellenists and Hebrews*, 117-22; cf. P. F. Esler, *Community and Gospel in Luke–Acts*, SNTSMS 57 (Cambridge: Cambridge University Press, 1987), 76-106.

26. The conflict between the "wicked priest" (Jerusalem?) and the "righteous teacher" of Qumran seems to have been an isolated affair. We have no evidence of a continuing persecution of the Qumran sect. See, e.g., J. C. VanderKam, *The Dead Sea Scrolls Today* (London: SPCK; Grand Rapids: Eerdmans, 1994), 102-4.

27. Peter Richardson, *Israel in the Apostolic Church* (Cambridge: Cambridge University Press, 1969), 45-46; Setzer, "'You Invent a Christ!'" esp. 316-17.

28. E. Bammel, "Jewish Activity against Christians in Palestine according to Acts," in *The Book of Acts in Its First-Century Setting*, vol. 4: *Palestinian Setting*, ed. R. Bauckham (Carlisle: Paternoster Press; Grand Rapids: Eerdmans, 1995), 357-63, is suggestive but all too brief.

of God and the name of Jesus Christ" (8:12). Miracles are performed through ritual use of Jesus' name (3:6, 16; 4:10, 30), and baptism is "in Jesus' name" and involves ritual invocation of his name as part of the rite (2:38; 22:16).

It is interesting that the Jewish Christians against whom Paul is portrayed as taking action are referred to simply as "those who invoke [*epikaleō*] Jesus' name" (9:14, 21), phrasing that both alludes to Old Testament references to calling upon (the name of) the Lord, and that connotes, thus, an action of equivalent cultic significance, a liturgical invocation of Jesus.[29] In the speech before Agrippa, Paul is pictured as characterizing his pre-conversion aim as "to do many things against the name of Jesus of Nazareth" (26:9). The statement in 26:11 that he sought to force Jewish Christians to "blaspheme" is probably to be taken as reflecting the idea that Jewish Christians were demanded to repudiate Jesus, perhaps even to join in cursing him (which seems to be reflected in 13:45; 18:6), a topic we shall return to later in connection with our discussion of evidence from Paul's epistles.[30] Those Jewish Christians who are punished by the authorities are pictured in Acts as regarding their suffering as "for the sake of the name" of Jesus (5:41). Jesus-devotion, including cultic actions concerned with him, seems to be central to the conflict with Jewish authorities, and the intensity of the opposition suggests that this devotional pattern was regarded as exceeding the rather generous range of acceptable Jewish religiousness.

To be sure, Luke-Acts is commonly dated a few decades later than the period portrayed in these references. But the attribution to Jewish Christians of a message and a devotional life in which Jesus figures prominently, and the portrayal of vigorous Jewish opposition focused on Jewish-Christian Christological claims and Jesus-oriented religious practices all agree with the reflections of the experiences of Jewish Christians that we find in GMatthew. Both in Luke-Acts and in GMatthew, Jewish Christians

29. E.g., Psalm 116:17: "I will offer to you a thanksgiving sacrifice and call on the name of the Lord." See also 116:13 (LXX 115:4); Gen. 4:26; 12:8; 13:4; 21:33; 26:25; 1 Kings 18:24. Note that Joel 2:28 (3:5 in Hebrew), which promises salvation to all who "call upon the name of the Lord *(Yahweh)*," is cited in Acts 2:21, and is probably to be seen as referring to cultic invocation of Jesus, who has now been made "Lord" (2:36), and whose name is efficacious for salvation (4:12).

30. On evidence of the cursing of Jesus (and Christians) in Jewish synagogues, see W. Horbury, "The Benediction of the *Minim* and Early Jewish-Christian Controversy," *Journal of Theological Studies* 33 (1982): 19-61.

of the first few years of the Christian movement are portrayed as practicing a religious devotion to Jesus that involves attributing to him powers and a status that are closely linked to God. Moreover, in Luke-Acts as well as in GMatthew, Jewish religious authorities are pictured as responding to Jewish Christians forcefully and in reaction against the role of Jesus in their message and religious practice. This agreement of Luke-Acts and GMatthew with GJohn indicates that more than one Christian group of the post-70 c.e. period was acquainted with this forceful Jewish opposition to Jewish-Christian devotion to Jesus.[31]

Jesus-Devotion and Jewish Opposition in Mark

The likelihood that vigorous Jewish opposition to the Jesus-devotion of Jewish Christians also characterized the pre-70 c.e. period is strengthened by evidence in the earliest of the Synoptics, Mark, commonly dated to 65-72 c.e.[32]

The Markan narrative of Jesus' "trial" before the Jewish authorities (14:53-64) is especially worth some further attention.[33] Two preliminary observations present themselves. First, although the temple-destruction charge is initially mentioned (14:57-58), the blasphemy charge is clearly the climax of the account and the basis given for Jesus' condemnation to death (14:64). Second, the blasphemy charge is in direct reaction to Jesus' oracular affirmations of his messiahship, divine sonship, and transcendent status ("the Christ the Son of the Blessed," 14:61; the "Son of Man" exalted at God's right hand who will preside in the eschatological triumph, 14:62).[34]

31. Although the texts are much later, we also have Jewish references to the prosecution of Jews for holding Jewish-Christian views and associations, probably to be set sometime in the Javnean period. See, e.g., R. T. Herford, *Christianity in Talmud and Midrash* (1903; Clifton, N.J.: Reference Book Publishers, 1996), esp. 137-45, on the prosecution of R. Eliezer for *Minuth*.

32. See, e.g., R. A. Guelich, *Word Biblical Commentary*, vol. 34A: *Mark 1–8:26* (Waco: Word Books, 1989), xxxi-xxxii.

33. Particularly useful is Donald Juel, *Messiah and Temple: The Trial of Jesus in the Gospel of Mark*, SBLDS 31 (Missoula, Mont.: Scholars Press, 1977); and J. Marcus, "Mark 14:61: 'Are You the Messiah-Son-of-God?'" *Novum Testamentum* 31 (1989): 125-41. See also J. R. Donahue, *Are You the Christ? The Trial Narrative in the Gospel of Mark*, SBLDS 10 (Missoula, Mont.: Scholars Press, 1973).

34. On Mark's Christology, see J. D. Kingsbury, *The Christology of Mark's Gospel* (Phila-

That is, the account of the Sanhedrin "trial" of Jesus in GMark is very much focused on this key religious issue. Either these Christological claims amount to a radical infringement upon the honor of God, or they are true.[35] This, I suggest, means that, as with GMatthew, GMark's first readers would have seen in the Sanhedrin trial a vivid dramatization and prefiguring of the conflicts that they knew through their own experience (or through reports from others), conflicts involving Jesus-devotion and the condemnations of it by Jewish religious authorities.

In fact, there are several good indications that the whole of the Markan narrative of Jesus' trial before the Council, Peter's denials in the courtyard, and Jesus' interrogation before Pilate were intended to speak to the experiences and concerns of GMark's first readers.[36] In GMark, followers of Jesus are called to be prepared for execution as part of their disciple-

---

delphia: Fortress Press, 1983); and J. Marcus, *The Way of the Lord: Christological Exegesis of the Old Testament in the Gospel of Mark* (Louisville: Westminster/John Knox Press, 1992), 37-40 and 145-46.

35. E. Bickerman ("Utilitas Crucis," in *Studies in Jewish and Christian History* [Leiden: E. J. Brill, 1986], 3:82-138) took the "blasphemy" in Mark 14:64 as meaning only a general affront (esp. 85-90), without the legal force of a capital crime. But, as Juel has noted (*Messiah and Temple*, 95-97), whatever the historical facts about Jesus' hearing before Jewish authorities, the Markan narrative clearly portrays the Jewish council as judging Jesus' claims to be blasphemy in the sense of deserving condemnation to death. See also H. W. Beyer, *Theological Dictionary of the New Testament*, 1:621-25, who warns that the narrow definition of *M. Sanh.* 7:5 was "not yet present in the time of Jesus" (621); he concludes that Jesus is pictured as bringing onto himself the charge of blasphemy by assuming "the prerogatives of God" (623). It should be noted that the LXX translation of Leviticus 24:15-16 (the key Old Testament reference to the sin of blasphemy) refers to "cursing" God *(kataraomai)* and to "pronouncing [*onomazō*] the name of the LORD," which suggests that blasphemy covered a certain spectrum of acts deemed to dishonor God sufficiently to justify death. Josephus (*Ant.* 4:202) refers to "him who blasphemes [*blasphēmēsas*] God" as worthy of stoning, and describes Essene courts as passing the sentence of death upon any blasphemer of God or of "the name of the lawgiver" (*War* 2:145). For a discussion of Qumran evidence about blasphemy, see L. H. Schiffman, *Sectarian Law in the Dead Sea Scrolls* (Chico, Calif.: Scholars Press, 1983), esp. 133-54.

36. C. P. Anderson, "The Trial of Jesus as Jewish-Christian Polarization: Blasphemy and Polemic in Mark's Gospel," in *Anti-Judaism in Early Christianity*, vol. 1: *Paul and the Gospels*, ed. P. Richardson (Waterloo: Wilfrid Laurier University Press, 1986), 107-25. Birger Gerhardsson ("Confession and Denial before Men: Observations on Matt. 26:57-27:2," *Journal for the Study of the New Testament* 13 [1981]: 46-66) illustrates how the Matthean accounts of Peter's denial and Jesus' trial were also probably intended to give contrasting examples for readers who could face trial for their faith.

ship to Jesus, and are warned about denying Jesus to save their lives (8:34-38). Also, it is, I think, well accepted that Mark 13 is crucial material for characterizing the concerns of the author and the experiences and prospects of the intended readers.[37] There, in addition to warnings about religious deceivers (13:5, 21-22) and about getting prematurely excited or discouraged over dramatic events (vv. 7-8, 13b-23, 30-32), we have a section that links the gospel mission of Christians with the prospect of suffering for their faith (vv. 9-13). Jesus' followers will face "councils" *(synedria)* and beatings in synagogues, and they will be interrogated before "governors and kings" precisely on account of their faith in him (*heneken emou*, v. 9b). When brought to trial, they are not to try to defend themselves but instead are to use the occasion to testify to their accusers (v. 9b), recognizing that the Holy Spirit speaks through their testimony (v. 11).[38] They will face hatred, betrayal by family members, and possibly even death, all on account of Jesus (v. 13). The fervency and specificity of these passages suggest that the author was writing for readers who knew such experiences, either directly or indirectly, and were in danger of facing similar sufferings in their immediate future. This means that the narratives of Jesus' arrest and trials would have been intended to have a practical, existential force and would have been read accordingly.

Indeed, it is interesting to read the Markan trial narratives in the light of 13:9-13. Just as Jesus warns of being brought before Jewish authorities (councils and synagogues) and Gentile authorities (governors and kings), so Mark's narrative has both a formal Jewish trial before the Council and a formal hearing before the governor Pilate. Just as Jesus instructs his followers not to prepare speeches of self-defense but to say only what they are "given," in the faith that the Spirit speaks through them,[39] so in the trial

---

37. Cf. B. Lindars' mistaken claim that Mark's circumstances were unconnected to the warnings in 13:9-13. See "The Persecution of Christians in John 15:18-16:4a," in *Suffering and Martyrdom in the New Testament*, ed. W. Horbury and B. McNeil (Cambridge: Cambridge University Press, 1981), 51-52.

38. Note also references to the Spirit and confession and acclamation of Jesus in 1 Corinthians 12:3; Romans 8:15-16; Galatians 4:6.

39. Cf. Matthew 10:19; Luke 21:15; 12:12. The varying expressions all picture speaking with a prophetic authority and impulse. What is to be spoken, however, is very likely a Christological confession, which Jesus models before the Sanhedrin. This is confirmed by such references as 1 John 4:1-3. See also V. H. Neufeld, *The Earliest Christian Confessions*, NTTS 5 (Grand Rapids: Eerdmans, 1963), esp. 13-33.

narratives Jesus' silence before his accusers is stressed (14:60-61a; 15:2-5), and Jesus' only words are the forthright Christological affirmation of 14:62 and his noncommittal response to the politically slanted charge that Pilate asks about (15:2).[40] In short, the Markan account of Jesus' behavior seems intended to present Jesus' trials as inspiring prototypes for the readers.[41]

The Markan story of Peter's denial, which is closely linked with the account of Jesus' trial by the Sanhedrin, has features that appear to have been intended to make it directly instructive to the situation of the first readers.[42] *Three times* Peter is asked if he is not in fact a follower of Jesus, an interesting detail that may reflect Roman court practice attested with reference to the interrogation of Christians under Pliny.[43] The repeated use of the term "deny" in the absolute, without an object (*arneomai*, 14:68, 70), may be intended to allude to warnings about denying Jesus attested elsewhere in the Jesus-tradition, and is probably directed to behavior in settings of Jewish or Roman arraignment (e.g., Matt. 10:33; Luke 12:9; cf. Rev. 2:13; 3:8). Also, it is likely that Peter's cursing (*anathematizein*, likewise in absolute form) in 14:71 is to be taken as a cursing of Jesus,[44] an action men-

---

40. The variant reading, *sy eipas hoti egō eimi* ("you say that I am he"), is probably influenced by the Matthew 26:64 parallel. The motif of Jesus' silence finds an analogy in Josephus's description of Jesus ben Ananias, who likewise made no attempt to speak in self-defense (*War* 6:300-305).

41. Marcus, *The Way of the Lord,* 169; Anderson, "The Trial of Jesus as Jewish-Christian Polarization," 115; Neufeld, *The Earliest Christian Confessions,* 146.

42. G. W. H. Lampe, "Church Discipline and the Interpretation of the Epistles to the Corinthians," in *Christian History and Interpretation: Studies Presented to John Knox,* ed. W. R. Farmer, C. F. D. Moule, and R. R. Niebuhr (Cambridge: Cambridge University Press, 1967), 337-61, esp. 355-58; D. Daube, "Limitations on Self-Sacrifice in Jewish Law and Tradition," *Theology* 73 (1969): 291-304.

43. Pliny, *Epp.* 10.96.3. Although Pliny's interrogations (*ca.* 110 C.E.) took place about forty years later than the probable date of Mark, it is quite likely that the threefold opportunity to recant mentioned by Pliny was an established practice, as suggested by A. N. Sherwin-White, *Roman Society and Roman Law in the New Testament* (Oxford: Oxford University Press, 1963; reprint, Grand Rapids: Baker, 1978), 25-26. Brown discusses the question of whether Mark framed the threefold denial or inherited it from pre-Markan tradition (*The Death of the Messiah,* 1:610-14, 620-21, favoring the latter). Note also *Mart. Pol.* 9:3, where Polycarp is urged to "revile" (*loidoreō*) Christ, as well as swear by Caesar's "genius" (9:2; 10:1), acclaim Caesar as Lord, and offer incense (8:2).

44. So Lampe, "Church Discipline and the Interpretation of the Epistles to the Corinthians," 357; H. Merkel, "Peter's Curse," in *The Trial of Jesus,* ed. E. Bammel, SBT 13 (London: SCM Press, 1970), 66-71; G. Bornkamm, "Das Wort Jesu vom Bekennen," in *Geschichte und*

tioned by Pliny as something required of those arraigned as Christians, and also a feature of some early Jewish responses to the Christological claims of Jewish Christians.[45] Thus, in ironic fashion, Peter's cowardice before the servants in the courtyard is portrayed in terms intended to suggest associations with the more formal denial of Christ in a synagogue or Roman court setting, and as a stark contrast to Jesus' positive example.[46]

We may ask, therefore, whether the Markan account of Jesus' Sanhedrin trial also may have some direct association with the experiences of the intended readers. The blasphemy charge certainly portrays the religious and theological disagreement between Christian and Jewish views of Jesus that would have been known to GMark's first readers.[47] That is, the account reflects the conflict over Jesus-devotion between Christian Jews and Jewish religious authorities, whatever one may think about the historicity of the events in the life of Jesus.[48] This is not, however, merely an account of a disputation, but more specifically a trial before Jewish authorities, with the Christological issue front and center, and with the result being the charge of blasphemy. With others, I propose that the account not only dra-

---

Glaube I (Munich: Kaiser, 1968), 25-36, esp. 36; Gerhardsson, "Confession and Denial before Men," 54-55; and Brown, *The Death of the Messiah,* 1:605. Cf. Beyer, *Theological Dictionary of the New Testament,* 1:355, and K. E. Dewey, "Peter's Curse and Cursed Peter (Mark 14:53-4, 66-72)," in *The Passion in Mark,* ed. W. Kelber (Philadelphia: Fortress Press, 1976), 101 n. 19.

45. See Horbury, "The Benediction of the *Minim* and Early Jewish-Christian Controversy," 53-54, 59-61, who builds upon Lampe, "Church Discipline and the Interpretation of the Epistles to the Corinthians," 358-60; and Lampe, "'Grievous Wolves' (Acts 20:29)," in *Christ and Spirit in the New Testament,* ed. B. Lindars and S. Smalley (Cambridge: Cambridge University Press, 1973), 253-68. See also the discussion of 1 Corinthians 12:3 later in this chapter.

46. The indication of Peter's restoration in 16:7 may likewise have been intended with practical relevance for the original readers. See Lampe, "Church Discipline and the Interpretation of the Epistles to the Corinthians," 358; and Brown, *The Death of the Messiah,* 1:621-26.

47. Anderson, "The Trial of Jesus as Jewish-Christian Polarization," 125.

48. Cf. E. P. Sanders, *Jesus and Judaism* (London: SCM Press, 1985), 296-301; T. A. Burkill, "The Trial of Jesus," *Vigiliae christianae* 12 (1958): 1-18; E. E. Ellis, "Deity-Christology in Mark 14:58," in *Jesus of Nazareth: Lord and Christ,* ed. J. B. Green and M. Turner (Carlisle: Paternoster; Grand Rapids: Eerdmans, 1994), 192-203; and two other essays in the same volume: D. L. Bock, "The Son of Man Seated at God's Right Hand and the Debate over Jesus' 'Blasphemy,'" 181-91; and G. N. Stanton, "Jesus of Nazareth: A Magician and a False Prophet Who Deceived God's People?" 164-80. See also B. Witherington, *The Christology of Jesus* (Minneapolis: Fortress Press, 1990), 256-62; C. A. Evans, *Jesus and His Contemporaries* (Leiden: E. J. Brill, 1995), 407-34; Brown, *The Death of the Messiah,* 1:530-47.

matizes the theological issue dividing Jews and Christians in the time of GMark and earlier, but also reflects the actual experiences of Jewish Christians called to account before Jewish authorities for their devotion to Christ and charged with blasphemy.[49]

The author of GMark must have expected his readers to recognize the validity of the dominical warning about being brought before Jewish councils and synagogues (13:9) through their knowledge of such experiences. Thus, arraignments of Jewish Christians before Jewish authorities must be dated no later than the probable time of the writing of Mark's Gospel, ca. 65-72 C.E. In fact, given that the Jewish-Christian heritage of Mark's readers seems to lie in their past, and that the intended readership is likely to have been heavily Gentile in make-up, the experiences of being arraigned before synagogue authorities on charges of blasphemy must derive from some time before the date of GMark.

That is, even before the expulsion of the Johannine Jewish Christians from their synagogues, the putative force of Gamaliel II's *Birkhat ha-Minim*, and the efforts of Javnean rabbis to limit the variations in Jewish belief and practice,[50] Christian Jews were probably experiencing the sort of condemnations for blasphemy reflected in the Markan narrative of Jesus' Sanhedrin trial. To be sure, these synagogue actions were localized and ad hoc, whereas in the post-70 C.E. period there appears to have been an effort toward a more consistently applied sanction against Jewish Christians.[51]

The Jesus-devotion manifest in the Markan Sanhedrin trial narrative is sufficient to have brought Jewish charges of blasphemy. As J. Marcus has argued, Mark 14:61-62 is to be taken as a claim to "participation in God's cosmic lordship" and an "approach to equality with God."[52] Such

49. Brown, *The Death of the Messiah*, 1:558-59; Burkill, "The Trial of Jesus," 9-10.

50. On the aims of the Javnean rabbis, see S. J. D. Cohen, "The Significance of Yavneh: Pharisees, Rabbis, and the End of Jewish Sectarianism," *Hebrew Union College Annual* 55 (1984): 27-53; Cohen, *From the Maccabees to the Mishnah* (Louisville: Westminster John Knox Press, 1987), esp. 214-31. Cf. Kimelman, "The Birkat Ha-Minim and the Lack of Evidence for an Anti-Christian Prayer in Late Antiquity," in *Jewish and Christian Self-Definition*, vol. 2, ed. E. P. Sanders (London: SCM Press, 1980), 226-44; Horbury, "The Benediction of the *Minim* and Early Jewish-Christian Controversy"; and G. Alon, *The Jews in Their Land in the Talmudic Age (70-640 C.E.)*, vol. 1, trans. G. Levi (Jerusalem: Magnes Press, 1980), 288-307.

51. This distinction is also suggested by Lindars, "The Persecution of Christians in John 15:18-16:4a," 50-51.

52. Marcus, "Mark 14:61," 139.

an exaltation of a human figure probably drew fire from scrupulous Jews as compromising "the incommensurateness and unity of God."[53] In order for the Markan account of the condemnation of Jesus to "ring true" and be meaningful to the intended readers of 65-72 C.E., the blasphemy charge had to have been recognized as an experienced or vividly remembered reality.

It is all the more likely that Jews would have responded with cries of blasphemy to the kind of Christological claims we have in Mark 14:61-62, for these Christological claims were accompanied by a devotional practice in which the exalted Jesus was invoked, hymned, and acclaimed in gathered cultic settings within the first couple of decades of the Christian movement.[54] It is important to emphasize that *this devotional practice* set apart Christian Christological claims from the honorific rhetorical treatment of other divine-agent figures, such as Moses, Enoch, and Michael. We have no indication of an equivalent organized devotional practice directed toward any of these figures among those Jews who imaginatively portrayed this or that heroic figure in exalted roles. In fact, the praxis of early Christian devotion to the exalted Jesus in public cultic actions would have made it difficult for others to resist the conclusion that those who expressed the sort of Christological claims we find reflected in Mark 14:61-62 really did regard the heavenly Jesus as participating in the divine prerogatives and status. Their religious life, as well as their rhetoric, would have communicated a "binitarian mutation" in comparison with more traditional Jewish monotheistic practices.

Pauline Evidence

From the letters of Paul, we have still earlier indications that the religious claims and devotional practices of Jewish Christians were deemed deeply problematic by some Jewish authorities. There is first of all Paul's own

53. Marcus, "Mark 14:61," 141. From some time later than GMark, Jewish sources indicate that a direct association of a human figure with God's lordship could be regarded as outrageous by scrupulous Jews. Marcus ("Mark 14:61," 140-41) cites the account of R. Jose's rebuke of R. Akiba over his assertion of the Messiah's heavenly enthronement in *b. Sanh.* 38b. See also A. F. Segal, *Two Powers in Heaven: Early Rabbinic Reports about Christianity and Gnosticism,* SJLA 25 (Leiden: E. J. Brill, 1977).

54. Hurtado, *One God, One Lord,* esp. 100-114.

strenuous effort to stamp out the Jewish-Christian movement prior to the Christophany that made him an adherent.[55] The language Paul uses in Galatians 1:13-15 to refer to his pre-Christian efforts against the Jewish-Christian movement conveys a fierce dedication. The verbs "persecute" *(ediōkon)* and "destroy" *(eporthoun)* both connote harsh, even violent actions. The latter term in particular signifies much more than disputation. As M. Hengel states, "This is the use of brute force," as illustrated by the use of the term to describe the anti-Jewish violence of Antiochus Epiphanes (4 Macc. 4:23; 11:4).[56] In the same context, Paul refers to being a superlative zealot *(perissoterōs zēlōtēs)* for his ancestral traditions (1:14), an allusion to the biblical character Phinehas, and to the ancient Jewish theme of direct and forceful action on the part of devout Jews against any Jew seen to engage in open actions that challenge the core religious commitments of the Torah.[57]

Thus, those against whom Saul of Tarsus directed his zeal were engaging in some kind of behavior sufficiently outrageous and radical as to call for strong measures. As Torrey Seland has shown, the particular violations deemed to require this Phinehas-type action were idolatry, apostasy, seduction by false prophets, and perjury.[58] It seems most probable, therefore, that Saul of Tarsus engaged in the determined effort to destroy the Jewish-Christian movement because he saw it as manifesting one or more of these major religious crimes. The following factors make this a reasonable position.

In Paul's references to his momentous religious change from persecutor to adherent of the Jewish-Christian movement, we have indications of

---

55. See M. Hengel, *The Pre-Christian Paul* (London: SCM Press; Philadelphia: Trinity Press International, 1991), 62-86, esp. 70-72; Hultgren, "Paul's Pre-Christian Persecutions of the Church," 97-111; and Simon Légasse, "Paul's Pre-Christian Career according to Acts," in *The Book of Acts in Its First-Century Setting*, vol. 4: *Palestinian Setting*, 365-90.

56. Hengel, *The Pre-Christian Paul*, 71-72, discusses the use of the Greek word *portheō* in Luke-Acts and Josephus (the quote is from p. 72). See also C. Spicq, *Theological Lexicon of the New Testament* (Peabody, Mass.: Hendrickson, 1994), 3:141-42.

57. Numbers 25:1-13; Josephus, *Ant.* 4.145-58; Philo, *Spec. Leg.* 1.54-57; Donaldson, "Zealot and Convert," 672-74; Torrey Seland, *Establishment Violence in Philo and Luke: A Study of Non-Conformity to the Torah and Jewish Vigilante Reactions* (Leiden: E. J. Brill, 1995), esp. 42-74; Seland, "Saul of Tarsus and Early Zealotism: Reading Gal. 1:13-14 in Light of Philo's Writings," *Biblica* 83 (2002): 449-71.

58. Seland, *Establishment Violence in Philo and Luke*, 37-42, 101-82. Prime examples of Phinehas-like zeal are 1 Maccabees 2:15-26; 3 Maccabees 7:10-15.

where the central issues lay.[59] Paul describes the key religious experience as a revelation of Jesus as God's Son (Gal. 1:15-17), that is, a "Christophany" in which Jesus is revealed to Paul in such a way as to convince him of Jesus' uniquely exalted status.[60] Likewise, in another undeniably autobiographical passage, Philippians 3:4-16, Paul contrasts his pre-conversion life of Pharisaism (v. 5) and zealous persecution of Jewish Christians (v. 6; note again the Phinehas allusion) with "the knowledge of Christ Jesus my Lord" (v. 8). He goes on to describe his present religious orientation as a fervent commitment to Christ, and he counts all his previous causes for boasting as nothing "on account of Christ" (v. 7), for whom he has willingly undergone the loss of it all (v. 8). He now seeks to "gain Christ" (v. 8), to "be found in him" (v. 9), to know Christ, experiencing the "power of his resurrection and the fellowship of his sufferings" (v. 10).

In both of these passages, Paul clearly portrays his change in religious views as his embrace of a very exalted view of Jesus and an intense religious devotion focused on Jesus. Given that his religious change also led Paul to become a part of the young Christian movement, the logical inference is that this movement shared basically the same devotion to Jesus that his "conversion" led him to embrace.[61] Furthermore, Paul ceased acting against Jewish Christians precisely as a result of a revelation of Jesus' exalted status, which suggests that exalted Christological claims and associated religious practices were the major objectionable features of the Christian movement that drew Paul's ire prior to conversion.

It is, of course, entirely likely that the full range of causes for Paul's pre-conversion persecution of Jewish Christians included other factors as well. Part of Paul's pre-Christian zeal may have been directed against what

---

59. Donaldson, "Zealot and Convert," 655-82, gives a summary of proposals about the causes of Paul's persecution of Jewish Christians.

60. See J. D. G. Dunn, "'A Light to the Gentiles': The Significance of the Damascus Road Christophany for Paul," in *The Glory of Christ in the New Testament: Studies in Christology in Memory of George Bradford Caird*, ed. L. D. Hurst and N. T. Wright (Oxford: Clarendon Press, 1987), 251-66; Seyoon Kim, *The Origin of Paul's Gospel*, WUNT 2/4 (Tübingen: J. C. B. Mohr [Paul Siebeck], 1981); C. C. Newman, *Paul's Glory-Christology: Tradition and Rhetoric*, NovTSup 69 (Leiden: E. J. Brill, 1992); K. O. Sandnes, *Paul — One of the Prophets?* WUNT 2/43 (Tübingen: J. C. B. Mohr [Paul Siebeck], 1991); and Larry W. Hurtado, "Convert, Apostate, or Apostle to the Nations? The 'Conversion' of Paul in Recent Scholarship," *Studies in Religion* 22 (1993): 273-84.

61. It is commonly accepted, for example, that Romans 1:3-4 reflects "pre-Pauline" Christological tradition, which confesses both Jesus' Davidic descent and his divine sonship.

he saw as a dangerously sectarian group whose claims amounted to a challenge to all other bases for understanding who the people of God are (e.g., the Torah). That is, Jesus-devotion may well have been tied up with issues about who the people of God were, and about what was required to serve God aright, which should perhaps be seen as corollaries of the Christological issues.[62] But, for the reasons we have considered here, it seems most likely that the Jesus-devotion of Jewish Christians was central in the matters under explicit dispute.

We may have some confirmation of this in passages where Paul conveys the view of Jesus he came to hold as a believer, among which 2 Corinthians 3:12–4:6 certainly must be considered. Here Paul laments the inability of unbelieving Jews (3:14-15) and others (4:4) to see "the glory of the Lord [Jesus]" (3:18), who is the very image of God (4:4); and he contrasts this inability with the illumination that leads Christian believers to reverence Jesus in these terms. In the contrast between the hardened minds of unbelieving Jews and the disclosure that comes "in Christ" (3:14), "when one turns to the Lord" (3:16), we perhaps have an echo of his own radical change of views about Christ.

The point I want to emphasize, however, is that Paul presents the exalted view of Jesus affirmed here as the shared understanding of believers, about which he appears to expect no controversy within the circle of Christian fellowship. Paul offers the Christological claims of this passage not as some truth granted especially to him, but as the common view of Jesus characteristic of those "in Christ."[63] This makes it likely that the Jesus-devotion of this passage basically reflects the religious stance that he formerly could not accept and felt obliged to oppose vigorously. It is not difficult to see why such an extraordinarily exalted view of Jesus would have elicited the determination to destroy the Christian movement. The attribution of divine glory to Jesus, a mere mortal who had been executed under a cloud of charges, in the eyes of Saul of Tarsus, could easily have seemed a blasphemous stance that required urgent Phinehas-type action.

To cite one more relevant passage, we may turn to Philippians 2:6-11. It is not necessary here to engage the many questions about whether this is a

---

62. This is the main point Donaldson argues in "Zealot and Convert," esp. 678-80, and in *Paul and the Gentiles: Remapping the Apostle's Convictional World* (Minneapolis: Fortress Press, 1997), esp. 273-92.

63. Cf. Kim, *The Origin of Paul's Gospel*, 44-50, 100-136, who attributes considerable Christological innovation to Paul.

Pauline adaptation of an anonymous hymn, or, if so, whether the hymn derives from Aramaic-speaking or Greek-speaking Christian circles. For our purposes, the first important point is the religious claim and devotional practice reflected in this passage, particularly the audacious claim that Jesus has uniquely exalted status as *Kyrios*, and thus is entitled to receive universal obeisance. This universal acclamation is described in language borrowed from Isaiah 45:23, a clear allusion that seems intended to associate the universal acclamation of Jesus the *Kyrios* with the acclamation of God, perhaps even to make the acclamation of Jesus as *Kyrios* the fulfillment of the Isaiah passage.[64] Moreover, it is commonly accepted that this future universal acclamation of Jesus as *Kyrios* was ritually anticipated in the regular cultic devotional life of many early Christian groups (e.g., Rom. 10:9-10; 1 Cor. 12:1-3).

The second point to make is that Paul presents this astonishing devotional stance as an uncontested premise for the ethical instruction he gives, which is the real focus of the letter.[65] That is, Paul presents this exalted view of Jesus as something about which he expects no controversy, something he does not need to defend or explain. By the time of this epistle (ca. 61 C.E.?), the Jesus-devotion reflected in this passage had become so commonplace as to require no introduction. Whatever the linguistic provenance of any material that Paul is quoting here, there is no hint that the passage has any new or distinguishing feature of Christian belief and practice. There seems every reason to conclude that the passage probably reflects the exalted Christological claims and innovative devotional practice of the earliest years of the Christian movement, the sort of Jesus-devotion that elicited the outrage of the pre-Christian Paul.

That is, there was certainly Jewish opposition specifically against early Jewish-Christian Jesus-devotion well before 70 C.E. and the Gospel of John. The pre-Christian Paul himself becomes an important example of devout Jews being outraged by the Christological claims and practices of Jewish Christians. As A. J. Hultgren has pointed out, there is no evidence that early Jewish Christianity, not even the "Hellenist" group, set itself against the Torah, so the assumption that Paul's pre-Christian

64. See esp. Takeshi Nagata, "Philippians 2:5-11: A Case Study in the Contextual Shaping of Early Christology," Ph.D. dissertation, Princeton Theological Seminary, 1981.

65. On Paul's characteristic hortatory use of Christological material, see S. E. Fowl, *The Story of Christ in the Ethics of Paul: An Analysis of the Function of the Hymnic Material in the Pauline Corpus*, JSNTSup 36 (Sheffield: JSOT Press, 1990).

persecution of Christian Jews was motivated by such a factor is ill-founded.[66] In Galatians 1:23, Paul refers to his persecution as an attempt to destroy "the faith," which points to the beliefs, the religious claims of the Jewish Christians.

To take Paul's persecution of Jewish Christians as at least in large part prompted by their Jesus-devotion also fits the traditions preserved in Acts. As noted earlier, Acts describes Saul of Tarsus as moving against those who "call upon" the name of Jesus, which is a clear reference to cultic invocation of Jesus as one would invoke a deity (Acts 9:14, 21). This implies that the offensiveness of these Jewish Christians had to do very much with their Christological claims and a devotional practice that could have been taken as an idolatrous deviation.[67]

We also know that Paul was not the only devout Jew moved to oppose Jewish Christians. First Thessalonians 2:14-16 mentions the "churches of God in Judea" suffering persecution from their fellow Jews.[68] There is also Paul's mention of being "persecuted for the cross of Christ" in Galatians 6:12, which may well refer to opposition from non-Christian Jews.[69] As confirming evidence, we can note Josephus's account of the incident where the high priest Ananus brought James, the brother of Jesus, and certain other

66. Hultgren, "Paul's Pre-Christian Persecutions of the Church," 97-104. Even Hengel, who seems interested in crediting the "Hellenists" with more innovative views of Torah and Temple than the "Hebrews," admits that we may not attribute to the Hellenists a rejection of the Torah or an active mission to Gentiles as causes of Paul's pre-Christian persecutions (*The Pre-Christian Paul*, 79-84). Attributions of radical creativity and distinctiveness to these "Hellenists" have received a telling critique from Hill, *Hellenists and Hebrews*.

67. Examples of cultic actions involving Jesus' name include Acts 7:59; 22:16. See W. Heitmüller, "*Im Namen Jesu*": *Eine sprach- und religionsgeschichtliche Untersuchung zum Neuen Testament, speziell zur altchristlichen Taufe*, FRLANT, 1/2 (Göttingen: Vandenhoeck & Ruprecht, 1903); S. New, "The Name, Baptism, and the Laying on of Hands," in *The Beginnings of Christianity*, ed. F. J. Foakes Jackson and K. Lake (1932; Grand Rapids: Baker, 1966), 5:121-40.

68. B. A. Pearson ("1 Thessalonians 2:13-16: A Deutero-Pauline Interpolation," *Harvard Theological Review* 64 [1971]: 79-94) has offered an influential case for the view that the passage is a later interpolation. Cf. K. P. Donfried, "1 Thessalonians 2:13-16 as a Test Case," *Interpretation* 38 (1984): 242-53; Ingo Broer, "'Antisemitismus' und Judenpolemik im Neuen Testament: Eine Beitrag zum besseren Verständnis von 1 Thess. 2:14-16," *Biblische Notizen* 29 (1983): 59-91; and R. Jewett, *The Thessalonian Correspondence: Pauline Rhetoric and Millenarian Piety* (Philadelphia: Fortress Press, 1986), 36-42.

69. Robert Jewett, "The Agitators and the Galatian Congregation," *New Testament Studies* 17 (1970/71): 198-212.

Jewish Christians before the Sanhedrin on charges of serious violation of the Torah and had them executed by stoning.[70] Such a punishment was restricted to radical violations of the Torah, such as idolatry and teaching Israel to stray from God. And, of course, there is the ironic fact of Paul, the onetime persecutor of Jewish Christians, himself subsequently being on the receiving end of severe opposition from Jewish authorities more than once, as mentioned in 2 Corinthians 11:23-26. Here, Paul refers to receiving synagogue floggings on five occasions, and mentions a stoning as well.

The "forty lashes minus one" represents a serious punishment for serious religious crimes.[71] We are not told the charges for which Paul was flogged, and so various possibilities have been mentioned, such as "consorting with Gentiles and eating forbidden food."[72] But I contend that such a proposal presupposes a far greater Halakhic uniformity among Diaspora Jews than seems to have been the case. Consorting with Gentiles would have been almost unavoidable for urban Jews in Diaspora cities, and it is widely accepted that Gentiles frequented Diaspora synagogues as visitors and religious inquirers. It is much more likely, thus, that Paul was deemed guilty of one or more serious crimes particularly associated with his being an exponent of Christian beliefs and practices. If Paul's persecution of Christian Jews was motivated at least in part by their Jesus-devotion, it seems a safe inference that his own troubles in synagogues also had something directly to do with holding a religious stance similar to that of those he formerly persecuted himself.

His proclamation of full enfranchisement of Gentile Christians into the elect people of God without requiring them to make a full conversion to Jewish observance of the Torah (including, for males, circumcision) certainly brought opposition from some other Christian Jews, as seems indicated in Galatians 5:11-12, and other Jews as well may have found this a cause for taking action against Paul. But we have good reason to think that this was by no means the only factor in the action taken against him. We have already noted references to Jewish Christians being hauled before

70. Josephus, *Ant.* 20:200-201. Execution by stoning suggests that the charges (whatever their validity) involved major offenses such as apostasy or idolatry or perjury.

71. *M. Makkoth* mentions a variety of offenses that make a Jew liable to this punishment, but we cannot be sure how much Mishnah here represents actual jurisprudence of the first-century synagogue courts. See also Philo, *Spec. Leg.* 2.28.

72. E.g., C. K. Barrett, *The Second Epistle to the Corinthians* (London: Adam & Charles Black, 1973), 296-97.

synagogues and councils on account of Jesus' name. We also have the Acts reference (mentioned earlier) to the pre-Christian Paul directing his efforts "against the name of Jesus of Nazareth," which included attempts to force Jewish Christians to "blaspheme," which probably means demanding them to curse Jesus (Acts 26:9, 11).[73]

We may have direct Pauline confirmation that there was this kind of bitter Jewish opposition to the Jesus-devotion of early Jewish Christians, including Paul, in 1 Corinthians 12:3, where he contrasts the Christian confession "*Kyrios Iēsous*" ("Jesus is Lord") with the cursing of Jesus, "*Anathema Iēsous.*" As has been argued by a number of scholars, the latter expression probably derives from real situations in which Jesus was cursed and placed under divine judgment among Jewish opponents of the Christian movement.[74] The cursing of Jesus (and Christians) is explicitly alleged later by Justin,[75] and Pliny mentions being informed by unnamed sources that cursing Christ was an effective test to distinguish a true Christian, intelligence that may well be based on Jewish synagogue practice.[76] Also, we noted earlier the likelihood that Peter's cursing in Mark 14:71 has to do with cursing Jesus.

---

73. In 1 Timothy 1:13 the pre-Christian Paul is described as a "blasphemer, a persecutor and a man of violence [*hybristes*]." "Blasphemer" here probably pictures Paul as having vilified Jesus, perhaps cursing Jesus, in his pre-conversion activities.

74. O. Cullmann, *The Earliest Christian Confessions,* trans. J. K. S. Reid (London: Lutterworth, 1949), 28-30; Neufeld, *The Earliest Christian Confessions,* 44, 63-64, 101; Lampe, "'Grievous Wolves' (Acts 20:29)," 251-68; J. D. M. Derrett, "Cursing Jesus (1 Cor. XII.3): The Jews as Religious 'Persecutors,'" *New Testament Studies* 21 (1975): 544-54; Horbury, "The Benediction of the *Minim* and Early Jewish-Christian Controversy," 53-54; J. M. Bassler, "1 Cor. 12:3 — Curse and Confession in Context," *Journal of Biblical Literature* 101 (1982): 415-18; Setzer, *Jewish Responses to Early Christians,* 138-42. Cf. other suggestions from J. C. Hurd, *The Origin of 1 Corinthians,* 2d ed. (London, 1965; reprint, Macon, Ga.: Mercer University Press, 1983), 193; G. D. Fee, *The First Epistle to the Corinthians* (Grand Rapids: Eerdmans, 1987), 578-82; B. A. Pearson, "Did the Gnostics Curse Jesus?" *Journal of Biblical Literature* 86 (1967): 301-5; and W. C. Van Unnik, "Jesus: Anathema or Kyrios," in *Christ and Spirit in the New Testament,* 113-26.

75. *Dial.* 47:4; 95:4; 108:3; 133:6; *1 Apol.* 31; cf. *Dial.* 31.

76. Pliny, *Epp.* 10:96. English translation and notes can be found in, *A New Eusebius,* ed. J. Stevenson (London: SPCK, 1974), 13-15; Latin text with German translation in P. Guyot and R. Klein, *Das frühe Christentum bis zum Ende der Verfolgungen, Band 1: Die Christen im heidnischen Staat* (Darmstadt: Wissenschaftliche Buchgesellschaft, 1993), 38-41, commentary 320-23. See 322 n. 11: "Die maledictio Christi war bereits seit frühester Zeit für die Juden ein Unterscheidungsmerkmal von den Christen. . . ."

Moreover, the use of *anathema* to mean a "curse" (rather than an oath) in the formula in 1 Corinthians 12:3 suggests a Jewish provenance.[77] Paul's reference to the crucified Jesus as "having become accursed for us [*genomenos hyper hēmōn katara*]" (Gal. 3:13) is often taken as Paul's adaptation of a Jewish anti-Jesus polemic in which he was portrayed as accursed by God. The reference to the crucified Jesus as a *skandalon* (offense) to Jews (1 Cor. 12:3) may be further evidence.[78] So there are good supporting reasons for the view that the *"Anathema Iēsous"* phrase in 1 Corinthians 12:3 reflects Jewish polemics directed against Jewish-Christian Jesus-devotion. Such a curse formula may indeed represent the sort of "blasphemy" of Jesus — that is, denials and vilifications of Jesus that Jewish Christians were pressured to utter according to Acts 26:11, as we noted earlier.[79]

In measuring the Jewish opposition to Jesus-devotion in the time of Paul, the force of the *Anathema Iēsous* should not be minimized. It denotes placing Jesus under divine curse and judgment. As analogy, we have only to note Paul's own use of *anathema* in Galatians 1:8-9, where he angrily hurls this searing threat against anyone who might promote a message contrary to his gospel. This *anathema* represents divine judgment against the false teacher in the spirit of Deuteronomy 13:1-5; 18:20. In Romans 9:3 *anathema* is the dire extremity Paul is willing to face if it would produce the salvation of his people. The *anathema* upon anyone who has "no love for the Lord [Jesus]" in 1 Corinthians 16:22 may in fact have been formed

77. The term is used in the Greek Old Testament (LXX) to translate *cherem* and thus connotes something/someone put under the ban or delivered up to wrath. See J. Behm, *Theological Dictionary of the New Testament*, 1:354-55; H. Aust and D. Müller, *New International Dictionary of New Testament Theology*, 1:413-14; also Philo, *Vit. Mos.* 1:253. Derrett, "Cursing Jesus (1 Cor. XII.3)," suggests *meharam* as the Hebrew term used in the synagogue formula (551 n. 9). For examples of pagan usage and meaning of *anathema*, see James H. Moulton and George Milligan, *The Vocabulary of the Greek New Testament* (1930; Grand Rapids: Eerdmans, 1952), 33; and A. Deissmann, *Light from the Ancient East* (1927; reprint, Grand Rapids: Baker, 1965), 95-96. Later examples show Christian and Jewish influence. See G. H. R. Horsley, *New Documents Illustrating Early Christianity* (North Ryde, NSW: Macquarie University, 1981), 99-101.

78. See D. Sänger, "'Verflucht ist jeder, der am Holze hängt' (Gal. 3:13b): Zur Rezeption einer frühen antichristlichen Polemik," *Zeitschrift für die neutestamentliche Wissenschaft* 85 (1994): 279-85; G. N. Stanton, "Aspects of Early Christian-Jewish Polemic and Apologetics," *New Testament Studies* 31 (1985): 377-92; and Stanton, "Jesus of Nazareth: A Magician and a False Prophet Who Deceived God's People?"

79. See especially the careful discussion in Neufeld, *The Earliest Christian Confessions*, 63-64.

in reply to the *anathema* known to have been pronounced upon Jesus in non-Christian Jewish circles.[80]

This kind of bitterly negative treatment of Jesus is most adequately accounted for by taking the measure of the exalted view of Jesus held by Paul and presumed by him as typical of fellow Christians. In short, *"Anathema Iēsous"* is probably an outraged Jewish reaction against what were seen as blasphemous Christological claims and utterly inappropriate cultic devotion to Jesus.

Conclusion

From the Synoptics, including GMark, the earliest, we have clear references to sharp conflicts over Jesus-devotion between Jewish followers of Jesus and Jewish religious authorities. These conflicts, which include charges of blasphemy and indications of synagogue trials, must be dated no later than the composition of these texts. From Paul's letters we have still earlier evidence of bitter Jewish opposition to Christian Jews in the earliest decades of the Christian movement, going back to his own vigorous efforts to stamp out the movement. This opposition, from devout defenders of Jewish religious practices who were concerned with the uniqueness of God, seems to have been directed against the Jesus-devotion of Christian Jews, because it was seen as a dangerous development.

In the earliest decades, however, it is quite likely that Jewish opposition was varied in nature and in causes. For example, although it was acceptable to exalt a great figure of the past recognized by the Jewish tradition, such as Moses, to give equivalent treatment to Jesus, a figure of their own time who was regarded by some as a false teacher and who did not enjoy broad respect outside the circle of his followers, would have seemed silly and offensive, all the more so since these followers even put Jesus above the great figures of Israel's past. There may have been howls of outrage, perhaps even cries of "blasphemy."

But in the eyes of at least some devout Jews the outrage went even further. The Christological assertions reflected in the New Testament texts that we have examined connote a divine-like status for Jesus in the devo-

---

80. Cf. G. Bornkamm, "The Anathema in Early Christian Lord's Supper Liturgy," in *Early Christian Experience* (London: SCM Press, 1969), 161-79.

tional life of many early Christians, and in addition to the Christological claims of early Christian Jews, their devotional practices would have poured fuel on the fire. Lofty honorific claims could be made for mortals, particularly the "greats" of the biblical tradition. But scrupulous Jews characteristically drew back from accompanying the honorific rhetoric with open cultic devotion directed to these great figures. Within the first years, however, Christian believers (still mainly Christian Jews) put Jesus with God at the center of their devotional life, including their worship practices, and this would have made their "binitarian" devotion seem not merely offensive but dangerous for the wider religious integrity of Judaism. In these cases, charges of "blasphemy" connoted an accusation of infringement on the uniqueness of God, the most important teaching of the Torah among devout Jews of the Roman period. The violent efforts of Saul of Tarsus, for example, may have been prompted by the conviction that Jesus-devotion was both a serious transgression in its own right and a possible encouragement to other Jews to take similar steps with other divine-agent figures.

Whatever the intentions of the Christian Jews whose Jesus-devotion elicited the opposition we have surveyed, it may be that Jewish religious opponents saw earlier and more clearly than the Jewish Jesus-devotees themselves that their devotion was a significant "mutation" in Jewish monotheistic practice.

CHAPTER EIGHT

Religious Experience and Religious Innovation in the New Testament

It is clear that earliest Christianity was characterized by a rich and varied assortment of religious experiences, ranging all along a continuum from the quiet and inward to the dramatic and outward categories. The rhetoric of the New Testament attributes all these Christian religious experiences to the Spirit of God, the "Holy Spirit." The success of earliest Christianity and its appeal and credibility in the eyes of converts seem to have been very heavily connected to its ability to provide religious experiences that corresponded to its rhetoric of being "gifted," "filled," "anointed," and "empowered" by the Spirit of God.[1] To cite but one example indicating the importance of the experience of the Spirit for early Christians, in Galatians 3:1-5 Paul cites the Spirit-experiences of the Galatians as evidence of the validity of their conversion apart from observance of the requirements of Jewish Torah.[2] In this discussion, in addition to emphasizing the general importance of religious experiences in early Christianity, I particularly

---

1. See, e.g., Luke T. Johnson, *The Writings of the New Testament: An Interpretation* (Philadelphia: Fortress Press, 1986), 85-114. "The key to Christianity's success lies not in its teaching but in its experience of power" (87).

2. On the importance of Spirit-experiences in this epistle, see C. H. Cosgrove, *The Cross and the Spirit: A Study in the Argument and Theology of Galatians* (Macon, Ga.: Mercer University Press, 1988).

This chapter is a revised text of my 1998 T. W. Manson Memorial Lecture that I delivered October 29, 1998, at the University of Manchester, United Kingdom. It was subsequently published in the *Journal of Religion* 80 (2000): 183-205. I thank the journal editor and publisher (University of Chicago Press) for permission to republish my essay, here slightly re-edited for this book.

want to argue that scholarly study of early Christianity should include the recognition that among the important chief historical factors that helped generate the religious innovations of the movement were powerful religious experiences perceived by the recipients as "revelations." This is not likely to be received by all without dispute, so I shall attempt to lay a case that I hope will at least provide a basic cogency for my thesis.

In the first part of this chapter, I shall survey attitudes toward the subject of religious experience in the New Testament. In the next part I shall review the studies of social scientists that help us to appreciate the efficacy of revelatory religious experience as a frequent factor in generating religious innovations. In the final part I shall discuss indications in the New Testament that revelatory religious experiences were significant factors in generating perhaps the most distinctive religious innovation characteristic of early Christianity: the cultic veneration of Jesus.

The Treatment of Religious Experience in Biblical Scholarship

The religious experiences attested in the sources for early Christianity have not always been done justice in scholarly studies. Scholarly work on the New Testament as we have come to know it has been shaped and driven mainly by theological interests and has mined the New Testament for support for and illumination of Christian beliefs and doctrines. Scholarly study was sharpened in theological dispute between Protestant and Catholic camps, and particularly within the Protestant tradition between more traditionalist and more modernizing versions of religious belief. In the controversies emerging in the Enlightenment and thereafter, scholars were more concerned to explore the historical bases for Christian beliefs and the influences that might have shaped them. Some sought to show that Christian beliefs and practices were very much shaped by and derived from non-Christian sources, particularly "pagan" religious traditions, in order to argue against the continuing validity of those beliefs and practices.[3] On the other hand, those scholars more sympathetic toward traditional beliefs seem often to have accepted the premise that heavy indebtedness to non-

---

3. On the polemical interests at work in the emergence of a modern critical approach to the New Testament, see J. Z. Smith, *Drudgery Divine* (Chicago: University of Chicago Press, 1990).

Christian traditions would call into question the validity of Christian tradition, and so they sought to resist the idea that early Christian beliefs and practices were deeply indebted to pagan traditions.

All of these scholarly developments were very understandable in light of the historical factors that motivated and shaped them. But the scholarly traditions, the issues, the apparatus of scholarship, and the questions and approaches were all focused on the religious *thought* of the New Testament, the concepts and doctrines, and comparatively less attention was given to the nature and importance of religious experience.

In the late nineteenth and early twentieth centuries, however, studies appeared that were more concerned with exploring the nature of the religious experiences reflected in the New Testament. Hermann Gunkel's classic study of the Spirit in Paul is commonly regarded today as a watershed publication.[4] Adolf Deissmann is noted also for emphasizing that early Christianity was foremost a religious movement of worship and religious experience and that it should not be approached as primarily a doctrinal development.[5] In English-speaking scholarship as well there were studies of this period that showed an interest in the religious experience of the early church.[6] But the influence of the dialectical theology movement on biblical scholarship after World War I renewed a focus on the doctrines of the New Testament. The historical-critical work of this period was heavily devoted to form criticism of the Gospels and to related attempts to trace the history of the traditions reflected in New Testament writings.[7]

---

4. Hermann Gunkel, *Die Wirkungen des heligen Geistes nach der populären Anschauung der apostolischen Zeit und die Lehre des Apostels Paulus* (Göttingen: Vandenhoeck & Ruprecht, 1888). The continuing significance of this study is reflected in its translation into English: *The Influence of the Holy Spirit,* trans. R. A. Harrisville and R. P. Quanbeck (Philadelphia: Fortress Press, 1979).

5. Adolf Deissmann, *Paul: A Study in Social and Religious History* (1911; English trans., 1927; reprint, New York: Harper & Bros., 1957).

6. P. Gardner, *The Religious Experience of St. Paul* (London: Williams & Norgate, 1911); H. B. Swete, *The Holy Spirit in the New Testament* (London: Macmillan, 1909), and *The Holy Spirit in the Ancient Church* (London: Macmillan, 1912). H. W. Robinson's *The Christian Experience of the Holy Spirit* (New York and London: Harper & Bros., 1928) is a more broad-ranging theological discussion but shows interest in religious experience in the early part of this century.

7. It is interesting to note that there apparently was a similar lapse in social-scientific study of religious experience in the same period — indeed, in the social-scientific study of religion in general. See comments to this effect in Rodney Stark, "A Taxonomy of Religious

In more recent years, however, we have seen a renewal of interest among New Testament scholars in studying the religious experiences of the earliest churches. This scholarly interest appears to have been stimulated in part by the Pentecostal and charismatic movements, which make a great deal of the Christian experience of the Holy Spirit and seek to associate the modern experiences cultivated in these circles with the experiences referred to in the New Testament. J. D. G. Dunn's 1970 book, *Baptism in the Holy Spirit*, is a clear example of this newer scholarly interest.[8] In particular, there have been several books on the phenomenon of prophecy in the New Testament.[9]

Two books may be cited as especially valuable. Dunn's *Jesus and the Spirit* ambitiously attempts a portrayal of the religious experience of Jesus and the earliest Christian communities.[10] This study must be regarded as essential reading for anyone today interested in a broad-ranging, sympathetic, but scholarly discussion of religious experience in the New Testament. More recently, Gordon Fee's massive work on the Holy Spirit in the epistles of Paul (967 pages!) combines detailed exegetical treatment of all references to the Spirit in Paul's letters and an enthusiastic synthesis of Paul's understanding of the Spirit.[11]

There has also been a spate of studies in recent years approaching New Testament references to powerful "mystical" experiences in the light of an-

---

Experience," *Journal for the Scientific Study of Religion* 5 (1965): 97-116, and Stark's citation of C. Y. Glock in "The Sociology of Religion," in *Sociology Today*, ed. R. K. Merton, L. Broom, and L. S. Cottrell Jr. (New York: Basic Books, 1959), 153-77.

8. J. D. G. Dunn, *Baptism in the Holy Spirit: A Re-examination of the New Testament Teaching on the Gift of the Spirit in Relation to Pentecostalism Today*, Studies in Biblical Theology, 2d series (London: SCM Press, 1970).

9. See, e.g., David Hill, *New Testament Prophecy* (Atlanta: John Knox Press, 1979); W. A. Grudem, *The Gift of Prophecy in 1 Corinthians* (Washington, D.C.: University Press of America, 1982); D. E. Aune, *Prophecy in Early Christianity and the Ancient Mediterranean World* (Grand Rapids: Eerdmans, 1983); C. B. Forbes, *Prophecy and Inspired Speech in Early Christianity and Its Hellenistic Environment*, WUNT, 2/7 (Tübingen: J. C. B. Mohr, 1995); T. W. Gillespie, *The First Theologians: A Study in Early Christian Prophecy* (Grand Rapids: Eerdmans, 1994).

10. J. D. G. Dunn, *Jesus and the Spirit: A Study of the Religious and Charismatic Experience of Jesus and the First Christians as Reflected in the New Testament* (London: SCM Press; Philadelphia: Westminster Press, 1975).

11. Gordon D. Fee, *God's Empowering Presence: The Holy Spirit in the Letters of Paul* (Peabody, Mass.: Hendrickson, 1994). Fee includes a good deal of exhortation to the modern churches to seek renewal along the lines of the place of the Spirit reflected in Paul's letters.

cient Jewish mystical traditions.[12] These studies have tended to focus on references in Paul to visionary experiences, with particular attention given to 2 Corinthians 12:1-10, where he seems to give an autobiographical account of an ascent into the heavens. But there has also been significant recent scholarly attention given to Paul's "conversion" experience, which he refers to as a "revelation" of Christ that changed him from a persecutor of Jewish-Christian groups to a dedicated promulgator of the Christian message.[13] To mention one notable publication, Seyoon Kim's forcefully argued study portrays Paul's Damascus road experience as a Christophany, a visionary revelation of Christ in glorious form, that also conveyed to Paul his sense of mission and the basics of his distinctive message.[14]

Nevertheless, it is still the case that New Testament scholarship tends to ignore or give little attention to religious experiences in describing and analyzing the features of Jesus and earliest Christianity. Even the recent attention given to the social and cultural characteristics of the early churches has tended to focus on other aspects and other questions, such as the economic levels of early Christians, the roles exercised by women, and organizational structures or rituals.[15] This reluctance or inability to come to

12. See, e.g., John Bowker, "'Merkabah Visions' and the Visions of Paul," *Journal of Semitic Studies* 16 (1971): 57-73; Peter Schäfer, "The New Testament and Hekhalot Literature: The Journey into Heaven in Paul and in Merkabah Mysticism," *Journal of Jewish Studies* 35 (1984): 19-35; A. F. Segal, "Heavenly Ascent in Hellenistic Judaism, Early Christianity, and Their Environment," in *Aufstieg und Niedergang der römischen Welt*, ed. H. Temporini and W. Haase (Berlin: W. de Gruyter, 1980), vol. 23, pt. 2:1333-94; and Segal, *Paul the Convert: The Apostolate and Apostasy of Saul the Pharisee* (New Haven: Yale University Press, 1990); and J. D. Tabor, *Things Unutterable: Paul's Ascent to Paradise in Its Greco-Roman, Judaic, and Early Christian Contexts* (Lanham, Md.: University Press of America, 1986).

13. I have surveyed the relevant publications in an earlier essay: "Convert, Apostate, or Apostle to the Nations? The 'Conversion' of Paul in Recent Scholarship," *Studies in Religion/ Sciences religieuses* 22 (1993): 273-84.

14. Seyoon Kim, *The Origin of Paul's Gospel*, WUNT, 2/4 (Tübingen: J. C. B. Mohr, 1981). In my view, however, Kim's attempt to make the single Damascus road experience the source event of all the basics of Paul's theology places too much weight on this one visionary experience and does not adequately allow for Paul's references to having had many visions and revelations (e.g., 2 Cor. 12:1, 7). Cf. J. D. G. Dunn, "'Light to the Gentiles': The Significance of the Damascus Road Christophany for Paul," in *The Glory of Christ in the New Testament: Studies in Christology in Memory of George Bradford Caird*, ed. L. D. Hurst and N. T. Wright (Oxford: Clarendon Press, 1987), 251-66.

15. E.g., the justly praised study by W. A. Meeks, *The First Urban Christians: The Social World of the Apostle Paul* (New Haven: Yale University Press, 1983), has no significant treat-

terms with the religious experiences reflected in the New Testament is the main complaint issued by Luke Johnson in a recent study, *Religious Experience in Earliest Christianity: A Missing Dimension in New Testament Studies.*[16] Johnson advocates a phenomenological approach, which employs comparisons with religious experiences in other times and cultures and, without assenting to the faith claims of those whose religious experiences are studied, accepts that religious devotees see their experiences as an encounter with divine realities. He offers stimulating analyses of early Christian baptism, glossolalia, and sacred meal practices to illustrate the gains of the general approach he advocates.

But among New Testament scholars there seems to be a continuing widespread reluctance to attribute much causative significance to religious experiences in the innovations that mark the development of early Christianity. Having argued that "revelatory" religious experiences such as visions and prophetic inspiration were an important historical factor in the appearance of innovative insights, beliefs, and devotional practices in the earliest Christian period, I have experienced the reluctance of some scholars to grant this view.[17] Paul Rainbow, for example, has rejected my proposal, asserting that religious experiences can only confirm previously derived beliefs and convictions and are not themselves causative factors in the emergence of new or altered beliefs and devotional practice.[18] To cite another instance, an anonymous assessor of one of my research grant applications in Canada described as "problematic" my view that there are religious experiences that help generate modifications in belief systems, asserting instead that "such religious experiences are themselves generated by socio-religious changes and so function as legitimating devices to ease the transition from the old to the new," and he proposed that it thus made

---

ment of the religious experiences that characterized early Christian groups. See also the survey of scholarship by Bengt Holmberg, *Sociology and the New Testament: An Appraisal* (Minneapolis: Fortress Press, 1990).

16. Luke Johnson, *Religious Experience in Earliest Christianity: A Missing Dimension in New Testament Studies* (Minneapolis: Fortress Press, 1998).

17. Larry W. Hurtado, *One God, One Lord: Early Christian Devotion and Ancient Jewish Monotheism* (Philadelphia: Fortress Press; London: SCM Press, 1988), esp. 117-22; see also my interaction with critics of my view in "Christ-Devotion in the First Two Centuries: Reflections and a Proposal," *Toronto Journal of Theology* 12 (1996): 17-33 (esp. 25-26).

18. Paul A. Rainbow, "Jewish Monotheism as the Matrix for New Testament Christology: A Review Article," *Novum Testamentum* 33 (1991): 78-91 (esp. 86-87).

more sense to "inquire into the social and cultural situation to which such supernatural experiences might be regarded as a *response.*"

In taking the "problematic" view I hold, I am not, however, alone. One prominent New Testament scholar (Dunn) lists tendencies that might bias our view of religious experience and issues a warning about "discounting the creative force of religious experience." Citing the Apostle Paul as an important case, Dunn insists that along with recognizing Paul's "debt to both Jew and Greek for the great bulk of his language and concepts," we also have to grant "the creative power of his own religious experience — a furnace which melted many concepts in its fires and poured them forth into new moulds. . . . Nothing should be allowed to obscure that fact."[19] In his study of scholarship on mystical experiences, Philip Almond notes that there is a connection between the nature of one's religious experience and "the content that informs it," but he also emphasizes that we must allow for "those experiences which go beyond or are at odds with the received context."[20] He specifically points to powerful religious experiences that "may lead too to the creative transformation of a religious tradition" and that are "capable of generating new interpretations of the tradition."[21] Later in this study he observes that though previously held religious beliefs may well shape the nature of mystical experiences, it is also true that "such experiences may be decisive in the formulation or revision of doctrinal frameworks."[22]

Similarly, Carl Raschke has proposed that revelation experiences involve "not the acquisition of an insider's perspective so much as an insight accruing from the *transposition of certain meaning systems*" and that this transpires "as part of a novel perceptual context within which the 'sense' of a host of related notions or the implications of certain common experiences can be reconstituted."[23] That is, the cognitive content of religious

---

19. Dunn, *Jesus and the Spirit,* 3-4 (quote on 4). We might also note Hermann Gunkel's comments against attempts during his day to make Paul's religious thought simply a borrowing from other sources: "The theology of the great apostle is the expression of his experience, not of his reading" (*The Influence of the Holy Spirit,* 100).

20. Philip C. Almond, *Mystical Experience and Religious Doctrine: An Investigation of the Study of Mysticism in World Religions* (Berlin: Mouton, 1982), 166-67.

21. Almond, *Mystical Experience and Religious Doctrine,* 168.

22. Almond, *Mystical Experience and Religious Doctrine,* 183.

23. Carl Raschke, "Revelation and Conversion: A Semantic Appraisal," *Anglican Theological Review* 60 (1978): 420-36, quotes on 424 and 422, respectively.

"revelations" is often, perhaps characteristically, a reformulation or reconfiguring of religious convictions.

In his recent study of Paul, Terence Donaldson draws upon Thomas Kuhn's now well-known analysis of "paradigm shifts," major reorientations that revolutionize scientific work, as a conceptual model for understanding how Paul's Damascus-road experience could have conveyed a fundamentally altered conviction about the significance of Jesus, which required and drove a "remapping" of Paul's whole "convictional world."[24] In Paul's case, this fundamental change in view about Jesus was not the disclosure of a totally new belief, for prior to his "conversion" Paul had been involved in combatting Jewish Christians whose exalted views of Jesus were likely a major reason for Paul's opposition to these groups. But it also appears that Paul's experience either conveyed or led to a conviction that he was personally commissioned to a mission to the Gentiles, which involved enfranchising them as members of God's elect on the basis of faith in Christ and without full conversion to Torah observance. The sense of this particular mission seems to have been a new "revelation" without true precedent in either the Jewish tradition or the emerging Christian movement.

Religious Experience in Social-Scientific Studies

In the social sciences there is recognition of the importance of religious experiences in defining and understanding religious movements.[25] There is also a comparatively greater recognition that "revelatory" religious experiences are often involved in the emergence of religious innovations. But the tendency among social scientists has been to regard such experiences as derivative phenomena, as the (dysfunctional) outcome of stressful social circumstances and the manifestation of psychopathology in the recipi-

---

24. Terence L. Donaldson, *Paul and the Gentiles: Remapping the Apostle's Convictional World* (Minneapolis: Fortress Press, 1997), esp. 43-49, 293-305.

25. The social-science literature on religious experience is now vast. Only a few items need be cited here as illustrative and heuristically useful. The classic pioneering study is of course William James, *The Varieties of Religious Experience* (1902; reprint, New York: Mentor Books, 1962). More indicative of recent work are the following: W. H. Clark, H. N. Malony, J. Daane, and A. R. Tippett, *Religious Experience: Its Nature and Function in the Human Psyche* (Springfield, Ill.: C. C. Thomas, 1973); Stark, "A Taxonomy of Religious Experience."

ents.[26] Thus, sociologists and anthropologists tend to focus on the social and cultural conditions that may be associated with religious experiences, and psychologists tend to look for personal psychological conditions that may be associated with them. It is very difficult to find social-science studies that approach religious experiences sympathetically and that address the questions of whether and how powerful religious experiences may themselves be causative factors in religious innovations.

Characteristically, social-science approaches assume one or another form of "deprivation theory," whether the deprivation is regarded as deriving from social and cultural conditions or individual conditions (e.g., extreme stress, sexual frustration, and so on).[27] Lying behind all such approaches, either explicitly or implicitly, is the outlook that religious experiences are "false consciousness" and dysfunctional responses to life. Powerful "revelatory" experiences are quite often taken as "hallucinatory" and delusional and, therefore, not of much significance in themselves.[28]

But there are a few scholars who have questioned this rather negative view of religious experiences and offer us some resources for understanding that there are religious experiences that seem to serve as the occasion for the emergence of sometimes significant innovations in religious traditions. That some kinds of religious experiences can have this effect is of course the repeated claim of prophet and founder figures throughout the centuries. The scholars whom I have in mind offer reasons for taking this sort of claim seriously and suggest theoretical models for understanding in

26. See, e.g., the forthright critique of this by Rodney Stark, "Normal Revelations: A Rational Model of 'Mystical' Experiences," *Religion and Social Order* 1 (1991): 239-51.

27. For a classic statement of "relative deprivation theory," see David Aberle, "A Note on Relative Deprivation Theory as Applied to Millenarian and Other Cult Movements," in *Reader in Comparative Religion: An Anthropological Approach*, ed. W. A. Lessa and E. A. Vogt, 3d ed. (New York: Harper & Row, 1972), 527-31. Note that Aberle himself admits that in fact deprivation theory is unable to "predict either the types of deprivations that lead to certain ideological formations, or the degree of deprivation which crystallizes a cult movement" (530). See also the critical comments by Holmberg, *Sociology and the New Testament*, 66-67.

28. See Stark, "Normal Revelations," esp. 239-41, 248-49, for criticisms of this bias by an eminent social scientist who has specialized in the study of religion. In an earlier essay as well, Stark criticized the simplistic assumptions governing much social-scientific study of religion, especially studies of religious innovation (e.g., new religious movements). See R. Stark and W. S. Bainbridge, "Three Models of Cult Formation," in their book *The Future of Religion: Secularization, Revival, and Cult Formation* (Berkeley and Los Angeles: University of California Press, 1985), 171-88.

general how religious experiences can be granted a causative role in religious innovations. To do so does not necessarily or always grant the validity of the religious claim being made (e.g., one does not have to subscribe to the beliefs that the experiences are taken to promote). All that is required for historical purposes is to grant that powerful religious experiences can themselves contribute significantly, sometimes crucially, to religious innovations and are not limited to serving as "legitimizing devices" for previously formed beliefs and practices. That is, we are concerned here primarily with the function and efficacy of revelatory religious experiences, not with their religious validity.

In his now classic essay, "Revitalization Movements," Anthony Wallace attempts a model of the processes involved in the emergence of major religious innovations such as new sects. In what he calls "mazeway reformulation," Wallace describes the restructuring of elements such as religious beliefs, which, he notes, usually happens in the mind of a prophet figure abruptly and dramatically as "a moment of insight" that is "often called inspiration or revelation." He observes, "With few exceptions, every religious revitalization movement with which I am acquainted has been originally conceived in one or several hallucinatory visions by a single individual."[29] Although Wallace operates with a Freudian outlook on religion, as illustrated in his use of the adjective "hallucinatory," he notes clear differences between revelatory religious experiences and the religious delusions of those suffering genuine mental disorders, and he acknowledges (with some surprise at this finding) that "the religious vision experience per se is not psychopathological but rather the reverse, being a synthesizing and often therapeutic process."[30] Wallace goes on to propose a process-model for understanding how the revelatory experiences of prophetic individuals can lead to the formation of new religious movements through the communication of the revelations, the organization of converts, adaptation to cultural patterns, and routinization.[31] In this essay we cannot explore further this social process, as we are primarily concerned with the initial "revelatory" experience.

Rodney Stark has categorized various types of religious experiences into four main types; his fourth "and least common" type is the "revelational."[32]

29. A. F. C. Wallace, "Revitalization Movements," *American Anthropologist* 58 (1956): 264-81; these citations are from 270.

30. Wallace, "Revitalization Movements," 272-73.

31. Wallace, "Revitalization Movements," 273-75.

32. Stark, "A Taxonomy of Religious Experience," 107-12.

For our purposes it is very interesting to note Stark's recognition of the capacity of such experiences to generate religious innovation, even to "contradict and challenge prevailing theological 'truths.'"[33] He also points to the capacity of such experiences to generate in the recipient a sense of personal divine commission and also to generate messages taken as directed to a wide public, "such as in the case of new theologies, eschatological prophecies, or commissions to launch social reforms."[34]

In a subsequent article, Stark focuses on religious experiences of "revelation," positing as "the most fundamental question confronting the social scientific study of religion: How does new religious culture arise?"[35] Lamenting a common social scientific bias against revelatory experience as psychopathology, Stark also expresses growing discomfort with his own earlier attempts to classify the emergence of new religious movements, acknowledging that these attempts had not allowed for "normal people" (Stark means mentally healthy people) to have "revelations sufficiently profound to serve as the basis of new religions."[36]

Noting that reports of religious experiences that convey new "revelation" are comparatively infrequent in comparison to lower-intensity religious experience, Stark proposes that "unusually creative individuals" might "create profound revelations" and attribute them to divine disclosure. For instance, Stark likens the experiences of revelation attributed to Muhammad to the way in which some composers (e.g., Mozart, George Gershwin, and Duke Ellington) are said to have "heard" complete musical melody lines, experiencing the tunes as having come to them from "out there."[37] Although he grants the possibility that revelations actually occur and that there is "an active supernatural realm closed to scientific exploration," Stark obviously is attempting to develop a theoretical model for the experience of revelation that does not require a prior acceptance of a supernatural agency behind the experience.[38] The important points for our topic are (1) that Stark defends the idea that certain powerful religious ex-

33. Stark, "A Taxonomy of Religious Experience," 108.

34. Stark, "A Taxonomy of Religious Experience," 110-11.

35. Stark, "Normal Revelations," 239.

36. Stark, "Normal Revelations," 240-41. The earlier study Stark refers to is W. S. Bainbridge and R. Stark, "Cult Formation: Three Compatible Models," *Sociological Analysis* 40 (1979): 283-95.

37. Stark, "Normal Revelations," 243-44.

38. Stark, "Normal Revelations," 241.

periences themselves can produce significant innovations in religious traditions, and (2) that such experiences, though shaped by social and cultural forces, are not merely continuations of religious ideas otherwise generated and are also not necessarily merely manifestations of psychopathology.

As does Wallace, Stark sketches a model of the process through which revelatory experiences of individuals might become the basis of religious movements or reformations of religious traditions. He proposes cogently that revelatory experiences are more likely to happen to "persons of deep religious concerns who perceive shortcomings in the conventional faith(s)," that persons are more likely to perceive shortcomings in conventional faith(s) during times of increased social crisis, that during such periods there is a greater likelihood of people being willing to accept claims of revelations, and that it is crucial to the success of the revelation that some others accept it.[39]

I find support in these studies for my contention that, just as it is a mistake to dismiss all revelatory experiences as psychopathology, so is it a mistake to ignore such experiences in explaining religious innovations in favor of social and cultural factors. For example, in describing indigenous Christian movements in Japan, Mark Mullins notes that cultural change and stress alone are not adequate explanation for these movements and agrees with Byron Earhart's judgment that "the innovative decision of the founder cannot be completely subsumed by either social factors or the influence of prior religious factors."[40] In a great many cases, the most significant "innovative decisions" of founder and reformer figures are attributed by them to powerful revelatory experiences.

In some cases, the revelation is so at odds with the conventional religious system(s) that what results is a new religion that cannot be accommodated within whatever variety is tolerated by the dominant religious system(s). Muhammad may be an example of this, with his fervent mono-

---

39. Stark, "Normal Revelations," 244-46.

40. Mark R. Mullins, "Christianity as a New Religion: Charisma, Minor Founders, and Indigenous Movements," in *Religion and Society in Modern Japan,* ed. Mark R. Mullins, Shimazono Susumu, and Paul Swanson (Berkeley: Asian Humanities Press, 1993), 257-72, esp. 264, citing H. Byron Earhart, *Gedatsu-Kai and Religion in Contemporary Japan: Returning to the Center* (Bloomington: Indiana University Press, 1989), 236. See also Earhart, "Toward a Theory of the Formation of the Japanese New Religions: The Case of Gedatsu-Kai," *History of Religions* 20, nos. 1 and 2 (1980): 175-97.

theistic stance over against the polytheistic traditions of his culture. But perhaps more often the revelation is (or is initially intended as) a major reformation or innovation within a dominant religious system. Mullins draws upon the "minor founder" category formulated by Werner Stark to deal with "innovations within a religious tradition."[41] The "minor founder" figure is "a charismatic individual who gives birth to a new religious movement in an effort to address the needs of a new type of member, while at the same time conceptualizing the movement as an extension, elaboration, or fulfillment of an existing religious tradition."[42] Of course, those who may have seen themselves as seeking reformation or innovations within their religious tradition — and thus can be thought of as "minor founder" figures — can be so firmly rejected by the tradition that their innovations eventuate in new religious traditions. This is likely the way we should understand the process by which the earliest revelations concerning Jesus issued into what eventuated as a new religion, Christianity.

If I may summarize the discussion to this point, I hope to have shown that it appears to be either ideological bias or insufficiently examined assumptions that prevent some scholars from taking seriously the idea that there are revelatory religious experiences that can directly contribute to religious innovations, sometimes even quite significant innovations. There are both religions scholars and social scientists who agree with this idea, which is based on historical examples and empirical study of recent and contemporary religious developments. That is, it is by no means idiosyncratic to attribute to powerful revelatory religious experiences the efficacy to generate significant religious innovations. Moreover, social scientists have proposed models for understanding the basics of how revelations issue in religious innovations, which in turn can become the basis of new religious movements within traditions, or even new religions.

---

41. Mullins, "Christianity as a New Religion," 265. Mullins cites here Werner Stark, *The Sociology of Religion: A Study of Christendom* (New York: Fordham University Press, 1970), 4:84.

42. Mullins, "Christianity as a New Religion," 265. Interestingly, Anthony Blasi has used the "minor founder" category to describe the Apostle Paul. See Blasi, *Making Charisma: The Social Construction of Paul's Public Image* (New Brunswick, N.J.: Transaction Books, 1991), 14-15, as cited in Mullins. See also Marilyn Robinson Waldman and Robert M. Braun, "Innovation as Renovation: The 'Prophet' as an Agent of Social Change," in *Innovation in Religious Traditions,* ed. M. A. Williams, C. Cox, and M. S. Jaffe (Berlin and New York: Mouton de Gruyter, 1992), 241-84.

Religious Experience and Innovation in the New Testament

In the remaining portion of this chapter, I wish to look further at indications that revelatory experiences were crucial contributing factors in producing the important religious innovations that mark early Christianity. It is neither possible nor necessary here to attempt anything approaching a comprehensive coverage of the relevant evidence. I shall restrict the discussion to one particular religious innovation that undeniably distinguishes early Christianity — the intense level of veneration of Jesus — and shall consider key considerations in the New Testament that revelatory experiences were crucial in generating this remarkable innovation. As mentioned earlier in this chapter, I have elsewhere drawn attention to the apparently singular nature of this innovation and have argued that powerful revelatory religious experiences must be reckoned with as one of the crucial causative factors behind it.[43] Here I will attempt to reinforce the argument by giving more detailed attention to the evidence of such experiences.

For our purposes, the earliest step in the phenomenon that we are investigating was the emergence of the conviction that the crucified Jesus had been raised from death and exalted to heavenly glory and rule. This conviction appears already in the very earliest Christian writings extant, and in these sources the conviction is already treated as a sacred tradition that goes back to the originating moments of the Christian movement. Moreover, this conviction is attributed primarily to the experiences of individuals who encountered the risen and glorified Christ.

In 1 Corinthians 15:1-11, in a letter written in the early 50s C.E. (scarcely twenty years into the Christian movement), the Apostle Paul recites as a sacred tradition the claim that Jesus died redemptively for sins and that he was "raised on the third day according to the scriptures" (v. 4). There follows a series of resurrection appearances to various people, and it is commonly recognized that these appearances are listed here as the basis for the traditional conviction that Jesus was resurrected. In the larger context of 1 Corinthians 15, Paul is defending the reality of a future resurrection of the elect, and he does this by linking this hope with the claim that Jesus has already been resurrected, making Jesus' resurrection the proof that the dead

---

43. Hurtado, *One Lord, One God*, esp. 93-128, on "the Christian mutation" in Jewish monotheistic devotion and its probable causes.

are to be raised. Thus, given that so much depends upon the resurrection of Jesus, the series of resurrection appearances must have been intended as the supporting witnesses for the claim that Jesus had truly been raised. There is no reference to an empty tomb. It would be exceeding the warrants of the passage to say that Paul knew of no tradition about the tomb. Whether he did or did not know of such reports, however, it is clear in the tradition he was taught and that he circulated among his churches that the resurrection appearances were the critical bases for the faith that God had raised Jesus from death.

These appearances must have been such as to contribute significantly to the specific convictions drawn from them. These convictions were not that Jesus somehow survived death by his own heroic strength, that his memory and influence continued to be inspiring among his followers, that he had been resuscitated back to mortal life, or that he had been given a martyr's commendation in heaven, or any of the other much more common postmortem views of heroic and beloved leaders that we encounter among their followers. All evidence indicates that the immediate convictions were (1) that God had released Jesus from death, so that it is Jesus who really lives, not merely his memory or influence; (2) that this divine act involved bestowing upon Jesus uniquely a glorious new form of existence, an immortal and eschatological bodily existence that marks him out in comparison with all the elect, including even the honored ancestors such as Moses, Abraham, and Elijah, all of whom await resurrection at the Last Day; (3) that Jesus had also been exalted to a unique heavenly status, presiding by divine appointment over the entire redemptive program; and (4) that his followers were now divinely commissioned to proclaim Jesus' exalted status and to summon people to recognize in his resurrection and exaltation the signal that an eschatological moment of redemption had arrived.[44] If we are to consider the resurrection appearances as crucial in generating earliest Christian claims, these experiences must have involved unusual and specific elements that helped shape the unprecedented convictions that mark the early Christian proclamation. That is, these experiences likely involved the sense of being encountered by a figure recognized

44. As illustrations of these convictions, note, for example, the early summary of Christian convictions in 1 Thessalonians 1:9-10, where Jesus' resurrection is connected with eschatological redemption. See also, e.g., Acts 2:32-36, 3:13-21, and 4:10-12. Although the speeches in Acts were composed by the author, his rhetorical aims required him to have sounded the themes that Christian readers would have recognized as traditional.

as Jesus but exhibiting features that conveyed to the recipients of the experiences the conviction that he had been clothed with divine glory and given heavenly exaltation.

I advocate taking seriously the resurrection appearances as efficacious in generating these convictions, not simply because the New Testament writers make this claim, but because historical investigation makes it evident that these convictions are unprecedented and clearly not appropriated from the religious matrix of the early Christian movement. Instead, these convictions constituted an innovation in religious belief. The earliest traditions attribute the innovation to powerful experiences taken by the recipients as appearances of the risen Christ. We have no historical basis for attributing the innovative convictions to some other source, and we have surveyed scholarly bases for accepting that there are "revelatory" experiences that can generate novel religious convictions. Whether one chooses to consider these experiences as hallucinatory, the projections of mental processes of the recipients, or the acts of God, there is every reason to see them as the historical ignition points for the Christological convictions linked to them.

As historical sources, the narratives of these appearances of the risen Jesus in the Gospels are later than Paul's letters and of course decades later than the time of the experiences that they claim to describe, and they likely exhibit the effects of a tradition-history and the particular emphases and aims of the individual authors. Basically, these narratives seem concerned to affirm the continuity of the Jesus encountered in the appearances with the Jesus who died. In other words, it would be naïve to press these Gospel narratives too much in details as a basis for reconstructing the actual nature of what was "seen" by those who claimed to have experienced resurrection appearances of Christ.[45] There are, however, good reasons to think that, whatever the details, the primary effect upon those who experienced these encounters was the strong sense that the crucified Jesus had been clothed with divine glory and given a heavenly status as the plenipotentiary of God.

In other passages in his letters, Paul refers to his own experiences that revealed to him the glorious status of Jesus and that transformed Paul from an opponent to an advocate of the early Christian faith.[46] In Gala-

---

45. For an accessible discussion of relevant matters, see R. E. Brown, *The Virginal Conception and Bodily Resurrection of Jesus* (New York: Paulist Press, 1973), 78-129.

46. See Hurtado, "Convert, Apostate, or Apostle to the Nations?"

tians 1:13-17, Paul refers to his pre-Christian religious commitment and describes his religious reorientation as the result of a divine revelation of "his Son" (v. 15). It appears likely that it is the same revelatory experience that Paul also refers to in 1 Corinthians 9:1 ("Have I not seen Jesus our Lord?"). Paul does not give us a detailed description of the event, preferring instead to focus on the convictions that it produced in him. It is quite plausible, however, that in 2 Corinthians 3:7–4:6 Paul draws upon his own revelatory experiences in portraying the move from unbelief in the Gospel to faith as "seeing the glory of the Lord," who is "the image of God" (3:16-18). Likewise, in his reference a few lines later to God having shone "in our hearts to give the light of the knowledge of the glory of God in the face of Jesus Christ," it seems entirely reasonable that Paul drew upon his own experience of sudden and powerful illumination, the Christophany that turned him from persecutor to devotee.

If this is accepted, then I suggest that Paul's revelatory experience involved a vision of Jesus in a glorious form that Paul perceived as the manifestation of divine glory resting upon (or reflected in) Jesus. Given that revelatory religious experiences seem to be shaped in some ways by the religious and cultural traditions of recipients, it is likely that Paul's revelation may have been shaped by biblical tradition of the glory of God manifested as bright light, Jesus' glorious status perhaps being experienced by Paul as a vision of Christ seen in radiant form.[47] It is not, however, necessary to attempt to recapture the visual details of Paul's experience. The important and undeniable thing is that Paul's embrace of Christian faith, his rather sudden transformation in religious convictions, was generated by a powerful religious experience that he took to be a divine revelation.

As mentioned earlier in this essay, in Paul's case, the cognitive content of the Damascus-road experience was not entirely innovative, overlapping in particular with the prior Christological convictions of early Christian Jews and, indeed, likely reflecting the Christological claims that had aroused Paul's earlier determination to oppose the Christian movement among Jews. But for Paul to come to see these Christological

---

47. For a more extensive discussion of allusions to Paul's revelatory experience in his letters, see, e.g., Kim, *The Origin of Paul's Gospel*. On the biblical/Jewish traditions associated with manifestations of divine glory, see esp. Carey C. Newman, *Paul's Glory-Christology: Tradition and Rhetoric*, NovTSup, 69 (Leiden: E. J. Brill, 1992).

claims as valid, to see Jesus as God's "Son," was for him a dramatic and compelling "revelation." Moreover, it seems that either in this experience or other revelatory experiences thereafter there came to Paul the additional conviction that he was divinely commissioned to conduct a special program of evangelization among Gentiles, a program with keen eschatological urgency and involving the exemption of Gentile converts from observance of the Torah. This conviction seems to have been a genuine and quite significant innovation, in both the Jewish and the emerging Christian traditions.[48]

Exactly how Paul came to this conviction, how in detail one or more revelatory experiences may have conveyed or stimulated it, is difficult to say with confidence. Seyoon Kim proposed that Paul arrived at the conviction that he was called to a Gentile mission through the Damascus-road vision of the glorified Christ and of the divine heavenly council (shaped by Paul's familiarity with the vision call in Isaiah 6), which included the experience of being summoned by God (after the fashion of Old Testament prophets) to proclaim the enfranchisement of the Gentiles.[49] Such a suggestion at the very least reflects the witness of numerous figures who claim to have heard a divine instruction to do this or that mission in the middle of a revelatory religious experience. It is certainly the case that Paul both saw himself and was seen by contemporaries, whether allies or critics, as conducting a distinctive mission to convert Gentiles to the Christian message.

Paul refers to the "mystery" *(mystērion)* that includes the "hardening" of "part of Israel" in unbelief, the ingathering of Gentile converts through his mission, and the subsequent salvation of all Israel through the banishment of their disbelief in the Gospel (Rom. 11:25-32). In Paul's usage, the term "mystery" is consistently used to refer to divinely disclosed information about the redemptive plan of God.[50] That is, in Paul's letters the term "mystery" signifies the cognitive content received through revelatory experiences, ideas not previously disclosed or known, cognitive content that in-

---

48. On Paul's Gentile mission, see esp. Donaldson, *Paul and the Gentiles.*

49. Seyoon Kim, "The 'Mystery' of Rom. 11:25-26 Once More," *New Testament Studies* 43 (1997): 412-29. On the likelihood that Paul's religious experience was shaped by his familiarity with Old Testament prophet traditions, see also Karl O. Sandnes, *Paul — One of the Prophets?* WUNT 2/43 (Tübingen: J. C. B. Mohr, 1991).

50. See 1 Corinthians 2:1, 7; 4:1; 13:2; 14:2; and 15:51 for examples. Note especially 1 Corinthians 13:2 and 14:2, where "mysteries" are referred to as disclosed and spoken through the experiential power of the divine Spirit.

cluded the innovative conviction that he was to spearhead a wholly new and eschatological mission to the Gentiles.

Scholars have tended to focus on Paul's Damascus-road vision of Christ, but it is well to remember that Paul mentions multiple "visions and revelations of the Lord" (2 Cor. 12:1). His most extended reference to such an experience is in 2 Corinthians 12:2-10, in which he speaks of being "caught up into Paradise," where he "heard things that are not to be told, that no mortal is permitted to repeat" (v. 4). Indeed, Paul claims that God has permitted him to be afflicted by Satan in his body to keep him humble, lest he become too proud about "the exceptional character of the revelations" he received in his visions (vv. 7-9). In Galatians 2:2, Paul refers to a trip to Jerusalem he took "in response to a revelation," which likely means that through some vision or prophecy he was directed to make the journey to confer with the Jerusalem leadership.

Paul's visions and revelations, thus, did not always involve major religious innovations, and could consist in directions about such mundane things as this conference trip. But this only shows how very much Paul (and other early Christians as well?) regarded visions and revelations as the source of cognitive content and inspiration. That is, within at least some circles of early Christianity there seems to have been a religious "micro-culture" that was both receptive to visions and revelations and highly appreciative of them as sources of direction in religious matters. This further reinforces the view that in these circles even major religious innovations could have been stimulated by particularly powerful experiences of this nature.

In terms of the religious scruples of the Jewish tradition, the most striking innovation in earliest Christianity is the treatment of the glorified Jesus as an object of cultic devotion in ways and terms that seem otherwise reserved for the God of Israel. In a 1988 book, I analyzed the reverential treatment of "principal agent" figures in Greco-Roman Jewish tradition (personified divine attributes, exalted Old Testament heroes, and principal angels), and I showed that though these figures can be described in the most amazingly exalted terms and can be attributed qualities and appearances that make it difficult to distinguish them from God, there is a clear reluctance to countenance the worship of these figures. There is an evident reservation of full cultic devotion for the God of Israel alone.[51] I also item-

---

51. Hurtado, *One God, One Lord*, esp. 17-92. By "full cultic devotion," I mean public,

ized six specific cultic actions of early Jesus-devotion that distinguish the reverence of Jesus from the reverential treatment of any of the Jewish principal-agent figures: hymns sung in the gathered worship setting both concerning Jesus and to him; prayer to Jesus and in his name; ritual use of Jesus' name in public cultic actions such as baptisms, exorcisms, excommunications, and so on; participation in the corporate sacred meal as "the Lord's Supper"; ritual "confession" *(homologein)* of Jesus in honorific terms; and prophecy uttered in Jesus' name and even as his spirit or voice.[52] I am encouraged to note that the many reviews of this book and the several studies that have interacted with my views essentially agree that the cultic devotion given to Christ is not paralleled in the Jewish tradition of the time.[53]

But what could have prompted such a major innovation in the devotional scruples and practices that the earliest Christian groups inherited from the Jewish tradition? To put the question a bit more pointedly, what might have moved Jews in touch with their religious tradition to feel free to offer to Jesus the kind of unparalleled cultic devotion that characterized early Christian religious practice? Given the evident strength of the scruple against infringing upon the uniqueness of the God of Israel by sharing the cultic reverence due to God with any other figure, I judge that the only option is to think that those members of the early Christian movement among whom there emerged the cultic devotion to Jesus that I have described must have felt compelled by God to reverence Jesus in ways otherwise reserved for God alone. The early Christians, however, were more concerned to proclaim Jesus' significance and to express their devotion to

---

corporate devotional practices that are intended as adoration and/or that engage the figure in ways otherwise reserved for God (e.g., prayers, hymns, and so on). Thus, there is a distinction between this public, corporate devotion or worship and the more secretive and private invocations of various names and beings that characterize "magical" materials such as amulets, among which there are, of course, Jewish examples.

52. Hurtado, *One God, One Lord,* 100-114.

53. I note in particular two important studies, which, though they both argue that the reverent treatment of angels in Jewish circles was a significant feature of religious life in those circles, acknowledge that the cultic devotion given to Jesus amounts to a substantially distinctive phenomenon: L. T. Stuckenbruck, *Angel Veneration and Christology,* WUNT 2/70 (Tübingen: J. C. B. Mohr, 1995); and C. E. Arnold, *The Colossian Syncretism,* WUNT 2/77 (Tübingen: J. C. B. Mohr, 1995). I have interacted with other reviewers and critics in my essay "First-Century Jewish Monotheism," *Journal for the Study of the New Testament* 71 (1998): 3-26 (Chapter Five of this book).

him than to provide explanations of how they came to the convictions that prompted them to do so. But what indications we have are that, from the earliest years of the Christian movement, individuals experienced what they took to be revelations sent by God that conveyed to them the sense that a right response and obedience to God demanded of them the cultic reverence of Jesus.

In addition to the allusions by Paul to his own revelatory experience of Jesus as reflecting divine glory, there are other New Testament passages that further support this. In the account in Acts 7 of the martyrdom of Stephen, he is pictured as being given a vision of "the glory of God, and Jesus standing at the right hand of God" (vv. 55-56). The enraged response of his fellow Jewish religionists that erupts when Stephen reports this vision (v. 58) suggests that its contents were taken by them as a blasphemous infringement upon the uniqueness of God. The details of the narrative may well derive from the author of Acts and may not be a direct account of the historical events the narrative purports to describe, but, even so, it is most logical to assume that the account reflects reports of visionary experiences of real Christians. If the author hoped that his first Christian readers would give the account credibility, it is likely that he would have described the sort of experiences that his readers had heard about and were prepared to treat seriously. Thus, the vision of Stephen may be taken by us as at least an indirect reflection of the sorts of visionary experiences that were reported among early Christians and were felt as divine disclosures of the exalted status of Jesus and the cultic honors due him.

In Stephen's vision, Jesus is seen in heavenly glory and stands in the position next to God, which in turn suggests his privileged and divinely approved status as God's plenipotentiary. Immediately thereafter, Stephen is pictured as praying to the heavenly Jesus (vv. 59-60), the very sort of specifically cultic devotion otherwise reserved for God in Jewish tradition. The collocation of the vision of the glorified Jesus and cultic devotional action contained in this passage reflects, I suggest, the original connection between the two, and also the impact of such visionary experiences in generating the "binitarian" devotional practice of the early Christian movement in which prayer and other cultic actions were directed to Jesus as well as to God in response to God's exaltation of Jesus to heavenly glory.[54]

54. Note, for example, that the universal acclamation of Jesus as "Lord" in Philippians 2:9-11 is to be done "to the glory of God the Father," reflecting the conviction that the cultic

It is commonly suggested that the narrative of the "transfiguration" of Jesus (depicted in Mark 9:2-8, Matthew 17:1-8, and Luke 9:28-36), though set within the earthly ministry of Jesus, may reflect the visionary experiences of the "post-Easter" Christian circles. Whatever the tradition-history of the episode, it is likely that early Christian readers would have taken the description of the transfigured Jesus, effulgent with divine light, as consonant with the sorts of revelatory visions of the risen and heavenly Jesus that were reported among them. Indeed, it seems to me likely that the Gospels' authors (and the prior Christians who may have shaped the story) intended the account to be read by, and in some sense perhaps validated for, readers in light of the revelatory religious experiences of the glorified Jesus that were witnessed to in the early Christian tradition.

In the book of Revelation we have another visionary scene that is even more clearly and specifically to be taken as affirming the propriety of giving worship jointly to God and Jesus. After claiming a visionary ascent into heaven (Rev. 4:1), the author then portrays two scenes of heavenly worship, the first focused on God the creator (4:2-11), the second marked by the appearance of the "Lamb" (Jesus) and the astonishing cultic reverence given to him along with God (5:1-14). The cultic devotion directed to the Lamb here includes hymnic praise by the same beings whose job is ceaselessly to praise God Almighty (5:8-10; cf. 4:8-11), plus hymnic adoration by all the heavenly host (5:11-12), followed by universal hymnic worship directed jointly to God and the Lamb (5:13-14). Chapters 4-5 of Revelation are crucial to the plan of the book and give a remarkable reflection of the Christian convictions of the author.[55] Jesus, the "Lamb," is given the same sort of cultic reverence as is given to God on the throne, and this reverence is offered by God's own heavenly courtiers and attendants in the heavenly throne room, actions that the readers were probably expected to take as ideally correct and paradigmatic for their own devotional life.

The point I wish to emphasize is that these chapters give us the description of a visionary experience of seeing heavenly realities, the cognitive con-

---

veneration of Jesus was understood by early Christians as obedience to God and not at all as detracting from the honoring of God.

55. Larry W. Hurtado, "Revelation 4-5 in the Light of Jewish Apocalyptic Analogies," *Journal for the Study of the New Testament* 25 (1985): 105-24; Lucretia Mowry, "Revelation 4-5 and Early Christian Liturgical Usage," *Journal of Biblical Literature* 71 (1952): 75-84; and Otto A. Piper, "The Apocalypse of John and the Liturgy of the Ancient Church," *Church History* 20 (1951): 10-22.

tent of which focuses on the adoration of the Lamb, which constitutes a remarkable innovation in the monotheistic tradition that is certainly the background of the author (and perhaps his readers).[56] To be sure, this innovation had begun well before the time of the writing of Revelation, so the author's heavenly ascent vision (if we grant that the text reflects a real experience) can hardly be taken itself as an example of religious experience generating innovations. I suggest, however, that not only the cognitive content of the vision but also the nature of the experience itself is traditional in Christian circles. That is, I propose that this literary description of a vision of Jesus' glory and the adoration of him in heaven with the approval of God reflects the content of the sort of *earlier* revelatory religious experiences that likely helped to generate the conviction that Jesus should receive the cultic reverence of Christian groups. The particular vision in Revelation 4-5 was not intended as a disclosure of radically new information but was offered to support and give vivid reinforcement to the "binitarian" devotional pattern that the original readers already knew and practiced.

It is relevant to note that the author of Revelation certainly manifests a belligerently conservative attitude toward cultic innovations. Not only does he oppose the worship of the "beast" by the general populace; he also condemns people in the churches who appear to advocate a more liberalized attitude toward participating in pagan religious practices. In Revelation 2:14 the church in Pergamum is criticized for having among themselves "some who hold to the teaching of Balaam," who sought to ensnare Israel into "eat[ing] food sacrificed to idols and practic[ing] fornication," and in 2:20-23 the church in Thyatira is rebuked for tolerating "that woman Jezebel, who calls herself a prophet and is teaching and beguiling my servants to practice fornication and to eat food sacrificed to idols." In both passages we probably have the author's rather polemical characterization of the teachings of some Christian individuals who encouraged Christians to relax or modify the more exclusivist Christian (and Jewish) devotional scruples that involved a refusal to participate in the civic cults and other pagan ceremonies and sacred meals that made up so much of the urban social life of the time.[57] Likewise, in Revelation 19:10 and 22:8-9,

---

56. Numerous things indicate the Jewish background of the author, including the name John, which is commonly accepted as the author's actual name. Unlike nearly all other examples of ancient apocalyptic writings, Revelation is not pseudonymous.

57. As we can tell from 1 Corinthians 8:1-3, 10:1–11:1, questions about such matters arose early and were not easy to answer.

the author reflects the traditional Jewish prohibition against worshipping even God's own angels, in the light of which the strong affirmation of the worship of Christ takes on even more significance.[58]

These things all indicate an author who is not a compromiser or receptive to liturgical innovations within the churches, beyond the innovation he has come to accept as authoritative (which was, by then, more traditional Christian teachings). Therefore, the worship of Jesus he pictures and clearly advocates, and the visions that assert the transcendent validity of offering this sort of devotion to Jesus, must likely all reflect very traditional phenomena for this author. This is why I suggest that we can take the literary account of the vision of Jesus' glory in Revelation 5 as reflective of much earlier visionary experiences of a similar nature. I contend that such early visions were likely among the factors that generated the convictions (1) that God had appointed the heavenly Jesus to a place of unique honor that rightly entailed his receiving the adoration of the heavenly host, and (2) that Christians who sought to obey God should shape their cultic devotional life accordingly by incorporating Jesus with God as the objects of their devotion.

Conclusion

We have noted that the binitarian cultic devotion of early Christianity was a unique and completely remarkable innovation in comparison with all else that we know of Jewish religious traditional practices of the time. This innovation did not, however, emerge in slow stages but seems already robustly underway and taken for granted in the letters of Paul, which date from scarcely more than twenty years into the Christian movement. Moreover, the innovation seems to have emerged among Jewish Christians — not later under the imagined influence of pagan converts less sensitive to the exclusivist monotheistic scruples of Jewish tradition.[59] In light of all this, again, the most reasonable view is that those who initiated this innovation in cultic practice must have done so under a profound sense of di-

---

58. Richard Bauckham, "The Worship of Jesus," in his *The Climax of Prophecy: Studies on the Book of Revelation* (Edinburgh: T&T Clark, 1993), 118-49; Stuckenbruck, *Angel Veneration and Christology,* esp. 245-66.

59. Again, see my book *One God, One Lord* for the evidence and fuller argument for these matters.

vine mandate. I see no evidence that any other Jewish religious movement of the period took any equivalent step in their devotional practice. There is no evidence of Jewish experimentation with cultic practices comparable to those we find reflected in the earliest New Testament writings.

To return to the key question, under what circumstances, then, could devout people from the ancient Jewish tradition have come to believe that God wished them to offer such cultic reverence to Jesus and, thus, to initiate this major innovation in traditional Jewish cultic practice? On the basis of the New Testament evidence we have surveyed, and on the basis of the studies of the connections between religious innovations and revelatory experiences summarized earlier, I submit that the most likely explanation is as follows. Within the early Christian circles of the first few years (perhaps even the first few weeks), individuals had powerful revelatory experiences that they understood to be encounters with the glorified Jesus. Some also had experiences that they took to be visions of the exalted Jesus in heavenly glory, being reverenced in cultic actions by the transcendent beings traditionally identified as charged with fulfilling the heavenly liturgy (e.g., angels, the "living creatures," and so on).[60] Some received prophetic inspirations to announce the exaltation of Jesus to God's right hand and to summon the elect in God's name to register in cultic actions their acceptance of God's will that Jesus be reverenced. Through such revelatory experiences, Christological convictions and corresponding cultic practices were born that amounted to a unique "mutation" in what was acceptable Jewish monotheistic devotional practice of the Greco-Roman period.

To grant my suggestion does not require that one accept the validity of either these convictions and this "mutation" or the claims of those whose religious experiences were taken as divine revelations. Nor, of course, is one required to doubt any of these things to conduct a scholarly analysis of them. Whatever our religious preferences (or even if some would-be sophisticates regard themselves as "beyond all that"), sound historical method requires that we understand the crucial role that has been played in notable religious innovations by powerful revelatory religious experiences. The particular cognitive content of such experiences may vary considerably from one religious innovation to another (cf. the beliefs that

---

60. Key pre-Christian biblical passages that reflected and stimulated traditions about such heavenly beings and their liturgical responsibilities include, of course, Ezekiel 1:4-28, Isaiah 6:1-5, and Daniel 7:9-10.

emerged from the Qumran "Teacher of Righteousness," Muhammad, Baha Ullah, Guru Nanak, and others documented in historical and social scientific studies).[61] But there seems to be a sufficient phenomenological similarity in the impact of such experiences upon individuals who have them, and in the efficacy of such experiences in forming religious ideas, beliefs, and convictions that can constitute significant religious innovations and can issue in new religious movements. Such powerful experiences also seem to have been crucial causative factors in the emergence of some of the most important distinguishing features of early Christianity, particularly the cultic veneration of the glorified Jesus, which represented a distinctive and highly significant "mutation" in Jewish monotheistic devotion.

61. In addition to these examples, see the analysis of Japanese indigenous Christian movements by Mullins, "Christianity as a New Religion," and descriptions of American native "Ghost Dance" and "Handsome Lake" movements, which were also initiated through revelatory religious experiences of individuals (T. W. Overholt, *Prophecy in Cross-Cultural Perspective* [Atlanta: Scholars Press, 1986], 101-41).

I n the preceding chapters I have been primarily concerned to underscore the important place that devotion to Jesus must have in any historical analysis of earliest Christianity. As well, I have attempted to set forth in brief scope a historical approach to early Jesus-devotion that is developed in dialogue with other scholars and that I believe does justice to the evidence.

I have argued that a remarkable level of devotion to Jesus erupted in the earliest years of the Christian movement and within circles of Jesus' followers who were shaped by Second-Temple Jewish traditions. That is, I contend, that in its earliest manifestations, devotion to Jesus has to be approached as a notable religious innovation within Second-Temple Jewish religion. To be sure, the tension generated by this innovation led to a rejection of it by the main body of Roman-era Jews, and the Jesus movement became what we know as Christianity. But in a certain sense, in its earliest stages, devotion to Jesus should also be seen in historical terms as forming part of the history of developments in Roman-era Judaism as well.

We have seen that for both Jewish and Gentile believers, the tensions created by their faith could have serious social costs. As we observed in Chapter Seven, within the first decades there sometimes was serious and determined opposition from within various local Jewish communities against fellow Jews whose devotion to Jesus was perceived as problematic. Gentile converts as well were subject to social and political consequences for their faith, largely, it appears, on account of its exclusivist demands.

To take account of this is to appreciate better how much it must have meant to participate with fellow believers in the conventicles that early Christian associations represented. In passages such as Philippians 2:6-11, we see a lyrical expression of early Christian devotion, and perhaps we catch a glimpse of the religious intensity that motivated believers in the early decades.

In Chapters Five through Eight I have offered studies of several phenomena and issues that are also crucially important for a historical understanding of Jesus-devotion. I have emphasized the nature and importance of Second-Temple Jewish concerns about the uniqueness of their God. This helps us to see more clearly that the "binitarian" shape of earliest Christian devotion really did represent an innovation of some significance. Moreover, although during his own historical lifetime Jesus' followers likely accorded him the sort of homage that was deemed fitting for a prophet or other figure seen as in some way a valid representative of God's purposes, we have noted that the more significant innovation comprised in treating Jesus as sharing in divine glory seems rather clearly to have emerged among circles of his followers after his execution.

In accounting historically for this significant innovation, it seems pertinent to include the effects of powerful "revelatory" religious experiences as a major factor. I have tried to show that this both reflects the findings of scholars about some other religious innovations and best accords with the evidence of earliest Christianity. However unfamiliar one might be with such experiences, they should be included in any adequate historical account of the emergence of devotion to Jesus.

I hope that the preceding studies will have communicated to readers something of the intriguing questions and hotly contested issues that justify and comprise the historical investigation of early devotion to Jesus. It may be somewhat unsettling for some Christians, at least initially, to explore the origins of Christian faith as a subject of historical inquiry. I trust, however, that Christians will see that a historical appreciation of the emergence of devotion to Jesus need not pose a challenge to continuing to revere Jesus as rightful recipient of devotion with God. Indeed, I hope that Christians will welcome any light that can be cast on the faith of their religious forebears from the earliest period of the Christian movement.

Likewise, I hope that readers who do not identify themselves with Christian faith will see that it can be an interesting adventure (perhaps almost equally unsettling, though for different reasons) to explore how devotion to Jesus as divine first emerged. Whether or not one shares in its continuing expression, devotion to Jesus has certainly proven to be one of the most significant and influential religious innovations in human history, helping to shape all subsequent Christian belief and practice.

Opening Remarks to the First Deichmann Annual Lecture Series

Horst-Heinz Deichmann

(Part of the Deichmann Program for Jewish and Christian Literature of the Hellenistic-Roman Era at Ben-Gurion University of the Negev, 22 March 2004)

Please allow me to say some words about my personal motivation and interest to establish this new annual lecture series as part of a new study program in the Department of Bible and Ancient Near Eastern Studies here at "our" university. As many of you know, my first visit to Ben-Gurion University was in 1988 for the inauguration of the Deichmann-Lerner Chair in Gynecology. During that ceremony I shared with you my impressions from a visit to Jerusalem, which in a way can also explain why I am an active supporter of this university since then, and why I am interested in the aforementioned program. Three stations in Jerusalem reflect cornerstones of my life and belief: the site of the crucifixion of Jesus in the Church of the Holy Sepulchre in the Old City, the Shrine of the Book in the Israel Museum with the famous Isaiah-scroll in its center, and Yad Vashem. Golgotha is, according to the Christian tradition, the place where the fulfillment of Isaiah 53, the famous chapter on the suffering servant of God, took place. That these words survived and were able to unfold their potential in the Jewish and Christian tradition we owe partially to people like the ones living in Qumran. Yad Vashem is the memorial of sin, especially the sin of the German people against the Jews as God's chosen people. Taking all three together, I understood that in Jesus there is forgiveness for what we did to the Jewish people, because Jesus died suffering in the service of God for our sakes, the sake of the sinners. But to enjoy the forgiveness that God planted in Jesus, we need your personal forgiveness, each of you, personally. Therefore I asked you to allow me to participate in your work here at Ben-Gurion University. That I am standing here in front of you more than fifteen years later is possible because you granted me forgiveness and gave me the opportunity to support and help this university.

That this new program is close to my heart as a Christian who is waiting for the Messiah to come you may understand. But let me add some additional reflections on why I think that there is an unbreakable bond between Jews and Christians from the beginning. I want to do this with words from the famous Swiss theologian Karl Barth (1886-1968), to whom I owe a lot, having heard him speak in 1946 in the destroyed faculty buildings of the Theological Seminar of the University of Bonn.

During the university service in the Schlosskirche in Bonn in the year 1933, in the very beginning of the Nazi regime, the Reformed Professor of Systematic Theology took his sermon on Paul's letter to the Romans 15:5-13 as an opportunity for his first public touching on the "Jewish questions." He said:

> It is not a matter of course that we belong to Jesus Christ and he to us. "Christ hath become a servant of the Circumcision for the sake of the truth of God, to confirm the promises which came unto the Fathers."[1] That is: Christ belonged to the people of Israel. This people's blood was in his veins, the blood of the Son of God. He took on the nature of this people when he took on humanity, not for the sake of this people, or because of the advantage of its blood and race, but for the sake of the truth, viz., for the sake of demonstrating the truthfulness and faithfulness of God. Because God had made a covenant with, and given his presence and the promise of an unparalleled redemption to, this and only this people: a stiff-necked and evil people [Ex. 32:9, etc.], but precisely this people — not to reward and lift up the Jews, but to confirm and fulfill this free, gracious promise of God "made to the Fathers," Jesus Christ became a Jew. He said once of himself that to the lost sheep of the house of Israel and only to them was he sent (Matt. 15:24; cf. 10:5-6). That means for us, who are not Israel, a locked door. If it is nevertheless open, if Christ nevertheless belongs to us too as we to him, then it must once again be true in a special sense that "Christ hath received us unto the praise of God." That this is so, we are reminded by the existence of the Jewish people to this very day.

Barth additionally cited the phrase from St. John's Gospel 4:22:

1. Romans 15:8.

"Salvation comes from the Jews" (John 4:22). Jesus Christ was a Jew. But in that, in the sins of the Jews, he bore and bore away the sins of the whole world including ours; the salvation from the Jews has come also to us.[2]

On reading Karl Barth's words today, we must necessarily observe the historical context. Barth preached in Germany at a time when the horrifying dimensions of the Nazi atrocities could not be predicted. Nevertheless, he has given clear and unambiguous evidence of solidarity with the Jewish people in making clear that the Christian church has its roots solely in God's promises to the people of Israel. Jesus of Nazareth, according to Paul, has then become the *Christ* for all peoples — that means for Jews and Gentiles — because of God's promises to the Jewish people. Everybody who belongs to the genuine church of Jesus Christ is therefore by no means allowed to oppose or to place himself above the first people of the promise. Let us again hear Paul: "If some of the branches [of the olive-tree Israel] have been broken off, and you, though a wild olive shoot, have been grafted in among the others and now share in the nourishing sap from the olive root, do not boast over those branches. If you do, consider this: You do not support the root, but the root supports you" (Rom. 11:17-18). When the first Gentiles became followers of Jesus Christ, the question arose: Is it necessary that these Goyim first convert to Judaism before they can be accepted as followers of the Jewish messiah? Connected with this was another question that moved Paul: Does God's loyalty to his people as people end when the message of Christ begins being spread among the nations? The Jewish thinker Jakob Taubes deals with this problem in his book *The Political Theology of Paul.* He writes:

But the word of God cannot just go awry! The word of God is after all true and firm, as the prayer of the Jews emphasizes daily. No, it didn't go awry. Because not all who descend from Israel *are* Israel. That is the key sentence. This means: this "all" according to the flesh is not identical to the "all" according to the promise. Not everyone. The apostle takes the

---

2. The sermon first appeared in K. Barth, *Die Kirche Jesu Christi,* Theologische Existenz heute No. 5 (Munich, 1933), 11-19. The sermon was republished, accompanied by a critical commentary, as part of the complete edition of Barth's works in K. Barth, *Predigten, 1921-1935,* ed. Holger Finze, Karl Barth Gesamtausgabe, Part 1: Predigten (Zürich: Theologischer Verlag, 1998). (I cite the English translation of this sermon by Charles Dickinson.)

election of Israel seriously. This is embarassing for modern Christianity, but that's the way it is. . . . Because he understands himself to be an apostle of the Jews to the Gentiles and understands this as a calling. In Galatians there is nothing about a conversion in the sense of being overwhelmed. Rather there is a calling: From the womb I have selected you, that's what it means in Jeremiah to be a prophet, and here it's what it means to be an apostle. Naturally this means: an apostle *from the Jews* to the nations.[3]

Very soon the church no longer understood this vocation, this conception of Paul himself. Within early catholic Christianity the theological heresy developed: The church was meant to be the new (spiritual) Israel. Israel, the old people of God, seemed to have lost its priority of selection as well as that of its salvation. In the early Middle Ages this conviction was often depicted allegorically, represented in stone by the victorious Ecclesia and the downcast Synagogue. This theologically abortive development has been wreaking much havoc and misery until today, and has been the reason for much blame to be attached to the Christian church. Unfortunately, the reformer Martin Luther did not reject this heresy. A two-thousand-year-long tragic history of the relationship and/or growing apart of synagogue and church, a history of great wrong vis-à-vis the Jewish people, must still be looked upon and reappraised, and genuine reconciliation must be sought.

A prerequisite for this kind of reconciliation is mutual understanding. This is the aim of the Deichmann Program for Jewish and Christian Literature of the Hellenistic-Roman Era, which concentrates on the literary heritage of the Jewish people from the third century B.C.E. till the second century C.E. Sometimes labeled as "intertestamental literature" (which admittedly is a Christian perspective), the manifold and diverse writings of this period are crucial for the understanding of the Jewish and emerging Christian history. I want to mention the main points to describe the field of the new program and the benefits that one can expect from dealing with it.[4]

---

3. Jakob Taubes, *The Political Theology of Paul,* trans. Dana Hollander (Stanford: Stanford University Press, 2004), 47-48 (italics original).

4. The core of the following text is based on a draft by Prof. Dr. Martin Hengel, Tübingen, which he sent to me on my request to help us in this project. It was first translated and modified by Dr. Roland Deines.

1. The so-called "intertestamental literature" comprises a body of the most important sources for Jewish history in the Second-Temple period. It starts with the translation of the five books of Moses into Greek in the third century B.C.E., and it ends in the second century C.E. with the beginning of the rabbinic literary corpus. In addition to the Septuagint (which includes some further writings not in the Hebrew Bible), there are many pseudepigraphical works in the form of apocalypses, patriarchal testaments, and wisdom literature. Along with them we have the famous library found in Qumran and at least two well-known and prominent Jewish authors: Philo of Alexandria as representative of the Diaspora, and Josephus Flavius as representative of *Eretz* Israel.

2. Most of this literature, whose volume exceeds that of the Hebrew Bible by far, got lost in the Jewish heritage from the third century C.E. onward. It was preserved mainly through the hands of early Christian scholars and later by monks in their monasteries. Partly as a result of this transmission, these original Jewish works have been revised, and there were some Christian alterations and additions to some of them. But very often it is unclear and highly disputed what constitutes a Christian addition and what could have been possible in a Jewish provenance. From this we learn how close Jewish and Christian sources come together, especially in matters of ethics, behavior, beliefs about the activity of God in history, afterlife beliefs, and hopes for the future. For example, the book of 1 Maccabees helped to shape the tradition of Christian martyrology, and the language of Philo from Alexandria is preparatory for what we call Christian "theology" from Origen (early third century C.E.) onward. The school of Origen, by the way, was in Caesarea, not too far away from here. And the Jewish historian Josephus is the most important witness for Jewish tradition of the first century C.E. in *Eretz* Israel, and is a contemporary of the writers of the New Testament.

3. So, Jewish history of the Second-Temple period is not possible without this "intertestamental literature" that was preserved mainly by Christians. But this is not the only contribution of the Christian heritage for the understanding of Jewish history. The writings of the New Testament and the other early Christian literature of this period are also part and parcel of the Jewish literature of the first and early second centuries C.E. The authors of the New Testament writings were

mostly if not all Jews, and the other early Christian writings are influenced mainly by Jewish thinking. These very close connections between "intertestamental" and early Christian literature form the main reason why we think that both scholarly fields should be studied together in one department and in one scholarly program: a program focusing on Jewish and Christian literature of the Hellenistic-Roman period. But keeping in mind that the differentiation between "Jewish" and "Christian" is in a way anachronistic for the period in question. If it would not be misunderstood in respect of a long scholarly tradition, the title "Jewish Literature of the Hellenistic-Roman Period" would be enough, because the New Testament is, from a historical perspective, part of the Jewish literary heritage. At least at the beginning, however, we accept the still existing division in "Jewish" and "Christian," but with the strong conviction that both belong — historically seen — together, and form the *one* corpus of Jewish literature in the Second-Temple period. The variety in this corpus is evidence of the creative Jewish thinking and its self-confidence in relation to the dominating Hellenistic-Roman culture in both *Eretz* Israel and the Diaspora. Beer-Sheva as a city between Alexandria and Jerusalem is an appropriate place for the study of this literature.

4. Christianity in its early stages, which means till the end of the first century C.E., was almost exclusively an inner-Jewish movement. The "parting of the ways" of Judaism and Christianity — to use a common but nevertheless problematic phrase — starts in the decades after the destruction of the Temple in Jerusalem in 70 C.E. It is superfluous to say that Jesus, Peter, John, Thomas, Matthew, Paul, and others were Jews. James, the brother of Jesus and for about two decades leader of the community in Jerusalem, was called *ha-zaddiq* ("the Just/Righteous") because of his loyalty to the Torah. The Jewish-Christian community whose roots go back to James existed at least until the seventh century and influenced even Muhammad. What we read in the New Testament is understandable to a large degree as purely Jewish. The longtime strongly overestimated pagan influence upon the New Testament — also accepted by most Jewish scholars dealing with early Christianity — we now understand better as influences of the Jewish-Hellenistic heritage. In addition to the Jewish-Hellenistic influence from the Diaspora, since the finding and editing of the Qumran scrolls, we see that even in *Eretz* Israel Judaism was much more

pluriform and creative than most scholars thought previously. The result from these studies during the last fifty years is the insight that Christianity owes most, if not to say all, to ancient Judaism.

5. Nevertheless, as we all know, the relations between Christianity and Judaism through the centuries are overshadowed by persecution, bloodshed, and many other atrocities. The first tensions are already visible in the New Testament itself, and they have the character of family conflicts, which are often the most painful. The tensions between what we may call "Christian Judaism" and rabbinic Judaism are at the beginning comparable to the rivalries between the Pharisees and the Sadducees, or the Pharisees and the Essenes, or the quarrels between Jews and Samaritans. "Christianity" in the beginning was a Jewish-messianic movement with many things in common with its Jewish matrix. But also from its beginnings it has had at the same time a universal horizon nurtured by the hopes of the prophets that at the End of Days all people will acknowledge the one and only God as creator and savior. For this universal hope early Christians were willing to open the fence that kept Israel apart from the nations. But even this would not have been possible and successful without the preparing of the ground done by the Diaspora synagogues. In their surroundings many Gentiles became proselytes or "God-fearers," or at least acquainted with the God of Israel and his moral teachings. In the beginning the seed of the Christian message grew up mostly on Jewish soil.

6. But formative Christianity, even in the periods when the tensions with Judaism loosened the historical relationship and interdependence of Christianity to its mother religion, never gave up the strong ties that bear inextinguishable Jewish marks. Of course, some tried to extinguish those marks. I mention only Marcion, who was the first but unfortunately not the last, who tried to remove from the New Testament everything that looked Jewish. Besides this, he also tried to convince the church to give up the Hebrew Bible, the so-called Old Testament in Christian tradition. But Marcion and all other Marcions since him never succeeded. The Church father Origen (from Alexandria and later from Caesarea), who was educated enough to learn from Jewish sages, and Jerome, who spent many years in Bethlehem translating the Bible into Latin, are just two of many ancient and modern Christian and Jewish scholars who were responsible for both parts of the Christian Bible, the Tanakh and the New Testament, which became the

most important books for the cultural development of Europe after the downfall of the Roman Empire. For Maimonides and other Jewish sages, the spreading of Christianity throughout the world was a kind of preparatory act for the age of truth, when all will recognize the God of Israel as the God of the Universe.

7. The Christian eschatology is, not surprisingly, a little bit different. But, indeed, only "a little bit," because Christian eschatology is formed by Jewish eschatology. In the New Testament there is no doubt that "salvation is from the Jews" (John 4:22), and that in the end "all Israel will be saved" (Rom. 11:26), because it is written, "The Deliverer will come from Zion." What Christians can find in Paul and the Gospel of John, Jews will find in the Mishnah, where it is stated, "All Israel has a share in the world to come" (*Sanhedrin* 10:1). Looking back to these texts from the perspective of what happened in Germany in the first half of the twentieth century is painful and shameful for Christians. What happened was not only a betrayal of the Jewish neighbor and compatriot living next door, but also a betrayal of the sources of Christianity. Nothing and nobody can heal these wounds. The only thing that remains possible for us to do is to prepare for our and the coming generations' opportunities for a better mutual understanding. One way — and I think not the worst — is to plough common ground together. One part of this common ground is the Jewish literature and the early Christian writings of the Second-Temple period and the decades immediately thereafter.

With the opening of the Deichmann Program for Jewish and Christian Literature of the Hellenistic-Roman Era at Ben-Gurion University, we want to pay our tribute to this common ground and give the opportunity to explore the ways in which the New Testament authors express their dependence upon the Tanakh. As fruits of this labor we are looking forward to a better understanding of Judaism and Christianity, more tolerance, and a generation who are able to respect and appreciate the distinctiveness of others as an enrichment for themselves. My personal hope is that these studies will help us both, Jews and Christians, to strengthen our hope of the Messiah to come.

Are There Good Reasons for Studying Early Christian Literature at Ben-Gurion University?

Roland Deines

L et me add some personal remarks to what Dr. Deichmann has already said. He invited me in the Summer of 2002 to join his vision for establishing a study program at Ben-Gurion University. The original aim was to teach and to research the close relations between the Tanakh and the New Testament. In the beginning, I confess, I was reluctant to accept this idea. I was not sure if there was a hidden agenda behind this scholarly project and if its real aim was an attempt to do some kind of missionary work under the flag of scholarship. I agreed to get involved in this undertaking only after this point was cleared up.

I am convinced that it is very promising as a *scholarly* project — and after one semester here at Ben-Gurion University, I am totally sure about it. I am, as some of you may know, by profession a New Testament scholar. For my generation the study of Jewish literature of the Second-Temple period and also of rabbinic literature is in a way a common procedure. Many of my colleagues have studied at least sometimes at a department of Jewish studies, either in Germany or somewhere else in Europe, North America, or Israel. The aim of these Jewish studies done by Christian scholars is no longer motivated or biased by the aim, open or hidden, to prove or to show the superiority of Christianity over against Judaism or something like this. The motivation is instead the insight that Christianity in its origins and developments is not understandable without its early Jewish "matrix." To study the literature and heritage of Judaism means for New Testament scholars first of all an enrichment of *our* understanding of the beginnings of Christianity as a Jewish messianic movement.

Teaching New Testament and early Christian literature at an Israeli university offers, therefore, a very welcome possibility to share these experiences in cross-cultural studies with others, and to give something back to a scholarly context to which I or, to speak less personally, to which the study of the New Testament owes a lot. Along with this motivation goes the strong conviction that the early Christian literature, including the New Testament as its starting point, can and has to be studied as one of the major sources for Jewish history and Jewish religious thinking in the Second-Temple period. I am convinced that the history and development of Judaism in the Common Era, in the same way or at least in a similar way as Christianity, is not understandable without its sibling. Both religions are rooted in the same ground of the Torah and the Prophets, but the trees that have grown up in this common soil are nevertheless different. To understand why the same ground can produce two very different kinds of offspring is a task that should be done together in friendship and mutual respect. That is what we are looking to do.

To bring this ambitious vision down to earth, we have already taken the first steps, and we hope to take more in the future. As you see on the invitations and posters for this lecture series, we call it now "The Deichmann Program for Jewish and Christian Literature of the Hellenistic-Roman Era." That means that we want to develop teaching and research in both fields, namely, early Jewish literature *and* early Christian literature, which is for the most part written by Jews or, in the case of Gentile authors, is nevertheless deeply connected with the Jewish literature. In the first term of this academic year (2003-2004), we started with teaching in both fields, and that continues in the second term. What we hope to have in the future are more possibilities to do research together on the common ground. To have with us during this week Professor Larry Hurtado is a promising beginning. My hope is that his lectures will stimulate students and teachers to get engaged in this field of research.

INDEX OF MODERN AUTHORS

INDEX OF SUBJECTS

INDEX OF SCRIPTURE
AND OTHER ANCIENT SOURCES